Proceedings
of the
United Nations Conference
on
Trade and Development

SEVENTH SESSION
Geneva, 9 July-3 August 1987

Volume I
Report and Annexes

UNITED NATIONS
New York, 1989

NOTE

Symbols of United Nations documents are composed of capital letters combined with figures. Mention of such a symbol indicates a reference to a United Nations document.

The designations employed and the presentation of the material in this publication do not imply the expression of any opinion whatsoever on the part of the Secretariat of the United Nations concerning the legal status of any country, territory, city or area, or of its authorities, or concerning the delimitation of its frontiers or boundaries.

*
* *

For the recommendations, resolutions, declarations and decisions adopted by the United Nations Conference on Trade and Development, see:

First session—*Proceedings of the United Nations Conference on Trade and Development,* vol. I, *Final Act and Report* (United Nations publication, Sales No. 64.II.B.11), pp. 18-65;

Second session—*Proceedings of the United Nations Conference on Trade and Development, Second Session,* vol. I and Corr.1 and 3 and Add.1 and 2, *Report and Annexes* (United Nations publication, Sales No. E.68.II.D.14), annex I, A, pp. 28-58;

Third session—*Proceedings of the United Nations Conference on Trade and Development, Third Session,* vol. I, *Report and Annexes* (United Nations publication, Sales No. E.73.II.D.4), annex I, A, pp. 53-114;

Fourth session—*Proceedings of the United Nations Conference on Trade and Development, Fourth Session*, vol. I and Corr.1, *Report and Annexes* (United Nations publication, Sales No. E.76.II.D.10), part one, sect. A, pp. 6-43;

Fifth session—*Proceedings of the United Nations Conference on Trade and Development, Fifth Session,* vol. I, *Report and Annexes* (United Nations publication, Sales No. E.79.II.D.14), part one, sect. A, pp. 6-50;

Sixth session—*Proceedings of the United Nations Conference on Trade and Development, Sixth Session,* vol. I, *Report and Annexes* (United Nations publication, Sales No. E.83.II.D.6), part one, sect. A, pp. 6-40.

TD/352 (Vol. I)

UNITED NATIONS PUBLICATION

Sales No. E.88.II.D.1

ISBN 92-1-112240-6

04500P

CONTENTS

Annexes

ABBREVIATIONS

ACP	African, Caribbean and Pacific Group of States
CFF	Compensatory Financing Facility
DAC	Development Assistance Committee (OECD)
ECDC	economic co-operation among developing countries
EEC	European Economic Community
FAO	Food and Agriculture Organization of the United Nations
GATT	General Agreement on Tariffs and Trade
GDP	gross domestic product
GNP	gross national product
GSP	generalized system of preferences
GSTP	Generalized System of Trade Preferences among Developing Countries
Habitat	United Nations Centre for Human Settlements
ICA	international commodity agreement or arrangement
IDA	International Development Association
IFAD	International Fund for Agricultural Development
ILO	International Labour Organisation
IMF	International Monetary Fund
IPC	Integrated Programme for Commodities
LDC	least developed country
MFA	Arrangement regarding International Trade in Textiles (Multifibre Arrangement)
MFN	most favoured nation
MTN	multilateral trade negotiations
ODA	official development assistance
OECD	Organisation for Economic Co-operation and Development
OPEC	Organization of the Petroleum Exporting Countries
SDR	special drawing right
TCDC	technical co-operation among developing countries
TNC	transnational corporation
UNCDF	United Nations Capital Development Fund
UNDP	United Nations Development Programme
UNEP	United Nations Environment Programme
UNV	United Nations Volunteers programme
WHO	World Health Organization

EXPLANATORY NOTES

The abbreviated title "*Proceedings . . .*" refers to *Proceedings of the United Nations Conference on Trade and Development* for the session indicated.

Statements made and summary records of the plenary meetings held at the seventh session of the Conference are contained in volume II, references to which are to *Proceedings . . ., Seventh Session*, volume II, *Statements and Summary Records* (United Nations publication, Sales No. E.88.II.D.2).

References to volume III are to *Proceedings . . ., Seventh Session*, volume III, *Basic Documents* (United Nations publication, Sales No. E.88.II.D.3).

References to dollars ($) are to United States dollars, unless otherwise specified.

A hyphen between years, e.g. 1981-1985, signifies the entire period, including the first and last years.

REPORT

OF THE UNITED NATIONS CONFERENCE ON TRADE AND DEVELOPMENT ON ITS SEVENTH SESSION

Preface

(i) In conformity with General Assembly resolutions 1995 (XIX) of 30 December 1964 and 41/169 of 5 December 1986, the seventh session of the United Nations Conference on Trade and Development was held at the Palais des Nations, Geneva, Switzerland, from 9 July to 3 August 1987.

(ii) The Trade and Development Board, in the exercise of its functions under General Assembly resolution 1995 (XIX), and in particular paragraph 21 thereof, served as a preparatory committee for the seventh session of the Conference. The Board began these preparations at the first part of its thirty-second session when, in decision 332 (XXXII), of 21 March 1986, having suggestions by the Secretary-General of UNCTAD regarding the provisional agenda for the seventh session of the Conference[1] and taking into consideration the views expressed by delegations[2] on the aims of the session, it requested the Secretary-General to pursue informal consultations on the Conference agenda.

(iii) At the second part of its thirty-second session, the Board, having considered the oral report by the Secretary-General of UNCTAD in response to decision 332 (XXXII) and noting that his consultations had been based on the papers submitted by delegations, requested him, in decision 336 (XXXII), of 17 June 1986, to continue consultations regarding the agenda on the basis of a paper, submitted by him and annexed to the decision, entitled "Point of departure for the elaboration of the provisional agenda for the seventh session of the Conference: unifying theme and main areas of concentration" and of earlier suggestions made by him and by delegations and regional groups. The Board further requested him to conduct informal consultations on the organization of the session and related matters. Subsequently, at the first part of its thirty-third session, in decision 341 (XXXIII) of 3 October 1986, the Board adopted the provisional agenda for the seventh session of the Conference, together with its understandings in annex II of that decision, and recommended that the session be held in Geneva.

(iv) The General Assembly, in its resolution 41/169, noted the adoption by the Trade and Development Board of the provisional agenda for the seventh session of the Conference, decided to convene the session at the United Nations Office at Geneva and called on all States members of UNCTAD to continue and intensify their preparations for the Conference with a view to ensuring that the session make a significant contribution to multilateral action for the revitalization of development, growth and international trade.

(v) In its decision 344 (XXXIII) of 3 April 1987, adopted at the second part of its thirty-third session, the Board endorsed organizational arrangements set out in an oral report by the Secretary-General of UNCTAD on the results of his consultations pursuant to Board decision 336 (XXXII) and remitted a number of outstanding organizational questions to its fifteenth special session. At that special session, in decision 346 (S-XV) of 20 May 1987, the Board took note of a further oral report by the Secretary-General of UNCTAD on outstanding questions, endorsed the arrangements set out therein, and thus concluded consideration of preparations for the seventh session of the Conference.

(vi) As part of the intergovernmental preparations for the Conference, a process of informal consultations among all members of UNCTAD, on the assessment of relevant economic trends and of global structural change, was undertaken under the aegis of the President of the Board after the special session, pursuant to decision 346 (S-XV). The President of the Board held seven open-ended informal meetings, with all regional groups and China present at each, and a round of bilateral consultations with the groups and China individually. The consultations were organized in such a way as to provide for maximum transparency, the widest possible participation, and a comprehensive exchange of views. As required by his mandate, the President summed up this informal pre-Conference assessment process. The summing-up, which was prepared by the President on his own responsibility, together with his letter of transmittal to the President of the Conference, was circulated to the Conference.[3]

(vii) As part of the preparations for the seventh session of the Conference, a number of regional intergovernmental meetings were held at the ministerial level: the Sixth Ministerial Meeting of the Asian Group of the Group of 77 at Dhaka, Bangladesh, from 14 to 16 March 1987, the Latin American Co-ordination Meeting at Ministerial Level prior to UNCTAD VII, at San José, Costa Rica, from 16 to 20 March 1987, and the Conference of African Ministers Responsible for Trade and Development Preparatory to UNCTAD VII at Addis Ababa, Ethiopia, from 16 to 18 March 1987.

(viii) The results of these meetings were considered at the Sixth Ministerial Meeting of the Group of 77, held at Havana, Cuba, from 20 to 25 April 1987, which was attended by the Secretary-General of UNCTAD. The Sixth Ministerial Meeting adopted the Havana Declaration[4] and the "Assessment and proposals by the Group of 77 relating to UNCTAD VII".[5]

(ix) The Council of the Organisation for Economic Co-operation and Development held a meeting at ministerial level on 12 and 13 May 1987 in Paris at

---

[1] TD/B/L.791.

[2] TD/B(XXXII)/CG/CRP.2-4.

[3] TD(VII)/BUR.1.

[4] TD/335, reproduced in annex V below.

[5] TD/330, reproduced in annex V below.

which matters relating to the seventh session of the Conference were discussed. A ministerial communiqué was issued and circulated to the Conference.[6]

(x) The Council for Mutual Economic Assistance held a meeting at ministerial level from 26 to 28 May 1987 in Moscow at which the final position of the member countries was drawn up. The approach of the socialist countries of Group D and Mongolia to the substantive items of the provisional agenda for the seventh session of the Conference was circulated to the Conference.[7]

(xi) The People's Republic of China circulated a position paper on issues to be considered at the Conference.[8]

(xii) The representatives of 141 States members of UNCTAD assembled at the Palais des Nations, Geneva, from 9 July to 3 August 1987 to take part in the seventh session of the Conference.[9]

(xiii) In the course of a special inaugural ceremony, the Conference was addressed by Mr. Javier Pérez de Cuéllar, Secretary-General of the United Nations, who presided, Mr. Pierre Aubert, President of the Swiss Confederation, and Mr. Lazar Mojsov, President of the Presidency of the Yugoslav Federal Republic and President of the Conference at its sixth session.[10]

(xiv) During the session the Conference was addressed by the following heads of State or Government: H.E. Colonel Denis Sassou Nguesso, President of the People's Republic of the Congo, Current Chairman of the Assembly of Heads of State and Government of the Organization of African Unity; H.E. Mr. Mohamed Hosny Mubarak, President of the Arab Republic of Egypt; H.E. Mr. François Mitterrand, President of the French Republic; H.E. Mrs. Gro Harlem Brundtland, Prime Minister of Norway, Chairman of the World Commission on Environment and Development; H.E. Mr. Pierre Aubert, President of the Swiss Confederation; H.E. Mr. Lazar Mojsov, President of the Presidency of the Yugoslav Federal Republic and President of the Conference at its sixth session; and H.E. the Hon. Robert G. Mugabe, Prime Minister of the Republic of Zimbabwe, Chairman of the Non-Aligned Movement; as well as by H.E. Mr. Tian Jiyun, Vice-Premier of the State Council of China; H.R.H. Crown Prince Hassan Bin Talal of the Hashemite Kingdom of Jordan;[11] and His Eminence Cardinal Roger Etchegaray, Chairman of the Pontifical Commission "Justice and Peace".

(xv) In the course of the session messages and good wishes were received from the heads of State or Government of: China; Cuba; German Democratic Republic; Holy See; Mongolia; Peru; Philippines; Poland; Romania; Union of Soviet Socialist Republics; and Viet Nam, and from the Minister of Foreign Affairs and Worship of Bolivia.[12]

(xvi) At the 215th meeting, on 28 July 1987, having heard a statement by the President, the Conference expressed condolences to the families of the 380 victims of the tragedy at the village of Homoine, Inhambane, Mozambique, among whom were numerous children, women and elderly persons.

---

[6] TD/334, reproduced in annex VI below.

[7] TD/333, reproduced in annex VI below.

[8] TD/331, reproduced in annex VI below.

[9] For the list of members of UNCTAD and of intergovernmental and other bodies represented at the seventh session of the Conference, see part three below, section K.

[10] The texts of these addresses are reproduced in annex III below.

[11] The texts of these addresses were issued at the Conference as TD/L.294, TD/L.289, TD/L.291, TD/L.293, TD/L.292, TD/L.286, TD/L.299, TD/L.304 and Corr.1, and TD/L.310, respectively. For statements and summary records, see volume II.

[12] The texts of the messages are reproduced in annex IV below.

Part One

ACTION TAKEN BY THE CONFERENCE

CONTENTS

A. FINAL ACT OF UNCTAD VII, RESOLUTIONS ADOPTED AND OTHER ACTION TAKEN BY THE CONFERENCE

1. *Final Act of UNCTAD VII*[1]

CONTENTS

---

[1] Adopted by the Conference at its 220th plenary meeting, on 3 August 1987. For statements, see part two below, paragraphs 13-21 and 23-58.

Introduction

1. The United Nations Conference on Trade and Development held its seventh session in Geneva from 9 July to 3 August 1987, under the presidency of the Hon. Bernard T. G. Chidzero, Minister of Finance, Economic Planning and Development of Zimbabwe. The representatives of 141 States members of UNCTAD participated. The Conference was addressed by its President, by the Secretary-General of the United Nations, Mr. Javier Pérez de Cuéllar, by the heads of State or Government of the Congo, Egypt, France, Norway, Switzerland, Yugoslavia and Zimbabwe, by H.R.H. Crown Prince Hassan Bin Talal of Jordan, by Ministers of 71 member States and by the Secretary-General of UNCTAD, Mr. K. K. S. Dadzie.[2] It received messages from 11 heads of State and Government.[3] The final week was devoted to the conclusion of the work of the session at the ministerial level, and 44 Ministers participated during this phase.

2. The main substantive item of the Conference agenda was the "revitalization of development, growth and international trade, in a more predictable and supportive environment, through multilateral co-operation: assessment of relevant economic trends and global structural change, and appropriate formulation of policies and measures, addressing key issues in the inter-related areas of resources for development, including financial, and related monetary questions; commodities; international trade; and problems of the least developed countries". This item was considered in the light of the related understandings.[4]

3. The Conference established four Sessional Committees to consider the four sub-items under the main agenda item: Committee I, on resources for development was chaired by Mr. M. Taniguchi (Japan); Committee II on commodities by Mr. C. Pérez del Castillo (Uruguay); Committee III on international trade by Mr. Chak Mun See (Singapore); and Committee IV on problems of the least developed countries, by Mr. M. Huslid (Norway). This consolidated text was prepared by the Contact Group of the President. The Rapporteur of the Conference was Mr. A. Ozadovski (Ukrainian Soviet Socialist Republic).

---

[2] See volume II.

[3] The texts of the messages are reproduced in annex IV below.

[4] See part three below, sect. E.

I. Assessment of relevant economic trends and of global structural change: findings and policy implications

4. The Conference undertook an assessment of relevant economic trends and of global structural change, as provided for in its agenda and in the related understandings.[5]

The findings of this assessment are as follows:

5. The world economy in the 1980s has been characterized by a slow-down in growth of demand and output, compared with the preceding two decades, generally lower rates of inflation, difficulties in many countries in adapting to structural changes, a mounting stock of debt, high real interest rates, inadequate net flows of financial resources, shifts in exchange rates, high and increasing levels of protection, commodity prices depressed to their lowest level in 50 years, terms-of-trade losses sustained by commodity-exporting countries, and a generally insecure economic environment in which millions of people still lack the basic conditions for a decent life.

6. In this difficult global economic situation, there has been a diversity of socio-economic experiences. Developed market-economy countries have succeeded in curbing inflation and in maintaining steady, albeit slow, growth, but unemployment levels are still high and external payments imbalances remain excessive in some of these countries. On account of their dominant share in world trade, the impact of their slow growth has been transmitted to other countries which have had to reckon with it as a significant factor in policy formulation. Growth has slowed also in socialist countries of Eastern Europe. Most developing countries have had to retrench; they have been unable to consolidate and build upon the economic and social progress which they had achieved during the two preceding decades. In the 1980s, the average per capita income of the developing countries as a whole fell further behind that of the developed countries. Indeed, per capita incomes declined in most countries in Latin America and in sub-Saharan Africa. Nevertheless, a number of more industrialized export-led economies of East Asia, and the larger Asian low income economies, have continued to grow appreciably.

7. Many developing countries continue to face serious debt problems. The main debt indicators remain at historically high levels, even for the poorer among them. Although most countries with debt-servicing difficulties have neither achieved a satisfactory growth momentum nor recovered their creditworthiness, the debt strategy has allowed some resumption of capital flows and growth in some developing countries. There continues to exist a need for more timely and effective mobilization of lending by commercial banks. In the context of expanding lending requirements for development, the multilateral financial institutions need to be provided with adequate capital resources to support growth and adjustment.

8. The roles of the external economic environment and of domestic policies and structural factors are recognized as contributory elements to the diversity of experiences of developing countries, but judgements differ with respect to the relative weights of these elements.

9. The 1980s have also been a time of complexity for economic policy-makers in both developed and developing countries. Increasing unpredictability has been manifested in the unilateral adoption of trade restrictions specific to countries and products, and in the appearance of massive and often distorting flows of funds within and across international currency and commodity markets. Associated with these phenomena have been interrelated problems arising from currency misalignments, persistent payments imbalances, an uneven distribution of international liquidity, and net outflows of financial resources from many developing countries.

10. Both policy-makers and entrepreneurs are being challenged by an acceleration in the pace of structural changes which are very difficult to harness. These changes can be traced to a number of underlying factors, the most important of which are the impact of scientific advance and applied technology, and government policy stances. These factors are affecting production, consumption and trade patterns; producing far-reaching developments in the service sector, particularly financial services, and in commodity markets; significantly altering employment patterns; and leading to shifts in international competitiveness.

11. Many countries—developed and developing alike, including the least developed countries—are investing substantial efforts in adjusting their economies to these new realities in pursuit of their national objectives. They are also reappraising the respective roles of the public and private sectors in the economy. However, although some have made progress in recent years in reducing or eliminating growth-retarding distortions and rigidities by enhancing the structural flexibility of their economies, much remains to be done.

12. The developed market-economy countries are committed to programmes of structural transformation to foster sustained non-inflationary growth, promote competition to accelerate industrial adjustment, facilitate job-creating investment, improve the functioning of labour markets, promote the further opening of internal markets, encourage the elimination of capital market imperfections, and reduce major imbalances between agricultural demand and supply.

13. Socialist countries of Eastern Europe have launched intensive policy reforms aimed at transforming the mechanisms of the national economy, improving the management of foreign economic relations and enhancing international competitiveness.

14. Many developing countries, recognizing the importance of their national policies in promoting social and economic development, are striving to: strengthen

---

[5] For this purpose, the Conference drew upon the documents before it, the statements made in plenary meeting, and the deliberations of its Sessional Committees.

their national capacities for mobilizing domestic resources, both financial and (through education and training) human; enhance the degree to which their economies can respond to efficient market signals; develop more flexible incentive systems for shifting prductive resources in line with dynamic comparative advantage; expand the scope for entrepreneurial initiative and enterprise development; devise incentives for the adoption of appropriate technologies; enhance the contribution of the public sector and broaden opportunities for management and technical education. Others have acknowledged the need to adopt similar policy approaches. At the same time, the implementation of such comprehensive adjustment measures has often been accompanied by high social and political costs.

15.   In view of the substantial and increasing interdependence in the world economy, both among countries and across the trade, money, finance and commodity sectors, national economic policies, through their interaction with the international economic environment, have become important factors influencing the development process. The more significant the country in terms of its economic weight, the greater is the effect of its policies on other countries. The structural characteristics of most developing economies leave them especially vulnerable to the impact of structural change and external shocks.

16.   Interdependence among countries has been increasing as the growth of world trade has outpaced that of world output. Furthermore, there has been a closer integration of the various sectors of the world economy. With the rapid diffusion of new technologies, the secondary and tertiary sectors have become more tightly integrated, as in the merger of many service activities with production processes.

17.   In the financial sector, a number of recent developments have accentuated the dependence of many countries upon their trade sectors. These have included the progressive dismantling of controls over international capital movements, the increasingly close connections between domestic and international financial markets, facilitated by the revolution in information and communications technology, the rise in the importance and the procyclical movement of international lending, the decline in net financial flows, and the scale of debt-servicing burdens compared with domestic savings capacities.

18.   The pursuit of export expansion by commodity-dependent developing countries to achieve balance-of-payments equilibrium and longer-term structural adjustment towards a more balanced, less vulnerable economic structure has failed to increase export earnings. In some instances, it has become a factor in generating over-supply, aggravating the effect on prices of weak demand. The sharp declines in commodity prices consequent thereon have resulted in losses of earnings, compounding the financial constraints. The least developed countries have been particularly affected in this regard.

19.   Attempts to expand export earnings have also been hampered in the agricultural sector and in many industries because the erosion of multilateral discipline has permitted the rise of protectionism, particularly of the non-tariff, selective and discriminatory form, restricting market access.

20.   In both these cases, the constraints on the ability of developing countries to increase their export revenues have further impaired their debt-servicing capacity. The resulting aggravation of the debt problem has, in turn, increased the calls on the resources of the multilateral financial institutions for meeting the financing needs of developing countries, in view of the slowness of the commercial banking sector to renew voluntary lending to these countries.

21.   Close interlinkages have also become apparent between the economy, population and the natural environment. The degradation of this environment associated with persistent poverty is being further worsened by the financial pressures on developing countries, which have led to the over-exploitation of natural resources and reductions in environmental programmes. Recognition is, however, growing that such degradation can be halted and reversed only by ecologically sustainable growth and by integrating environmental factors in development programmes.

22.   Current economic performance in some developed and developing countries as well as the imbalances which characterize the world economy suggest that the responsibilities and opportunities inherent in interdependence have been inadequately addressed by national and international policies.

23.   Indications have been given by the developed market-economy countries that they have a responsibility to ensure a better environment for the growth and exports of developing countries, primarily by fostering vigorous economies in an open multilateral trading system, correcting massive current-account imbalances, and achieving greater stability in exchange rates. Improved and sustained growth in the developing countries can, in turn, have a substantial positive impact on growth in the developed countries. In this regard, a number of developing countries now play an increasing role in the world economy by virtue of the strong growth in their industrial production, exports of manufactures and import capacity.

24.   Recent positive developments have included the broad acceptance of the need for support of growth-oriented adjustment in the developing countries, the successive commitments to macro-economic policy co-ordination by the seven major developed market-economy countries, the latest of which was made at their most recent summit meeting; the declaration by the socialist countries of Eastern Europe on ways and means to resolve global economic problems and overcome underdevelopment through multilateral co-operation; the recent decision by the Government of Japan to channel a portion of that country's external surplus to developing countries; the movement towards more co-ordinated and longer-term debt rescheduling in the context of the Paris Club; the launching of the Uruguay Round of multilateral trade negotiations; the new impetus to the process of entry-into-force of the Agreement Establishing the Common Fund for Commodities; the initiation of negotiations on a Global System of Trade Preferences among Developing Coun-

tries; and the adoption of the United Nations Programme of Action for African Economic Recovery and Development 1986-1990, envisaging measures by both the African countries and the international community. These developments were welcomed as evidence of a growing consensus that the revitalization of development, growth and international trade in an increasingly interdependent world is a common objective which requires continued co-operative efforts within a multilateral framework involving all States.

Implications for policy

25. Drawing upon these findings, the Conference considered their implications, and reached a number of general policy conclusions. These constitute a basis for continuing action by Governments, individually and collectively, and in the competent international organizations, in pursuit of the objective of revitalizing development, growth and international trade. If this objective is to be attained, Governments need to improve their capacities to manage the interrelationships among different economies and the interlinkages between various sectors and issues.

26. Thus, a reactivation of the development process in the developing countries, whose markets now absorb more than a quarter of the exports of the developed market-economy countries, would contribute to non-inflationary growth, employment and structural adjustment in the latter group of countries. It would in addition enhance the capacity of the indebted developing countries to meet their debt-service obligations to creditors in the developed market-economy countries. Faster growth and non-discriminatory trade liberalization in these countries would boost the economies of developing countries through strengthened commodity prices, improved market access and enlarged financial flows. The same processes would also support the efforts of the socialist countries of Eastern Europe to achieve trade-oriented growth, while the closer integration of these countries in international economic interchange would, in turn, contribute to global growth and stability.

27. If both national and international policies were growth-oriented and mutually reinforcing, interdependence would, in contrast to the experiences of the recent past, be a vehicle for transmitting and cumulating positive impulses. This implies the acceptance of joint responsibility to take convergent action. Such responsibility rests on all countries, collectively and individually, with each country contributing to the common objective in accordance with its capacities and weight in the world economy. At the same time, a shared approach to internationally agreed objectives must not involve any attempt to impose a unique model of national economic management for adoption by all countries. Account would need to be taken of the diversity of national objectives, of specific problems, of experience and of capacity to respond to changes in the external environment. In this context, the fundamental principle was stressed that each country has the primary responsibility for its own socio-economic and political development, and the right to adopt the economic,

social and political systems which it considers most appropriate.

28. The Conference emphasized that the Charter of the United Nations provided a basis for the conduct of relations among States in a manner that would promote the shared objectives of revitalizing development, growth and international trade in a more predictable and supportive environment through multilateral co-operation and thus also promote peace, security and stability. In a climate of greater security there would be increased opportunities for diverting resources from expenditures on armaments towards more socially productive uses, including development finance.

29. The Conference agreed that mutual benefit, common interest, equality, non-discrimination and collective responsibility, as well as recognition of the diversity of national paths to development, could be the basis of a constructive and action-oriented dialogue which would instil new strength into multilateral co-operation for development. In a particular conjuncture, such a dialogue would have to pay due regard to cyclical and structural trends and incorporate both international dimensions and the interactions between those dimensions and national factors and policies. It would also have to take into account the interrelationships between short-, medium- and long-term problems and solutions.

30. In the light of the foregoing considerations, the Conference reached a broad understanding on the need for:

(*a*) All countries to implement national and international policy measures to improve the environment for accelerated and sustainable development;

and in that context for:

(*b*) Major market-economy countries

  (i) To adopt co-ordinated policies to promote stable, sustainable, non-inflationary growth, consistent with their declared aims;

  (ii) To enhance the positive impact on development of measures to deal with their mutual imbalances;

  (iii) To strengthen mechanisms for the ongoing process of multilateral surveillance of economic policies;

(*c*) Developed market-economy countries and socialist countries of Eastern Europe:

  (i) To contribute to the strengthening of the production potential of developing countries, to improve access for imports from those countries and to undertake the consequential structural adjustments in agriculture and industry, where appropriate;

  (ii) To enhance the flow of public and private resources and to intensify economic assistance to developing countries, bearing in mind their particular resource needs: those of the poorer countries, notably the least developed countries and other countries in sub-Saharan Africa, those of the commodity-dependent countries and those of the heavily indebted countries;

(*d*) Developing countries, in fulfilment of their primary responsibility for their own development and in accordance with their respective national objectives and priorities:

   (i) To strengthen policies and measures to mobilize domestic financial and human resources, including indigenous private capital and entrepreneurship;

  (ii) To provide a suitable policy environment for external financial resources, public and private, as appropriate;

 (iii) To improve further the effectiveness of domestic and external resource use;

  (iv) To continue to improve their mutual economic co-operation in pursuance of the objectives of national and collective self-reliance;

   (v) To promote the development of human resources, in order to utilize their capacities most effectively.

31.   The Conference also agreed that this understanding would need to be complemented by co-operation among all countries to improve the systems, structures and arrangements which underpin international economic relations, particularly in the inter-related areas of money, finance and trade, making them more supportive of development and observing provisions related to differential and more favourable treatment for developing countries in trade. Although divergences remain concerning the modalities for such co-operation, it was nevertheless recognized that such matters should remain on the active agenda of the competent international forums, including UNCTAD.

32.   The Conference noted that many UNCTAD members proposed an international conference on money and finance for development with universal participation, with the aim of evolving a stable, effective and equitable monetary system. Other members did not agree to the need for such a conference and indicated that these issues were being, and should continue to be, dealt with satisfactorily in the Interim Committee of the International Monetary Fund and the Development Committee of the World Bank and IMF.

II.   Policies and measures

33.   In the context of the foregoing assessment and general policy conclusions and of the unifying theme of its agenda, the Conference reviewed key issues arising in the four areas listed in its agenda. The Conference agreed upon the need for a number of policy approaches and concrete measures in those areas, bearing in mind the interrelationships among those areas and among the policies and measures envisaged. This agreement is expressed in the following text, the elements of which are addressed, as appropriate, to Governments, to the intergovernmental bodies of UNCTAD and its Secretary-General, and to other international institutions.

A.   Resources for development, including financial, and related monetary questions

INTRODUCTION

34.   The stringency of external resources for many developing countries in recent years has posed difficult challenges for both multilateral co-operation and domestic economic management. The main challenges are: the debt problem; the adequacy of external financial resources; the mobilization of domestic savings and human resources; and the related monetary questions.

35.   Net resource inflows to developing countries have declined steeply since 1982. Commercial bank loans and net export credits have contracted sharply. Official development assistance flows have stagnated in real terms, though net disbursements of ODA by developed countries as a whole have advanced moderately. Many donors continue to remain below the target of 0.7 per cent of gross national product, as adopted. Foreign direct investment flows have fluctuated and remain at present depressed. Multilateral development finance has grown modestly. For many countries, net drawings from the International Monetary Fund have dropped sharply, to the extent that IMF is currently a net recipient of resources from developing countries as a whole.

36.   Many developing countries, particularly those having high debt-service ratios, have experienced a severe reduction of resources available for development. This has contributed to the reversal of economic and social progress in a number of countries, and to a slowing down of growth in the world economy.

37.   The objective of adjustment with growth can be realized only if all the parties concerned discharge their responsibilities. Such a process requires restoring economic activity in developing countries which will in turn enhance their ability to service debt. It also requires greater flows of external resources to developing countries, as investment and import volumes need to grow.

38.   There has been an evolving response of the international community to the debt problem. It recognizes the shared responsibility of the main parties concerned (developing debtor countries, developed creditor countries, private and multilateral financial institutions). The developed countries have the responsibility to help create a favourable economic environment through, *inter alia*, the promotion of growth and the expansion of trade. In the context of a favourable international economic and trade environment, the main elements are: the pursuit of programmes of economic adjustment and structural reform by developing countries, the enhancement of lending by multilateral and international financial institutions, particularly the World Bank, and the provision of external private financial flows in volume and terms appropriate to support the adjustment and reform efforts of developing countries, while promoting the growth of their economies.

39.   The debt problems of both those developing countries with lower per capita income, whose debt is mainly on concessional terms and largely with official

creditors, and those with higher per capita income, whose debt is mainly on market terms and largely with commercial creditors, are being addressed.

40. There has been some resumption of growth, correction of imbalances and progress in restoring the flow of resources to some countries. Many developing countries have made far-reaching changes in their macroeconomic and structural policies. In a number of cases, notable achievements have been recorded. However, the costs of adjustment have been heavy, and many countries with debt-servicing difficulties have yet to achieve a satisfactory growth momentum or recover their creditworthiness. Several debtor countries are experiencing interest payments on accumulated loans that are larger than net financial transfers through net new lending. Increased private financial flows have failed until now to materialize. Although debt-restructuring agreements have been concluded on a significant scale, with the involvement of international financial institutions, new financial inflows have been modest, and the external economic environment has improved little.

41. With regard to official development finance, certain efforts have been made by the international community to increase its volume, including the establishment of the World Bank Special Facility for sub-Saharan Africa; the agreement on the Eighth Replenishment of the International Development Association, although the amounts involved represent virtually no increase in real terms as compared to the combined resources of the Seventh Replenishment of IDA and the Special Facility for sub-Saharan Africa; the commitment by developed countries to mobilize additional resources for Africa in the context of the United Nations Programme of Action for African Economic Recovery and Development 1986-1990; and the setting up of the IMF Structural Adjustment Facility. Certain donor countries have taken steps to increase their contribution to development finance and improve its term and effectiveness.

42. The financing of development also requires enhanced mobilization of domestic financial and human resources. In some countries, current efforts to expand domestic savings and to improve the quality of investment in physical and human capital need to be increased and complemented by an improved external environment.

43. Finally, related monetary issues, especially with regard to multilateral surveillance, exchange rates, interest rates and liquidity needs of developing countries, have an important role to play in the concerted efforts towards revitalizing the development process.

1. DEBT PROBLEMS

44. The debt crisis is complex and an equitable, durable and mutually agreed solution will be reached only by an approach based on development, within the framework of an integrated, co-operative, growth-oriented strategy that takes into account the particular circumstances of each country. The response to the debt crisis should continue to evolve, through continuous dialogue and shared responsibility, and the strategy should be implemented with flexibility in an environment of strengthened international co-operation, bear-

ing in mind General Assembly resolution 41/202 of 8 December 1986. To that end:

(a) The various parties should co-ordinate their respective contributions in the context of medium-term development policies and programmes oriented towards adjustment and growth formulated by the country. Such programmes should examine the country's investment requirements and take into account important relevant factors of debt-servicing capacity, such as prospective export earnings, terms of trade, import requirements, GDP growth, and volume and terms of likely future financial flows;

(b) Policy advice should take into account the economic, political and social characteristics and needs of the country;

(c) Maturity, grace and, as appropriate, consolidation periods in official debt-restructuring arrangements should be tailored to the individual circumstances of individual countries, with due regard to the need to accord Governments and enterprises an adequate planning horizon. It is also desirable that consolidation, maturity and grace periods in private debt-restructuring arrangements should also be tailored to that end. Due consideration should be given to unforeseen changes in the country's external payments due to factors beyond its control;

(d) It is essential for debtor developing countries to pursue and intensify their efforts to raise savings and investment, reduce inflation and improve efficiency, taking into account their own individual characteristics and the vulnerability of the poorer strata;

(e) It is essential that external financing from official and private sources be increased on appropriate terms and conditions in support of these efforts;

(f) It is essential for the international economic environment to be made more stable and predictable in support of growth through efforts by the major market-economy countries, including strengthened multilateral surveillance, aimed at correcting existing external and fiscal imbalances, promoting non-inflationary sustainable growth, lowering real rates of interest, and making exchange rates more stable and markets more accessible;

(g) In view of the debt burden, it will be necessary to work out, in appropriate cases, judicious combinations of measures designed to reduce it. Debt-equity swaps and other non-debt-creating flows have a role to play. A further widening of the range of options needs to be explored and developed in terms of realistic and effective instruments including those devised by banks and debtors to take advantage of discounts prevailing in secondary markets;

(h) Commercial banks of developed countries should be encouraged, in accordance with the policies and procedures of those countries, to apply flexibility in debt-restructuring operations and in providing new loans to indebted nations, as well as in taking innovative measures according to individual circumstances;

(i) Export credit agencies should be flexible regarding early resumption or increases in cover for developing countries in support of their adjustment programmes;

(j) Terms and conditions of rescheduling operations should continue to be based on the realistic assessment of the financial situation of individual countries;

(*k*) The debt-service burden of the poorest countries, primarily in sub-Saharan Africa, that are undertaking adjustment effort should be eased by longer repayments and grace periods, especially in the Paris Club. Consideration should also be given to the possibility of applying lower interest rates to their existing debt;

(*l*) In respect of the ODA debt of poorer developing countries, developed donor countries which have not yet done so should implement in full Trade and Development Board resolution 165 (S-IX) of 11 March 1978;

(*m*) It is recognized that the problems of the poorer countries in sub-Saharan Africa are uniquely difficult and need special treatment. It is also recognized that, in dealing with Africa's external indebtedness, the magnitude and the servicing of its debt constitute a severe and continuing burden which restricts its economic recovery and long-term development; the international community, particularly the donor developed countries, reaffirms its agreement to adopt concrete measures, and the importance of increasing urgently ODA to Africa in accordance with the provisions of the United Nations Programme of Action for African Economic Recovery and Development 1986-1990.[6]

45. The Conference took note of the proposal of the Group of 24 endorsed by the Group of 77 to establish, within the Interim and Development Committees, a Committee of Ministers from developing and developed countries to take up the examination of the debt problem, including specific solutions for low income countries, particularly those in sub-Saharan Africa, and recommend appropriate measures. The Conference also noted the view of a number of participants that consideration of these important issues continues to remain under constructive discussion at the ministerial level within the Interim and Development Committees. They strongly encouraged the efforts within these Committees on the existing basis. The Conference also noted the view of other participants that an effective and equitable solution of the debt problem could be found only in the framework of a universal forum.

46. Some debtor developing countries are at present making interest and service payments that exceed net new lending to them. The objective of the co-operative debt strategy is to produce a situation where, in support of the process of structural adjustment, domestic resources and external resources (facilitated, *inter alia*, through export earnings, new financial flows and/or debt rearrangements) are sufficient to finance the country's import and investment requirements, in order to assist the country to reach on a sustainable basis its growth and development potential.

2. RESOURCES FOR DEVELOPMENT

(a) *External resources for development*

47. ODA will continue to play an important role for a large number of developing countries, especially for poorer and least developed countries. In compliance with the recommendations of the IMF/World Bank Development Committee's Task Force on concessional flows, developed countries should renew and make more effective their efforts to achieve, as quickly as possible, the internationally agreed target of 0.7 per cent of gross national product for total ODA and the targets for ODA directed towards the least developed countries as adopted in the Substantial New Programme of Action for the 1980s for the Least Developed Countries[7] and the International Development Strategy for the Third United Nations Development Decade.[8] At the same time, donor and recipient countries should together seek to ensure that aid is fully supportive of development efforts and that aid effectiveness is strengthened, *inter alia*, through improved co-ordination.

48. Multilateral financial institutions should play a central and growing role in supporting the growth and adjustment process, by providing both concessional and non-concessional finance and catalysing additional private capital flows. These institutions should be strengthened by endowing them with adequate resources and instruments to fulfil their tasks. Members of the World Bank should support a substantial and early general increase of its capital when needed to support quality lending and to enable the Bank to meet the increased needs for external resources of developing countries for adjustment and investment and for maintaining net lending at a reasonable level. Donors should meet expeditiously their commitments to the Eighth Replenishment of IDA and ensure that terms and conditions of IDA credits remain highly concessional.

49. Regional development banks and funds also need to be strengthened. They have an important role to play in support of development, investment and growth in developing countries. The resources of these regional development institutions should be maintained at adequate levels and reviewed as necessary. In particular, negotiations on a capital increase of the Inter-American Development Bank and a replenishment of the African Development Fund should be concluded as soon as possible.

50. All countries are called upon to participate actively in the future negotiations on the third replenishment of the International Fund for Agricultural Development and all contributors to the Fund are urged to make additional efforts to contribute to the Fund with a view to ensuring the highest possible level of resources while preserving the institution and its unique structure.

51. The conditionality criteria of international financial institutions should take into account, among other things, adverse changes in the external environment which affect the prospects for achieving necessary adjustment with adequate rates of growth and for protecting the poor segments of the population, as well as the necessary resources for development and the periods required for adjustment with growth. Increased co-operation between IMF, the World Bank and other multilateral financial institutions is welcomed but should not lead to cross-conditionality.

---

[6] General Assembly resolution S-13/2 of 1 June 1986, annex.

[7] *Report of the United Nations Conference on the Least Developed Countries, Paris, 1-14 September 1981* (United Nations publication, Sales No. E.82.I.8), part one, sect. A.

[8] General Assembly resolution 35/56 of 5 December 1980, annex.

52. Developed countries should effectively mobilize additional resources for Africa, in accordance with the commitments undertaken in the context of the United Nations Programme of Action for African Economic Recovery and Development 1986-1990.

53. Concern is expressed about the plight of low income countries and in this connection it is recognized that implementation of major reforms in these countries needs to be accompanied by additional financing on concessional terms. The Managing Director of IMF has proposed a tripling of the resources of the Structural Adjustment Facility. A significant increase in such resources over the three years from 1 January 1988 would be welcomed. It is urged that a conclusion of discussions on this proposal be reached by the end of 1987.

54. Both developed and developing countries should explore ways and means to encourage private capital flows to developing countries. Flows fostered through non-debt-creating instruments are particularly welcome. Foreign direct investment should be encouraged by the promotion of such flows by developed countries, and by improving as necessary the environment for investment in host countries, in accordance with their national policies and legislations, and development priorities. Governments of developed countries should encourage the revival of bank lending, in accordance with the practices and procedures in the developed countries concerned. Policies regarding export credits should allow such credits to make a meaningful contribution to the financing of investment programmes, under suitable terms and conditions.

55. Negotiations on the elaboration of the code of conduct on transnational corporations should be completed as soon as possible.

56. Continued efforts are needed to foster the flows of resources from developed to developing countries. The recent initiative of the Japanese Government to increase the transfer of financial resources to developing countries is welcomed. It is hoped that all developed countries will take appropriate steps to increase overall financial flows to developing countries.

57. The Conference notes with interest the proposal of the Japanese Government for establishing an independent high-level group of wise persons, with the support of interested countries and relevant international organizations, to examine ways and means to encourage the flow of financial resources to developing countries.

(b) *Domestic resources for development, including non-financial resources*

58. The future financing of development requires both higher flows of external finance and enhanced domestic resource mobilization. Domestic savings remain an essential means of financing development. Many developing countries have embarked upon rigorous programmes to expand domestic savings and increase the efficiency of investment. However, their capacity to save has been depresssed by external factors. Their efforts would be enhanced by an improved external environment with increased financial flows to developing countries, reduced debt service and improved terms of trade.

59. Growth of per capita incomes is necessary for increasing domestic savings. In many developing countries per capita consumption has been depressed; in some the declines have endangered social peace. Another important factor for increasing domestic savings is restoration of financial stability. However, domestic financial stability is difficult to attain when the external financial situation remains seriously disrupted.

60. In many countries, increased efforts are needed to improve the mobilization and use of domestic savings through, *inter alia*, ensuring an appropriate return to savers, as well as by strengthening the institutions and instruments for investment finance. In the same context, increased attention needs to be given to the quality of investment in the public as well as private sectors, so that due weight is given to projects that promise the highest pay-off, *inter alia*, in terms of foreign-exchange earnings or savings. Finally, fiscal disciplines require close attention in a number of developing countries, with a view to raising savings and investment in the public sector from their currently depressed levels. This may often call for a strengthening of public sector finances, increased investment in human resources and physical infrastructure, and other necessary measures.

61. Although such measures help to improve the mobilization of domestic resources in developing countries, they take time to bear fruit; their effectiveness will be enhanced by an improved external environment.

62. The fulfilment of human potential and the promotion of human well-being are the ultimate goals of the development process. In this context it is essential to mobilize fully human resources, recognizing, in particular, the role of women and the need to integrate women and development issues. Human resource development will lead to improvements in labour productivity, which depends on, among others, a series of factors, such as nutrition, health, housing, education, environment and quality of management. Qualified national specialists should be fully used as an important factor of social and economic development in developing countries.

63. A very large number of developing countries have made substantial progress in securing the full and effective participation of all strata of the population in the development process, in enhancing education, reducing illiteracy and improving the provision of social services. However, many developing countries have recently experienced a deterioration in several of the factors influencing the development of the human potential, as a consequence of cuts in government expenditures on health, education, and other basic social services, made necessary by their worsened economic situation.

64. Development of human resources in developing countries is primarily their responsibility. Developed countries are ready to support their efforts by providing, in particular, necessary financial and technical assistance through bilateral and multilateral channels.

(c) *Monetary questions as related to resources for development, including financial resources*

65. A stable international monetary environment is essential to foster global economic growth required to address effectively debt and development problems. Polices in the areas of debt and resources are more effective when supported by appropriate fiscal and monetary policies.

66. The balance-of-payments problems of developing countries are related to resource availability and use, exchange rates and policies, and the level of reserves. Difficult monetary and exchange rate reforms and policy adjustments have been made by many developing countries aimed at achieving a sustainable balance-of-payments pattern. Adequate availability of international liquidity is important for sustainable non-inflationary economic growth of the world economy, including the growth of developing countries. In this context the question of international liquidity must be kept under permanent review under the auspices of IMF.

67. Volatile exchange rates in the major market economies have contributed to economic imbalances in these countries and to uncertainty in international trade, investment and economic growth, and to the intensification of protectionism. A stable exchange-rate environment is conducive to balanced trade, investment and an open multilateral trade system. Co-operative efforts are being undertaken by Governments of countries with major currencies and aimed at promoting orderly behaviour and stability of exchange rates. Co-operation to stabilize exchange rates and promote growth should continue to be worked out in the context of strengthened multilateral surveillance with the assistance of IMF, in conformity with the growth objectives provided for in article 1 of its Articles of Agreement and taking into account trade and capital flows as well as fiscal balance.

68. International interest rates remain high in real terms, affecting investment and growth both in developed and developing countries. Governments' efforts in economic and fiscal policies and in the correction of external and domestic imbalances, particularly of major market economies, are helping to create an environment for a further decline in interest rates. A decline in interest rates, keeping in mind sustainable non-inflationary growth objectives, would help stimulate economic activity further in both developed and developing countries.

69. The continued examination within IMF of the question of allocation and functioning of special drawing rights with a view to enhancing their attractiveness as a reserve asset is welcomed. Most States members of UNCTAD reiterated the view that there is a long-term global need to supplement existing reserve assets on a continuous basis and that many countries have a need for reserve supplementation. They asked that IMF should agree on a new substantial special drawing right allocation. They stressed the costs and risks to the efficient functioning of the international monetary system of building reserve holdings through borrowing on international credit markets or through current-account surplus. Other States members, however, continue to believe that the condition for special drawing right allocation, that is, the existence of a long-term global need, had not been demonstrated.

B. Commodities

INTRODUCTION

70. Commodity prices in real terms are on the whole at their lowest level for half a century and over the short and medium term a major sustained improvement is not expected. The present situation has adversely affected, in varying degrees, all producing countries. Developing countries heavily dependent on exports of commodities have been particularly severely affected. In these countries the sharp declines in prices of commodities have resulted in losses in earnings, decline in capital investment and, in many of them, the accumulation of debt.

71. A complex interplay of factors has affected demand and supply and contributed to the downward pressure on prices. Such factors, which vary in their impact from one commodity to another, and from one country to another, are short, medium and long term in their origin and are induced by cyclical and structural factors, as well as by government policies. Among these various factors are moderate economic growth; fluctuating exchange and interest rates; the less intensive use of some commodities as a result of technological change, including recycling and the use of synthetics and substitutes; concentration of growth in recent years in sectors such as services and electronics in developed countries; increased productivity; support measures encouraging increased production and exports; protectionism; and the declining role of comparative advantage in primary agricultural products, minerals and metals.

72. As a result, changes have occurred in the patterns of production, consumption and trade. The share of non-fuel commodities in world trade in relation to world trade in manufactures has been following a declining trend. Developing countries' share in total imports of non-fuel commodities has been increasing; nevertheless, this increase has been concentrated in only a small number of developing countries. In addition, there has been an increase in the local processing of some commodities in some developing countries, but for a large number of them little or no progress has been made.

73. In view of this situation, there is a need to seek lasting solutions to deal effectively with the short-, medium- and long-term problems in the commodities area, and the Conference recognized that international co-operation between producers and consumers is necessary for the achievement of these objectives and should be strengthened. To this end, the Conference reaffirms the validity of its resolution 93 (IV) of 30 May 1976 and calls for the implementation of, *inter alia*, policies and measures as agreed below.

1. INTERNATIONAL COMMODITY AGREEMENTS/ARRANGEMENTS IN THE LIGHT OF THE WORLD COMMODITY SITUATION AND THE SITUATION OF INDIVIDUAL COMMODITIES

74. The Conference recognized the need for a better functioning of commodity markets and the desirability

of achieving stable and more predictable conditions in commodity trade, including the avoidance of excessive price fluctuations and the search for long-term solutions to commodity problems.

75. In this respect, there was agreement that, where appropriate and feasible, producer-consumer consultations and co-operation should be enhanced, strengthened or established. The Conference highlighted that there had been a long experience with international commodity agreements as a mechanism for greater stability and predictability in commodity markets. The adoption of Conference resolution 93 (IV) in Nairobi with its integrated approach to commodity problems had added a new dimension and scope to the work on international commodity agreements. Decision 23 (XI) of the Committee on Commodities[9] provides additional elements geared towards achieving a more effective functioning of international commodity agreements.

76. The Conference agreed that the operation and functioning of existing commodity agreements should be improved. The negotiation of new international commodity agreements or arrangements should cover the conclusion of agreements or arrangements containing, as appropriate, economic provisions, or developmental measures, or measures to improve market transparency, or a combination of such provisions and measures. Such agreements or arrangements should also receive the participation of as many important producing and consuming countries as possible.

77. The Conference also agreed to request the Secretary-General of UNCTAD to convene or to resume, in accordance with the results of comprehensive consultations with producers and consumers, *ad hoc* review meetings and/or preparatory meetings on individual commodities which are not covered by international commodity agreements/arrangements and which are included in the indicative list of resolution 93 (IV). Following these consultations, an appropriate schedule of meetings shall be prepared by the Secretary-General of UNCTAD for these purposes, for implementation by 1990 as far as possible.

78. Such meetings would, in the light of Conference resolution 93 (IV) and decision 23 (XI) of the Committee on Commodities and taking into account the particular characteristics and situation of each individual commodity, decide on the appropriate international action needed to solve the problems faced by these commodities in international markets.

2. THE COMMON FUND FOR COMMODITIES

79. The Conference noted that the prospects for the entry into force of the Agreement Establishing the Common Fund for Commodities[10] in the near future had improved with additional signatures and ratifications. The entry into force of the Common Fund Agreement might further the conclusion of international commodity agreements with economic provisions. A number of developmental programmes on individual commodities have already been approved or considered by producers and consumers for possible financing under the Second Account of the Common Fund.

80. It was urged that countries which had not taken action to sign the Agreement Establishing the Common Fund for Commodities and/or to deposit the necessary instruments of ratification, acceptance or approval should do so in the near future and that, once the entry-into-force conditions are met, efforts should be made as soon as possible by parties to the Agreement to ensure that the Common Fund is made operational.

3. DIVERSIFICATION, PROCESSING, MARKETING AND DISTRIBUTION

81. The Conference recognized that for most developing countries horizontal and vertical diversification of their economies, as well as increased participation in the processing, marketing and distribution, including transportation, of their commodities, is a long-term development objective towards which international co-operation between producers and consumers should be intensified.

82. The Conference noted that decisions on diversification are primarily the responsibility of developing countries. International assistance should be directed to viable diversification programmes within a broad economic policy framework and in a context of growth-oriented structural adjustment. Full account should be taken of the developmental objectives of each country and of dynamic comparative advantage considerations. In this context, an adequate expansion of official bilateral and multilateral resources, as well as private resources, including private investment, was called for to finance appropriate diversification projects and programmes, possibly through special facilities for this purpose. Diversification can help reduce vulnerability to changing market conditions and instability in commodity export earnings. The Conference also recognized the linkage between diversification efforts and market access conditions.

83. The Conference agreed on the need for adequate financial resources to implement diversification programmes, including processing, marketing and distribution activities.

84. Such medium-term and long-term financing should be complemented with technical assistance for the implementation of these programmes as well as for feasibility studies and infrastructural developments.

85. The Conference agreed that UNCTAD should assist in diversification as well as processing, marketing and distribution programmes, including the improvement of information flows to aid investment decisions, and technical co-operation projects and programmes, particularly for human resources development. It also agreed that the Working Party on Processing, Marketing and Distribution, including Transportation, of the Committee on Commodities, should continue to meet to pursue its work in the light of the orientations described above. Full support should be given to the International Trade Centre UNCTAD/GATT in the areas of market research, market development and promotion including training in the commodities field.

---

[9] See *Official Records of the Trade and Development Board, Thirty-second Session, Supplement No. 4* (TD/B/1085), annex I.

[10] United Nations publication, Sales No. E.81.II.D.8 and corrigendum.

4. Access to markets

86. The Conference noted that the Uruguay Round is an important opportunity to strengthen the multilateral trading system, to halt and reverse protectionism, to remove distortions to trade and thus to make, *inter alia*, a significant contribution to improve access to markets.

87. Achievement of these objectives will be important for improving the conditions for trade in commodities. In this respect, the Uruguay Round has defined objectives for negotiations in the areas of tropical products, natural resource-based products and agriculture. These objectives, and the general principles governing the negotiations as contained in part I, section B, paragraphs (i) to (vii), of the Ministerial Declaration on the Uruguay Round,[11] were underscored by the Conference.

88. The Conference also emphasized that greater market transparency is a factor in improving access to markets.

89. It was noted that technical assistance referred to in section C, subparagraph 105 (9) below, would also extend to the sectors referred to above. It was agreed that the UNCTAD secretariat should continue, under its existing mandates, to undertake analyses of issues relating to access to markets as they affect commodities.

5. Compensatory financing

90. The Conference recognized that commodity-related shortfalls in export earnings of developing countries were an important obstacle to their development efforts.

91. The need for strengthening and improving the existing Compensatory Financing Facility of IMF so as to facilitate increased drawings and broaden its coverage on concessional terms and more favourable conditions and to overcome its operational difficulties and rigidities, including access limitations, was stressed by developing countries. They also stressed the need for an additional facility because of the limited scope of the existing facilities. Therefore, in their view, the ongoing programme of work in UNCTAD aimed at establishing an additional facility to compensate developing countries for their shortfalls in commodity export earnings should be positively concluded. They recognized the value of existing arrangements in this field, such as the ACP-EEC Stabex,[12] and highlighted the desirability of other industrialized countries introducing other schemes.

92. The developed market-economy countries referred to the current review of the IMF-CFF, whose outcome was awaited. The view was expressed concerning the necessity of reconciling the short-term impact of compensatory financing with the long-term re-

quirements of commodity sectors in the context of overall development. Among them, the view was also expressed that export earnings shortfalls are essentially a short-term balance-of-payments issue, outside UNCTAD's operational mandate. Where balance-of-payments problems occur, they should be dealt with *in toto*, rather than on a commodity-specific basis through the existing competent international organizations. This approach minimizes distortive effects caused by addressing the symptoms of export earnings instability rather than their causes. On the other hand, others among them expressed the view that compensatory financing could be commodity-related and contribute to diversification in the area of commodities.

93. The Intergovernmental Group of Experts on the Compensatory Financing of Export Earnings Shortfalls is requested to take into account the implications of export earnings shortfalls and, when making its recommendations, to consider the various institutional options, bearing in mind the balance-of-payments and/or commodity-related approaches.

6. Synthetics and substitutes

94. The Conference recognized that this subject could be dealt with in a broader developmental context. It agreed that the programmes or actions should be focused towards improving the competitiveness of natural products with respect to synthetics and substitutes.

95. Technical and financial support should be extended towards this end. In this respect research and development activities, the identification of new end uses, improving the quality of natural products, market promotion and transfer of technologies, were mentioned.

96. The need for greater transparency in the markets of synthetics and substitutes as well as the beneficial effects of trade liberalization of natural products, both in raw and processed forms, were also highlighted.

7. Disposal of non-commercial stocks

97. The Conference underlined that disposal of non-commercial stocks should not disrupt commodity markets and should be done in consultation with producers, and where appropriate, commodity organizations, bearing in mind Conference resolution 155 (VI) of 2 July 1983, paragraph 14, and decision 4 (V) of 17 July 1970,[13] and decision 23 (XI),[14] paragraph 8, of the Committee on Commodities.

98. The Conference took note of the proposal of developing countries for an international code of conduct to halt the prevailing adverse effects on commodity markets. It also noted that guidelines on disposal also exist in GATT and FAO.

99. The Conference agreed that the situation of disposal of non-commercial stocks should be reviewed in the light of UNCTAD's mandates.

[11] GATT, *Basic Instruments and Selected Documents, Thirty-third Supplement* (Sales No. GATT/1987-1), p. 19.

[12] System of stabilization of export earnings established by the first Lomé Convention, concluded between the EEC and 46 ACP States on 28 February 1975, and reinforced by the second ACP-EEC Convention, concluded between the EEC and 58 ACP States on 31 October 1979 (see *Official Journal of the European Communities*, vol. 23, No. L 347 (22 December 1980)).

[13] See *Official Records of the Trade and Development Board, Tenth Session, Supplement No. 3* (TD/B/317), annex I.

[14] See footnote 9.

C. International trade

INTRODUCTION

100. The Conference has carried out extensive discussions on a wide range of international trade issues, as folows: (i) protectionism and structural adjustment, market access and policies affecting trade; (ii) systemic issues of international trade; (iii) enhancement of trade prospects for developing countries: technical assistance; and the Uruguay Round of multilateral trade negotiations; and (iv) trade relations among countries having different economic and social systems.

101. Structural rigidities and resistance to structural change have exacerbated protectionism, including sectors of particular export interest to developing countries. Subsidization of production and exports have resulted in major distortions in the world economy and misallocations of resources. It is generally recognized that expansion of trade has an important role in the process of economic development and there is a strong interrelationship between trade expansion and structural adjustment.

102. The international trading system is under a severe strain. Protectionist pressures and measures have proliferated and tendencies towards managed trade have intensified. International trade has been affected by restrictive trade policies and restrictive business practices. This is undermining the functioning of the international trading system and retarding the process of structural adjustment. These factors are having a serious impact on trade and particularly on the trade and development of developing countries.

103. Although the generalized system of preferences has played an important role in expanding the exports by developing countries, its objectives are not fully achieved.

104. The successful conclusion, within the agreed time-frame of the Uruguay Round of multilateral trade negotiations, is important for bringing about further liberalization and expansion in trade, for creating an improved multilateral framework for trade and for strengthening the effectiveness of GATT.

105. In this context the Conference agreed that:

(1) The commitments to halt and reverse protectionism, including those in Conference resolutions 159 (VI) of 2 July 1983, 96 (IV) of 31 May 1976, and 131 (V) of 3 June 1979, should be fully implemented, in particular taking into account the export interests of developing countries.

(2) The commitments relating to structural adjustment, in particular those contained in resolutions 96 (IV), 131 (V) and 159 (VI), should be fully implemented.

(3) The annual review of protectionism and structural adjustment in the Trade and Development Board should continue under the existing mandate and should be improved to have a wider coverage taking into account the specific interests of developing countries. The review should include analysis of the principal elements and effects of structural adjustment policies, including trade policies, and of the various policy options, keeping in mind the importance of resources and technology

in the process of development and national development priorities and objectives. In this context, the importance of a favourable international economic environment and relevance of domestic policies is recognized, in particular those policies which have a large influence on the world economy.

(4) Governments should consider, as part of their fight against protectionism, as appropriate, the establishment of transparent mechanisms at the national level to evaluate protectionist measures sought by firms/sectors, and the implications of such measures for the domestic economy as a whole and their effects on the export interests of developing countries.

(5) Preference-giving countries should continue to improve their autonomous GSP schemes, *inter alia*, through the expansion of product coverage and in strict compliance with multilaterally agreed principles relating to their generalized, non-discriminatory and non-reciprocal character. The Special Committee on Preferences should consider a study to be prepared by the secretariat in this regard.

(6) The Secretary-General of UNCTAD is requested to continue and strengthen the technical assistance programmes in the field of the GSP and is also requested to publish detailed information on the technical assistance programme. UNDP is invited to consider favourably the requests for providing adequate financial resources for this purpose.

(7) The Uruguay Round of multilateral trade negotiations has a critical role in the international trading system. The programme of negotiations covers a range of important subjects, whose balanced outcome should in the end develop a more open, viable and durable multilateral trading system and thereby contribute to promoting growth and development. The success of the multilateral trade negotiations will be greatly facilitated by a supportive international economic environment which should ensure mutually reinforcing linkages between trade, money, finance and development. The commitments on "standstill" and "rollback" made in the Uruguay Round should be fully respected and implemented.

(8) The Trade and Development Board should follow closely developments and issues in the Uruguay Round of particular concern to the developing countries.

(9) The Secretary-General of UNCTAD is requested to provide technical assistance to developing countries, on request, in connection with the Uruguay Round of multilateral trade negotiations so as to facilitate their effective participation in these negotiations. UNCTAD should render technical support which might be required in the negotiations. In doing so, it should consult with other relevant international organizations if necessary. UNDP is invited to consider favourably the requests for the provision of adequate financial resources to UNCTAD and to individual countries for this purpose.

(10) There should be improvement in the access to markets, particularly for the products of export interest to the developing countries, including manufactures and semi-manufactures. Fullest liberalization of trade in tropical products and in natural resource-based products should be aimed at. Escalation of tariff and non-

tariff barriers, particularly affecting the products of export interest to the developing countries should be reduced or eliminated.

(11) The work undertaken in the Uruguay Round of multilateral trade negotiations in this context is expected to make a significant contribution to improve the access to markets.

(12) The further liberalization of trade is an important objective for the trade in textiles and clothing. Modalities should be formulated which would permit the eventual integration of this sector into GATT on the basis of strengthened GATT rules and disciplines. The work undertaken in the Uruguay Round of multilateral trade negotiations in this context is expected to make a significant contribution.

(13) The removal of discriminatory restraints on exports particularly from developing countries is essential for liberalization.

(14) There is an urgent need to bring more discipline and predictability to world agricultural trade by correcting and preventing restrictions and distortions, including those related to structural surpluses, so as to reduce the uncertainty, imbalances and instability in world agricultural markets. Negotiations in the Uruguay Round shall aim to achieve greater liberalization of trade in agriculture and bring all measures affecting import access and export competition under strengthened and more operationally effective GATT rules and disciplines, taking into account the general principles governing the negotiations, as contained in part I, section B, paragraphs (i) to (vii) of the Ministerial Declaration on the Uruguay Round,[15] by:

(i) Improving market access through, *inter alia*, the reduction of import barriers;

(ii) Improving the competitive environment by increasing discipline on the use of all direct and indirect subsidies and other measures affecting directly or indirectly agricultural trade, including the phased reduction of their negative effects and dealing with their causes;

(iii) Minimizing the adverse effects that sanitary and phytosanitary regulations and barriers can have on trade in agriculture, taking into account the relevant international agreements.

(15) Special problems of the least developed countries should be kept in view while undertaking measures to improve market access.

(16) Problems specific to the land-locked and island developing countries should be kept in view while undertaking these measures.

(17) Observance of multilaterally agreed commitments with respect to trade in goods should not be made conditional on receiving concessions in other areas.

(18) In respect of restrictive business practices the ongoing work in UNCTAD should continue and be strengthened, particularly with a view to ensuring transparency and to defining consultations procedures. The UNCTAD secretariat should continue its technical

assistance programme in the field of restrictive business practices.

(19) UNCTAD should continue its useful work in the field of services under its existing mandate, as contained in Conference resolution 159 (VI) and Board decision 309 (XXX) of 29 March 1985. From the point of view of developing countries and in the context of overall development objectives, the Secretary-General of UNCTAD is requested:

(i) To analyse the implications of the issues raised in the context of trade in services;

(ii) To explore appropriate problematics for trade in services, keeping in view the technological changes in the field of services.

(20) UNCTAD is requested to continue its programmes of technical assistance to developing countries in the field of services. UNDP is invited to consider favourably the requests for the provision of adequate financial resources for this purpose.

(21) While providing technical assistance to developing countries, special attention should be paid to the needs of the least developed countries.

(22) The UNCTAD secretariat is requested to continue keeping member States informed on the progress and activities of the technical assistance projects and to prepare a detailed report on them annually in order to promote transparency.

(23) UNCTAD takes note that the Trade and Development Board has been requested to review and study in depth developments in the international trading system. In doing so, it could, respecting the principles of most-favoured-nation treatment and non-discrimination, make recommendations on principles and policies related to international trade, and make proposals as to the strengthening and improvement of the trading system with a view to giving it a more universal and dynamic character, as well as to making it more responsive to the needs of developing countries and supportive of accelerated economic growth and development, particularly that of developing countries.

(24) A stable and supportive international economic environment is essential for the smooth functioning of the international trading system, as the interrelationship between trade policies and other economic policies affecting growth and development is recognized. In this regard the policies in the areas of monetary and financial matters, technology, and in other relevant areas should be compatible and consonant with the international trading system.

(25) The UNCTAD secretariat should carry out further analytical work on developments in trade relations between countries having different economic and social systems, in particular East-South trade. This further work should be based on better and more transparent statistics and pay due regard to the product structure, geographical coverage and the respective roles played in this trade by various developing countries.

(26) The Trade and Development Board is requested, further to Conference resolutions 15 (II) of 25 March 1968, 53 (III) of 19 May 1972 and 95 (IV) of 31 May 1976, to examine the possibility of elaborating a programme for the further promotion of trade and

---

[15] See footnote 11.

economic co-operation among countries having different economic and social systems, in particular East-South trade. In so doing, the Board should bear in mind the work done on the informal text annexed to Conference decision 145 (VI) of 2 July 1983, and the ideas contained in TD/B/1104/Rev.1.[16]

(27) The Secretary-General of UNCTAD is requested to carry out the necessary consultations with Governments on further strengthening of trade relations among countries having different economic and social systems, in particular East-South trade.

(28) The socialist countries of Eastern Europe are requested: to contribute further to the efforts of the developing countries to diversify and intensify their economic relations towards attaining growth in the socialist countries' imports from developing countries including in manufactures and semi-manufactures; to make further improvements in their GSP schemes; to ensure the best possible terms and conditions of credits to the developing countries; to continue to provide and develop their economic assistance; to ensure, when financing and executing developing countries' projects, that due consideration be given to such flexible and efficient modalities as would promote viable economic and technical co-operation; to pay special attention to the specific needs and requirements of the least developed countries.

(29) Member States and the UNCTAD secretariat are invited, in co-operation with UNDP, as appropriate, to continue and further develop the necessary support for the implementation of projects and programmes of technical assistance to the developing countries, with particular reference to the needs of the least developed ones, in their trade and economic co-operation with the socialist countries of Eastern Europe.

D. Problems of the least developed countries, bearing in mind the Substantial New Programme of Action for the 1980s for the Least Developed Countries

INTRODUCTION

Some basic features of the general economic situation and trends in relation to least developed countries

106. The least developed countries are the poorest countries in the world. Their average GDP per capita is slightly higher than $200, which is less than one quarter of that of the developing countries as a whole and only about 3 per cent of that of the developed countries, in spite of relatively high growth in some least developed countries in the past few years. A high proportion of the population of the least developed countries lives in conditions of mere subsistence and often below it.

107. At the mid-term review of the Substantial New Programme of Action in 1985[17] it was noted with serious concern that since the adoption in 1981 of the Substantial New Programme of Action there had been a significant deterioration in the overall socio-economic situation of the least developed countries, the causes of which were external, domestic and environmental. GDP per capita declined from $220 in 1980 to slightly more than $200 in 1985. The share of least developed countries in the world economy and trade has been declining. The trends for the coming years, according to present assumptions, are also generally unfavourable. The continuous monitoring of the implementation of the Substantial New Programme of Action to date shows that, despite certain improvements in the situation of some least developed countries since 1985, negative economic and other factors have persisted.

108. Although least developed countries face widely differing circumstances and needs in terms of size, population, economic and social structure, literacy rate, etc., they generally have for a long time been lagging behind in growth and development compared with other countries and many of them seem to have entered a vicious circle of constraints, poverty and population explosion, with stagnation or even backsliding as a result.

109. Structural handicaps make the least developed countries particularly vulnerable to the external economic environment. On the whole this environment has been unfavourable to the least developed countries over the last few years. Of particular concern have been: (i) the historically low level of commodity prices which, *inter alia*, increased the serious debt-servicing problems of least developed countries; (ii) the mounting debt-to-GDP ratio; and (iii) insufficient external financial flows. Adverse weather conditions and natural calamities have in some cases further contributed to reducing output and already very low living standards. Many of these countries initiated structural adjustment programmes, policy changes or took other measures designed to make their economies more efficient in a manner consistent with their own national conditions and priorities. All these measures have begun to have positive effects in some of these countries. Complementary international support for these efforts, in the form of both multilateral and bilateral ODA, has resumed a rising trend, but there is a continuing need for additional efforts. Those developed countries which have not fully participated in efforts to assist the least developed countries should do so.

110. There was a consensus on the need for full and expeditious implementation of the Substantial New Programme of Action and of the recommendations of the mid-term review as adopted.[18] Some problems facing the least developed countries call for further study. In the light of the general background documents and discussions describing the serious situation of the least developed countries and its own fruitful discussion, the Conference reached the following conclusions aiming at an improvement of the economic and social conditions in the least developed countries.

[16] Note by the UNCTAD secretariat entitled "Objectives, guidelines and elements of a programme for further promotion of trade and economic co-operation among countries having different economic and social systems".

[17] For the report of the Intergovernmental Group on the Least Developed Countries on the mid-term review, see *Official Records of the Trade and Development Board, Thirty-second Session, Annexes,*

agenda item 7, document TD/B/1078. For the conclusions and recommendations submitted by the Intergovernmental Group, see part one of the report.

[18] *Idem.*

1. NATIONAL EFFORTS

111. It was reaffirmed that the least developed countries will continue to have primary responsibility for their overall development.

112. Many least developed countries have made efforts to improve the effectiveness of domestic resource mobilization and use, by strengthening economic and financial management. These efforts should be actively pursued.

113. Least developed countries should continue to implement adjustment programmes or take such other measures as are necessary in accordance with their long-term national social and economic objectives. In particular it appears imperative, taking due account of individual characteristics of each least developed country:

(*a*) To accelerate agricultural development and enhance food security;

(*b*) To design structural adjustment and diversification programmes or other more specific measures suited to each country's particular social and economic condition;

(*c*) To endeavour to mobilize fully the human resources through education and training in required skills;

(*d*) To strengthen the role of women in the development process;

(*e*) To take appropriate measures to encourage external financial flows;

(*f*) To promote appropriate economic incentive systems;

(*g*) To develop institutional arrangements to improve the efficiency of the public sector and encourage indigenous entrepreneurship;

(*h*) To give priority to the advancement of the poorest in the development policy and adopt measures to protect the most vulnerable parts of the population during adjustment;

(*i*) To take account of environmental issues;

(*j*) To develop and strengthen social and economic planning capability.

2. INTERNATIONAL EFFORTS

(a) *Financial and technical assistance*

114. In order to complement national efforts, international programmes of financial and technical assistance as well as other supportive measures from all donors are fundamental.

115. For aid to make a sustained contribution to development, it has to be geared to the support of overall policy objectives of growth-oriented programmes. At the same time, polices in least developed countries encouraging financial flows and enhancing aid effectiveness are desirable.

116. For the purpose of full and effective implementation of the Substantial New Programme of Action, donors are urged to enlarge susbstantially financial assistance to the least developed countries in a volume and on terms which correspond to their immediate and long-term development needs. The volume and forms of aid should be supportive of and commensurate with the growing requirements of the adjustment programmes and broader development efforts of the least developed countries.

117. ODA will continue to play a decisive role in least developed countries. In compliance with the Substantial New Programme of Action and the mid-term review conclusions as adopted, developed countries are requested to attain the internationally agreed targets of 0.7 per cent of GNP for total ODA and of 0.15 per cent of GNP for ODA to least developed countries or doubling their ODA to these countries as soon as possible. In this connection, the recommendations of the IMF/World Bank Development Committee's Task Force on Concessional Flows were recalled.

118. Multilateral development institutions should be strengthened by endowing them with adequate resources and instruments to fulfil their tasks. Members of the World Bank are invited to support an early general increase of its capital as needed to support quality lending. Donors should meet expeditiously their commitments to the Eighth Replenishment of IDA, keeping in view the critical importance of IDA for the least developed countries. Regional development banks and funds also need to be strengthened, and the adequacy of their capital and lending programmes should be kept under review.

119. The overall volume of multilateral assistance to the least developed countries through such channels as IDA, IFAD, regional development banks and their funds, UNDP, the special measures fund for the least developed countries, the United Nations Capital Development Fund, UNV, etc., should be adequate to meet the substantially increased development needs of the least developed countries; donors, including those who have not to date participated in these institutions, should channel a substantial part of their aid through these institutions and agencies. Relevant international institutions should continue their concerted efforts to increase the share of concessional assistance to least developed countries.

120. The proposal by the Managing Director of IMF for a significant increase in the resources of the Structural Adjustment Facility over the three years from 1 January 1988 is welcomed by those countries which are also members of IMF. It is expected that the realization of this increase would result in substantial benefits to the least developed countries. Discussions on this proposal ought to be concluded by the end of 1987. In this respect, those countries also welcome closer co-operation between the World Bank and IMF and note the increasing bilateral co-financing with the World Bank.

121. IMF is invited to continue to keep under review the principles on which its conditionality rests, in such a way as to reflect the peculiar social, economic and political priorities of the least developed countries. Relevant international institutions should continue their concerted efforts for the benefit of the least developed countries.

122. The international community should continue to support the efforts of least developed countries to increase their food production and improve distribution, and to provide financial and technical assistance for

research, exploration and development of energy resources; and should assist in maximizing capacity utilization of their productive economic units.

123. Donors should continue to provide emergency assistance and to contribute to the financing of costs involved in the management of relief operations in African and other least developed countries affected by food shortages and other emergencies.

(b) *Aid modalities*

124. Donor and recipient countries should together seek to ensure that aid is fully supportive of development efforts and that aid effectiveness is strengthened, *inter alia*, through improved co-ordination. In this regard, central responsibility for aid co-ordination lies with each recipient Government.

125. The international financial institutions and concerned donors should provide timely assistance to support the efforts of the least developed countries in implementing the required policy changes, taking into account the need to mitigate the possible adverse effects of such adjustment programmes, including the effects on the most vulnerable groups of the population, as well as the period required for adjustment with growth. The increasing co-operation between IMF, the World Bank and other multilateral financial institutions is welcomed, but should not lead to cross-conditionality.

126. Further steps should be taken by donors, in particular those who have not yet done so, to provide bilateral ODA to the least developed countries essentially in the form of grants and to provide loans on highly concessional terms.

127. Donors are urged to take the necessary steps to ensure that ODA loans and grants to least developed countries are untied to the maximum extent possible.

128. Donors and least developed countries should make efforts to minimize the time-lag between aid commitment and disbursement. To this end, advance payments should be made whenever appropriate. In this regard, donors were urged to ensure greater predictability of disbursement.

129. It is recommended that donors should further increase, where appropriate, their participation in local and recurrent cost financing. Adequate provisions should also be made for allowing a progressive take-over of recurrent costs by least developed countries.

130. Donors are recommended particularly to support domestic adjustment measures of least developed countries, to provide aid in more flexible forms, in particular balance-of-payments support, and at a sectoral level for rehabilitation and improved maintenance, as well as for longer-term development objectives.

131. Technical assistance should be provided to strengthen the capacities of least developed countries to establish and implement their own policies and programmes and to address the basic structural rigidities of their economies. There is scope for joint international action in the area of technical assistance in support of improved management capacity and infrastructures.

132. Efforts should be made to harmonize and simplify existing aid procedures.

133. The positive contribution of the non-governmental organizations to the development of least developed countries, as well as in providing valuable disaster relief, was recognized. The Governments of least developed countries and donors were called upon to encourage active participation of the local population, both women and men, through non-governmental entities. The non-governmental organizations were invited to comply with national policies and legislation of the host countries while preserving their character and to contribute to the development priorities of the least developed countries, co-operating with appropriate authorities and organizations in order to implement effective development programmes. The non-governmental organizations of the donor countries were invited to reinforce their role in consciousness-raising in their countries of origin and in mobilizing increased private and public resources for the benefit of the least developed countries.

(c) *Debt problems of the least developed countries*

134. The debt and debt-servicing situation of the least developed countries has remained serious and in many cases worsened in past years. The ratios of debt to GDP and of debt service to exports have increased in the case of some least developed countries to unmanageable levels. Major causes include the depressed export earnings, which have impaired the debt-servicing capacity of the least developed countries, including those which are heavily dependent on commodities. Their debt-servicing burden constitutes for many of them a hindrance to their development process. Problems of the least developed countries' debt to the multilateral financial institutions were also recognized.

135. The Conference notes with satisfaction that a number of donor countries have responded favourably to section A of Trade and Development Board resolution 165 (S-IX) of 11 March 1978 by cancellation of ODA debt or other equivalent measures, and firmly invites other donors, which have not yet done so, to implement fully commitments undertaken in purusuance of the resolution, keeping in mind paragraph 71 of the Substantial New Programme of Action.

136. The debt-servicing burden of the poorest countries, including least developed countries, the majority of which are in sub-Saharan Africa, which are undertaking adjustment efforts, should be eased by longer repayments and grace periods, especially in the Paris Club. Consideration could also be given to the possibility of applying lower interest rates to their existing debts.

137. The Conference further notes that the repayments of debt to the multilateral assistance institutions is one of the elements in the overall debt-service burden of least developed countries. Those institutions should continue to take into account the financial requirements in their lending programmes to the least developed countries.

138. Substantially increased concessional finance, essentially in grant form, is required to enable least developed countries to resume growth so as to cope with their debt problems in the long run. This task should be

pursued both bilaterally and by international financial institutions.

139. Measures should be taken, particularly by debtor countries, to facilitate non-debt-creating capital flows, especially direct investment to least developed countries.

140. Measures to alleviate the debt-servicing burden for the least developed countries should be supplemented and strengthened by technical assistance, as appropriate, as well as by measures in other fields such as trade, commodities, etc.

(d) Country review mechanism

141. The Conference noted the improvements registered in the country review meetings, which are the mechanisms for the periodic review and implementation of the Substantial New Programme of Action. Nevertheless, the need for a further strengthening and improvement in order to make them more effective was recognized. These reviews should take place at appropriate intervals at the initiative of the interested least developed countries, which may seek assistance from the lead agency for its aid group in organizing them. UNDP and the World Bank, as the lead agencies, should expand their technical assistance to the least developed countries to enable them to prepare appropriately for these meetings. Donor countries should be represented at an adequately high level. The meetings should facilitate an increased and improved flow of assistance through a better dialogue and co-ordination between least developed countries and their development partners. The Secretary-General of UNCTAD is requested to continue to prepare, on a regular basis, reports on the situation in least developed countries as well as the implementation of the Substantial New Programme of Action.

(e) Land-locked and island developing countries among the least developed countries

142. In line with section B-VIII of the mid-term global review of progress towards the implementation of the Substantial New Programme of Action for the 1980s for the Least Developed Countries:[19]

(a) Transit countries should intensify co-operation with the land-locked countries among the least developed countries to alleviaite the transit problems;

(b) Concerned donors, while providing technical and financial assistance to land-locked and island countries among the least developed countries, should particularly focus on capital input in infrastructural development;

(c) International bodies, in particular UNDP and the United Nations regional commissions, should continue to support those least developed countries with measures required to alleviate their specific transit-transport and communications problems.

(f) Commodities/international trade

143. The least developed countries have greatly suffered from vulnerability to declines in the prices of their

---
[19] See footnote 17.

basic commodity exports. Being commodity-dependent countries, least developed countries have felt the most severe impact of the commodity price situation. In this context, depending on the nature and intensity of specific country and commodity circumstances, the least developed countries should endeavour to promote economically appropriate diversification of their economic structures, both vertically and horizontally.

144. The international community should support these efforts through improved co-operation in the commodities sector aiming at, *inter alia*, better market transparency, increased market access and reduced trade distortions, recognizing the need for a better functioning of commodity markets and the desirability of achieving more stable and more predictable conditions in commodity trade. Sustained efforts should be made to provide aid for structural measures, and technical assistance in support of improved management capacity and infrastructure.

145. Steps should be taken to further develop the trade relations with least developed countries and, in this context, the importance for certain countries of intergovernmental long-term agreements was underlined.

146. The special needs of the least developed countries should be taken into account when implementing relevant aspects of the Integrated Programme for Commodities.

(i) Compensatory financing

147. The commodity-related shortfalls in export earnings of least developed countries are an important obstacle to their development efforts. Therefore, there was a recognition that the compensatory finance questions deserve full consideration, in particular as they relate to the least developed countries.

(ii) Access to markets

148. It is recognized that beneficial action is already undertaken by developed countries to provide market access for the products of least developed countries in the context of their GSP schemes. All other developed countries which have not yet done so should make similar efforts. Steps should be taken by developed countries to further improve GSP or most-favoured-nation treatment for products of particular interest to least developed countries and to eliminate or reduce quantitative restrictions and other non-tariff measures affecting such products. Moreover, in the framework of the multilateral trading system the promotion of South-South trade through the GSTP, particularly for the benefit of the least developed countries, and through regional integration could make an important contribution to the expansion of trade among developing countries. Progress towards promotion of subregional trade should be enhanced through activities of technical and economic co-operation among developing countries. All other international trade flows should also be further developed.

149. As mentioned in part I, section B, paragraph (vii), of the Ministerial Declaration on the Uruguay Round adopted in September 1986, "special attention shall be given to the particular situation and problems of the least developed countries and to the need to en-

courage positive measures to facilitate expansion of their trading opportunities. Expeditious implementation of the relevant provisions of the 1982 Ministerial Declaration concerning the least developed countries shall also be given appropriate attention."[20]

150. Least developed countries are invited to utilize fully the opportunities which are already available in the field of market access, in particular under GSP schemes. Increased technical assistance should be given to the least developed countries, *inter alia*, through the International Trade Centre UNCTAD/GATT and UNCTAD, for promotion of trade and expansion of production facilities for export and to help improve their capacity to benefit from existing preferential arrangements in favour of developing countries.

151. Developed countries and international organizations should also assist the least developed countries to create economically appropriate industries for on-the-spot processing of raw materials and food products, and the development of integrated projects for the expansion of exports and to provide adequate resources to overcome supply bottlenecks.

152. The developed countries in a position to do so should assist the least developed countries in entering into long-term arrangements for exports, as called for in the Substantial New Programme of Action.

(g) *Global review and appraisal of the implementation of the Substantial New Programme of Action*

153. The Conference welcomes the generous offer made by France and, in line with General Assembly resolution 40/205 of 17 December 1985, the Conference recommends that a United Nations conference at a high level on the least developed countries should be convened in 1990 to appraise and review the implementation of the Substantial New Programme of Action for the 1980s for the Least Developed Countries.

---

[20] See footnote 11.

III. Orientations for the future

154. The policies and measures delineated by the Conference in the different areas of its agenda, being interrelated, should be pursued in such a manner as to make their effects mutually reinforcing. The appropriate international forums should keep under review the interrelationships among these policies and measures, together with their implementation and the need to adapt and strengthen them in the light of changing circumstances. As a universal forum with a focus on trade and development, which also encompasses the interlinkages of a wide range of issues, UNCTAD can make a significant contribution to this process.

155. The constructive dialogue which took place at the seventh session of the Conference has been an important step in heightening awareness and sharpening perceptions of problems arising from the complex interactions among national policies adopted by Governments, internationally accepted rules and disciplines, and the operation of markets. This dialogue should be continued in the intergovernmental machinery of UNCTAD so as to enhance these perceptions and thus assist in providing fresh impetus to policy formulation and to multilateral co-operation for development. With this in mind, the Trade and Development Board should consider how best to strengthen its regular review of the interdependence of economic issues.

156. The Final Act contains several explicit and implicit orientations for the future work of the UNCTAD secretariat, including its activities of research, policy analysis, conceptual innovation and technical co-operation. These orientations will be acted upon in the coming months by the Secretary-General of UNCTAD, in the first instance in the context of the UNCTAD submission for the 1988-1989 programme budget of the United Nations, and by the relevant intergovernmental bodies of UNCTAD.

157. The Conference agreed that multilateral economic co-operation should be a continuing endeavour from which important benefits could be expected for the development process and for the world economy as a whole. Acknowledging this imperative, member States pledge themselves to a reinvigorated effort to strengthen multilateral co-operation to promote and give effect to policies aimed at revitalizing development, growth and international trade, and to enhance the effectiveness of UNCTAD as an important instrument of international economic co-operation.

2. Resolutions adopted by the Conference

CREDENTIALS OF REPRESENTATIVES TO THE CONFERENCE
(*Agenda item 5*)

RESOLUTION

168 (VII). Credentials of representatives to the seventh session of the Conference[1]

The United Nations Conference on Trade and Development

Approves the report of the Credentials Committee.

220th plenary meeting
3 August 1987

---

[1] For statements, see part three below, paragraphs 10-20 and 22.

OTHER BUSINESS
(*Agenda item 9*)

RESOLUTION

169 (VII). Economic situation in the occupied Palestinian territories[2]

The United Nations Conference on Trade and Development,

Recalling Conference resolution 109 (V) of 1 June 1979,

Recalling also resolution 239 (XXIII) of the Trade and Development Board of 9 October 1981,

Recalling further Conference resolution 146 (VI) of 2 July 1983,

---

[2] The Conference adopted this resolution by a roll-call vote of 80 to 2, with 32 abstentions. Malta did not participate in the vote. The voting was as follows:

In favour: Afghanistan, Algeria, Argentina, Bahrain, Bangladesh, Benin, Bhutan, Bolivia, Botswana, Brazil, Bulgaria, Burma, Burundi, Byelorussian Soviet Socialist Republic, China, Colombia, Comoros, Cuba, Cyprus, Czechoslovakia, Democratic Kampuchea, Democratic People's Republic of Korea, Democratic Yemen, Ecuador, Egypt, Ethiopia, Gabon, German Democratic Republic, Ghana, Hungary, India, Indonesia, Iran (Islamic Republic of), Iraq, Jamaica, Jordan, Kenya, Kuwait, Lebanon, Libyan Arab Jamahiriya, Madagascar, Malaysia, Mexico, Mongolia, Morocco, Mozambique, Nepal, Nicaragua, Niger, Nigeria, Oman, Pakistan, Philippines, Poland, Qatar, Republic of Korea, Romania, Rwanda, Saudi Arabia, Senegal, Singapore, Somalia, Sri Lanka, Sudan, Syrian Arab Republic, Thailand, Togo, Trinidad and Tobago, Tunisia, Turkey, Ukrainian Soviet Socialist Republic, Union of Soviet Socialist Republics, United Arab Emirates, United Republic of Tanzania, Venezuela, Viet Nam, Yemen, Yugoslavia, Zaire, Zimbabwe.

Against: Israel, United States of America.

Abstaining: Australia, Austria, Belgium, Cameroon, Canada, Costa Rica, Côte d'Ivoire, Denmark, El Salvador, Finland, France, Germany, Federal Republic of, Greece, Guatemala, Honduras, Ireland, Italy, Japan, Liechtenstein, Luxembourg, Netherlands, New Zealand, Norway, Panama, Paraguay, Peru, Portugal, Spain, Sweden, Switzerland, United Kingdom of Great Britain and Northern Ireland, Uruguay.

For statements, see part two below, paragraphs 60-79 and 81-88.

Mindful of General Assembly resolution 39/223 of 18 December 1984,

Aware of the European Community decision of 27 October 1986 concerning goods and products of the occupied Palestinian territories,

Seriously concerned at the refusal of the Israeli occupation authorities to permit the export of Palestinian goods and products to the European Community market,

Rejecting the Israeli occupation and its restrictions hampering the development of the Palestinian national economy including its trade sector,

1. *Welcomes* the establishment of the Special Economic Unit (Palestinian people) in UNCTAD;

2. *Welcomes also* the European Community decision to give Palestinian goods and products preferential access to its market on the basis of a Palestinian certificate of origin;

3. *Strongly deplores* the obstruction by the Israeli occupation authorities of the implementation of the above-mentioned decision;

4. *Strongly deplores also* the Israeli obstruction of the establishment of a commercial seaport in the occupied Gaza Strip, which would give Palestinian goods and products direct access to external markets;

5. *Recognizes* the need to establish a centre for marketing and exporting Palestinian goods and products, in co-operation with the Palestine Liberation Organization;

6. *Requests* UNCTAD to provide advice on the establishment of the centre referred to above;

7. *Urges* all States to facilitate access of Palestinian goods and products to their markets;

8. *Urges* all States, United Nations bodies, governmental and non-governmental organizations to continue

providing assistance to the Palestinian people, in close co-operation with the Palestine Liberation Organization, to enable them to develop their national economy, including the trade sector, free of occupation;

9. *Calls for* giving UNCTAD staff and experts access to the occupied Palestinian territories;

10. *Requests also* the Secretary-General of UNCTAD to report periodically to the Trade and Development Board and the General Assembly, through the Economic and Social Council, on the progress made in the implementation of the present resolution.

220th plenary meeting
3 August 1987

3. *Other action by the Conference*

COMMODITIES
(*Agenda item 8* (b))

At the 220th (closing) meeting, on 3 August 1987, the Conference adopted the following proposal (TD/L.317):

The United Nations Conference on Trade and Development

Notes the signature and/or ratification, during the Conference, of the Agreement Establishing the Common Fund for Commodities[1] by Bulgaria, Côte d'Ivoire, Peru, and the Union of Soviet Socialist Republics, and the announcements by Costa Rica,

Madagascar, Portugal and Thailand of their intention to deposit their instruments of ratification in the very near future;

Notes also the announcement of the decision by Switzerland "to share in the efforts of the international community with regard to compensatory financing by committing funds for the poorest countries most dependent on commodity export earnings which have suffered from the highest deficits in their commodity exports in Switzerland";

Notes the proposal of the Government of Japan (TD/L.315) to assist in a programme for the purpose of improving the processing of commodities in developing countries.

---

[1] United Nations publication, Sales No. E.81.II.D.8 and corrigendum.

4. *Decisions taken by the Conference*

(a) Periodic review by the Conference of the lists of States contained in the annex to General Assembly resolution 1995 (XIX)[1]

1. In conformity with paragraph 6 of General Assembly resolution 1995 (XIX) of 30 December 1964, which provides that the lists of States contained in the annex to the resolution "shall be reviewed periodically by the Conference in the light of changes in membership of the Conference and other factors", the Conference, at its 201st plenary meeting, on 9 July 1987, reviewed the lists contained in the annex to that resolution, as amended.[2] The Conference approved the inclusion, in the appropriate lists, of the following States which had become members of UNCTAD since the sixth session of the Conference:

In list A: Brunei Darussalam.

In list C: Saint Kitts and Nevis.

2. The lists of States members of UNCTAD given in the annex to General Assembly resolution 1995 (XIX)

have accordingly been amended by this decision. The amended lists are set out below:

A

Afghanistan	Fiji
Algeria	Gabon
Angola	Gambia
Bahrain	Ghana
Bangladesh	Guinea
Benin	Guinea-Bissau
Bhutan	India
Botswana	Indonesia
Brunei Darussalam	Iran (Islamic Republic of)
Burma	Iraq
Burundi	Israel
Cape Verde	Jordan
Central African Republic	Kenya
Chad	Kuwait
China	Lao People's Democratic
Comoros	Republic
Congo	Lebanon
Côte d'Ivoire	Lesotho
Democratic Kampuchea	Liberia
Democratic People's Republic	Libyan Arab Jamahiriya
of Korea	Madagascar
Democratic Yemen	Malawi
Djibouti	Malaysia
Egypt	Maldives
Equatorial Guinea	Mali
Ethiopia	Mauritania

---

[1] See part three below, paragraph 38.

[2] Paragraph 1 of General Assembly resolution 1995 (XIX) provides that "the members of the United Nations Conference on Trade and Development shall be those States which are Members of the United Nations or members of the specialized agencies or of the International Atomic Energy Agency".

Mauritius
Mongolia
Morocco
Mozambique
Namibia
Nepal
Niger
Nigeria
Oman
Pakistan
Papua New Guinea
Philippines
Qatar
Republic of Korea
Rwanda
Samoa
Sao Tome and Principe
Saudi Arabia
Senegal
Seychelles
Sierra Leone
Singapore
Solomon Islands

Somalia
South Africa
Sri Lanka
Sudan
Swaziland
Syrian Arab Republic
Thailand
Togo
Tonga
Tunisia
Uganda
United Arab Emirates
United Republic of Cameroon
United Republic of Tanzania
Upper Volta
Vanuatu
Viet Nam
Yemen
Yugoslavia
Zaire
Zambia
Zimbabwe

Brazil
Chile
Colombia
Costa Rica
Cuba
Dominica
Dominican Republic
Ecuador
El Salvador
Grenada
Guatemala
Guyana
Haiti
Honduras

Jamaica
Mexico
Nicaragua
Panama
Paraguay
Peru
Saint Kitts and Nevis
Saint Lucia
Saint Vincent and the
  Grenadines
Suriname
Trinidad and Tobago
Uruguay
Venezuela

D

Albania
Bulgaria
Byelorussian Soviet Socialist
  Republic
Czechoslovakia
German Democratic Republic
Hungary

Poland
Romania
Ukrainian Soviet Socialist
  Republic
Union of Soviet Socialist
  Republics

B

Australia
Austria
Belgium
Canada
Cyprus
Denmark
Finland
France
Germany, Federal Republic of
Greece
Holy See
Iceland
Ireland
Italy
Japan
Liechtenstein

Luxembourg
Malta
Monaco
Netherlands
New Zealand
Norway
Portugal
San Marino
Spain
Sweden
Switzerland
Turkey
United Kingdom of Great Britain
  and Northern Ireland
United States of America

(b) Designation of intergovernmental bodies for the purposes of rule 80 of the rules of procedure of the Conference and rule 78 of the rules of procedure of the Trade and Development Board[3]

At its 201st plenary meeting, on 9 July 1987, the Conference decided to designate the undermentioned intergovernmental bodies for the purpose of participation in its proceedings under rule 80 of its rules of procedure and in the deliberations of the Board under rule 78 of the rules of procedure of the Board:

International Tropical Timber Organization;
International Textiles and Clothing Bureau.

C

Antigua and Barbuda
Argentina
Bahamas

Barbados
Belize
Bolivia

---

[3] See part three below, paragraph 39.

(c) Calendar of meetings for the remainder of 1987[4]

At its 220th plenary meeting, on 3 August 1987, the Conference adopted the following calendar of meetings for the remainder of 1987.

CALENDAR OF UNCTAD MEETINGS FOR THE REMAINDER OF 1987[5]

	Date
Fourth Meeting of Governmental Experts on the Reverse Transfer of Technology*	31 August-9 September
United Nations Sugar Conference, 1987[6]	10-11 September
Working Party on the Medium-term Plan and the Programme Budget, thirteenth session (second part)	14-17 September
Intergovernmental Group of Experts on the Compensatory Financing of Export Earnings Shortfalls,* second session	14-25 September

---

[4] See part three below, paragraph 40.

[5] Meetings marked with an asterisk are deductible from the provision for "Working parties, study groups and expert groups". Unless otherwise indicated, all meetings will be held in Geneva. All meetings listed are subject to a written notification, which is normally dispatched six weeks before the opening date.

[6] To be held at the headquarters of the International Sugar Organization in London.

Date

Ad hoc Intergovernmental Group of Senior Officials on Co-operation among Developing Countries in the area of Shipping, Ports and Multimodal Transport*	21-25 September
Trade and Development Board, thirty-fourth session, first part	5-16 October
Intergovernmental Group of Experts on Iron Ore, second session.........................	2-6 November
Committee on Tungsten, nineteenth session	9-13 November
Intergovernmental Group of Experts on Restrictive Business Practices, sixth session...	11-20 November
Preparatory Meeting on Copper..	16-20 November
Working Group on Rules of Origin, eleventh session[7]...	23-27 November
Joint UNCTAD/IMO Intergovernmental Group of Experts on Maritime Liens and Mortgages and related subjects, third session[8]	30 November-11 December

Meetings for which the dates are undetermined

Duration

Trade and Development Board, sixteenth special session[9] (Board decision 317 (S-XIV))	2 weeks
Working Party on the Medium-term Plan and the Programme Budget, fourteenth session	1 week
Group of Governmental Experts on the Economic, Commercial and Developmental Aspects of the Industrial Property System in the Transfer of Technology to Developing Countries,* second session	1 1/2 weeks
Intergovernmental Group of Experts on Definitions and Methodology employed in the UNCTAD Data Base on Trade Measures,* second session	1 week
Meeting of Representatives of Interested Governments on Bulk Cargo Shipments* (Conference resolution 120 (V), paragraph 5)	1 week
Ad hoc Intergovernmental High-level Group of Experts on the Evolution of the International Monetary System,* second session	1 week
Group of Governmental Experts on the Concepts of the Present Aid and Flow Targets,* fourth session	1 1/2 weeks
Permanent Sub-Committee on Commodities (if required)	1-2 weeks
Permanent Group on Synthetics and Substitutes (if required)	1 week
Second Preparatory Meeting on Bauxite	1 week
Seventh (third part) or Eighth Preparatory Meeting on Copper	1 week
Resumed Sixth Preparatory Meeting on Cotton	1 week
(Preparatory) Meeting on Hard Fibres..	1 week
Third Preparatory Meeting on Manganese..	1 week
Third Preparatory Meeting on Phosphates	1 week
Meeting of Tea-Exporting Countries on Quota Allocation and Minimum Export Standards...	3 days
Fourth Preparatory Meeting on Tea[10]..	1 week
International Nickel Study Group: Inaugural Meeting[11]	1 week

*

*   *

Commodity conferences and other commodity meetings	As required (up to 26 weeks)
Working parties, study groups and expert groups	As required (up to 3 1/2 weeks)

---

[7] To be reviewed in the light of one group's insistence that assurances be provided on an adequate degree of expert representation.

[8] To be held at, and serviced by, UNCTAD, at Geneva, using the services assigned to the Working Group on Shipping Legislation.

[9] To decide on requisite follow-up action in respect of the Intergovernmental Group of Experts on the Compensatory Financing of Export Earnings Shortfalls, including the possible convening of a negotiating conference on an additional complementary facility.

[10] Subject to the satisfactory conclusion of the Meeting of Tea-Exporting Countries on Quota Allocation and Minimum Export Standards.

[11] Reimbursable meeting. Listed for information. Consultations are to be held to determine the dates of this meeting.

B. INDEX TO OBSERVATIONS AND RESERVATIONS ON THE FINAL ACT OF UNCTAD VII AND ON THE RESOLUTIONS ADOPTED BY THE CONFERENCE

Part Two

SUMMARY OF PROCEEDINGS

1. At the opening meeting of the seventh session (201st plenary meeting), the United Nations Conference on Trade and Development was addressed by the Hon. Bernard T. G. Chidzero, Minister of Finance, Economic Planning and Development of Zimbabwe and President of the Conference (TD/L.284),[1] and by Mr. K. K. S. Dadzie, Secretary-General of UNCTAD (TD/L.276).[2]

2. For its consideration of the substantive items of the agenda, the Conference had before it the report of the Secretary-General of UNCTAD entitled "Reviving multilateral co-operation for growth and development" (TD/329).[3] The report covered the major issues to be considered by the Conference and explored possible results in the different areas covered by agenda item 8.

3. The Conference also had before it the report of the UNCTAD secretariat entitled "Revitalizing development, growth and international trade: assessment and policy options" (TD/328/Rev.1)[4] together with an "Executive Summary" (TD/328/Rev.1/Add.1).[5] The report consisted of five chapters, and their statistical appendices, relevant to the agenda topics, as follows: chapter I, "Development and change: The recent dynamics of global interdependence", comprising sections on the state of development, the external environment and developing countries' trade, and the changing world economy and national policies; chapter II, "Resources for development, including financial, and related monetary questions", comprising sections on development resources in the 1980s and the question of debt, and reviewing issues for the future; chapter III, "Commodities", comprising sections on commodity exports and the development perspective, salient developments in commodity markets, factors affecting the demand and supply for commodities, and other factors affecting commodity prices, prospects for commodities, the state of international action on commodities, and *problématique* and policy options relating to future actions aimed at achieving the objectives of the Integrated Programme for Commodities; chapter IV, "International trade", comprising an overview and sections on protectionism and structural adjustment, the international trading system, services, and trade relations among countries having different economic and social systems; chapter V, "Problems of the least developed countries", bearing in mind the Substantial New Programme of Action for the 1980s for the Least Developed Countries", comprising sections on economic and social trends, national policies in selected areas and international action, together with conclusions and policy options.

4. The *Trade and Development Report, 1987*[6] was available to the Conference and provided an up-to-date view of the world economic situation and, in discussing the impact of technological change on international competitiveness, an additional perspective on relevant economic trends and global structural change.

5. The Havana Declaration (TD/335)[7] was presented to the Conference as representing the position of the Group of 77 on the issues before it, and an assessment and proposals by the Group of 77 relating to the seventh session of the Conference was circulated (TD/330 and Corr.1 and 2).[8] Further documents were submitted by: the Permanent Mission of China, containing a position paper of the People's Republic of China on issues to be considered at the seventh session of the Conference (TD/331);[9] the delegation of Poland, on behalf of the countries of Group D and Mongolia, entitled "Approach of the socialist countries members of Group D and Mongolia to the substantive items of the provisional agenda for the seventh session of the Conference" (TD/333 and Corr.1);[10] and the United Kingdom of Great Britain and Northern Ireland, on behalf of Group B, containing a ministerial communiqué of the Council of the Organisation for Economic Co-operation and Development (TD/334).[11]

6. Communications were also circulated by the delegation of the Union of Soviet Socialist Republics, containing a document entitled "Basic provisions for a fundamental reform of economic management" approved by the June 1987 Plenum of the Central Committee of the Communist Party of the Soviet Union (TD/337), and a description of the economic and technical assistance of the USSR to developing countries (TD/341); by the delegation of the Democratic People's Republic of Korea, containing the Pyongyang Declaration and Plan of Action on South-South Co-operation, adopted by the Extraordinary Ministerial Conference of Non-Aligned Countries on South-South Co-operation (TD/339); by the delegation of Nicaragua, containing a resolution adopted without a vote by the 77th Conference of the Inter-Parliamentary Union, entitled "The

---

[1] See volume II.

[2] *Ibid.*

[3] Reproduced in volume III.

[4] *Idem.*

[5] *Idem.*

[6] United Nations publication, Sales No. E.87.II.D.7.

[7] Final document of the Sixth Ministerial Meeting of the Group of 77, held at Havana, Cuba, from 20 to 25 April 1987; reproduced in annex V below.

[8] Reproduced in annex V below.

[9] Reproduced in annex VI below.

[10] *Idem.*

[11] *Idem.*

Contribution of Parliaments to: the achievement of fair international trade in all its aspects, including trade in agricultural products; the elimination of tariff and other barriers; a better understanding of the socio-economic impact of protectionism, in particular on the developing countries'' (TD/340); by the delegation of the Socialist People's Republic of Albania, containing a declaration with regard to TD/333 (TD/343); and by the delegation of Czechoslovakia entitled ''Economic assistance provided by the Czechoslovak Socialist Republic to developing countries and national liberation movements in 1986'' (TD/345).

I. General debate

(Agenda item 7)

7. The general debate was opened at the 202nd meeting of the Conference, on 10 July 1987, and was concluded at the 219th meeting, on 30 July 1987. In the course of the general debate, the Conference was addressed by heads of delegation of members of the Conference as well as by the executive heads or representatives of a number of regional commissions and specialized agencies of the United Nations and by heads of department of the United Nations Secretariat, representatives of intergovernmental bodies and observers for non-governmental organizations, and by other representatives and observers.[12] At the 209th meeting, on 15 July 1987, the Conference heard a statement by Mr. Gamani Corea, former Secretary-General of UNCTAD (TD/L.298).[13]

------

[12] For the list of statements made, see annex II below.

[13] See volume II.

II. Revitalizing development, growth and international trade, in a more predictable and supportive environment, through multilateral co-operation: assessment of relevant economic trends and of global structural change, and appropriate formulation of policies and measures, addressing key issues in the following interrelated areas:

(*a*) **Resources for development, including financial, and related monetary questions;**

(*b*) **Commodities;**

(*c*) **International trade;**

(*d*) **Problems of the least developed countries, bearing in mind the Substantial New Programme of Action for the 1980s for the Least Developed Countries**

(Agenda item 8)

8. Item 8 was considered by the Conference in plenary meeting in conjunction with the general debate.

9. At the 205th meeting, on 13 July 1987, the Conference decided to refer the four sub-items of item 8 to four Sessional Committees for consideration and report.

10. During the session, proposals were submitted by Cuba, on behalf of the States members of the Group of 77, regarding policies and measures in the areas of: resources for development, including financial, and related monetary questions (TD/L.312); commodities (TD/L.313); and international trade (TD/L.314).

11. At the 220th (closing) meeting, on 3 August 1987, the reports of Sessional Committees I, II and IV were introduced by the respective Chairmen and that of Sessional Committee III by the Rapporteur. At the same meeting, the Conference took note of the reports of the four Sessional Committees and decided that these should be incorporated in the report on its seventh session (see chapter V below).

12. At the same meeting, the *President* introduced a draft consolidated text (TD/L.316 and Add.1-6), which had been elaborated in the President's Contact Group on the basis, *inter alia*, of the contributions of the Sessional Committees and represented the substantive outcome of the consideration of item 8. The Contact Group had recommended that the text be entitled ''Final Act of UNCTAD VII''.

13. The representative of *Jamaica* recalled that, in the informal negotiations on the text on resources in the Final Act, his delegation had on two occasions indicated that the text as it finally emerged did not reflect the delegation's instructions, although at a certain stage it had appeared that it would do so. Jamaica—as well as perhaps more than 50 other countries—had not seen its concerns reflected in the text on resources. The policy statement by the representative of Jamaica at the opening of the Conference[14] had contained a section headed ''Debt and development: the experience of small middle-income developing countries'' and it had drawn attention to a proposal by the Prime Minister of Jamaica which sought to ensure that the developing

------

[14] For a summary of the statement, made at the 203rd plenary meeting, see volume II.

debtor countries received the necessary and sufficient financial resources to enable them to grow out of the present crisis. The Jamaican proposal built on the widely accepted growth and development oriented strategies, and the key element was "the targeted reduction of debt ratios to sustainable levels over a programmed period, which would release sufficient disposable resources to achieve targeted growth." The Jamaican delegation believed that that additional element to the debt strategy would allow all developing debtor countries to receive the external resources needed to achieve sustainable growth and thereby development.

14.   He recalled further that one of the documents emanating from the informal negotiations contained a paragraph (para. 4) which had read as follows:

"The objective of bringing indebtedness and debt-servicing capacity into line with one another in the context of adjustment with growth can only be realized if all the parties concerned discharge their responsibilities. Such a process requires higher levels of external resources availabilities as investment and import volumes will need to grow substantially."

In the informal negotiations he had stated that that text was acceptable to the Group of 77 and to his own delegation. Subsequently, in another informal setting in which he had not participated, that text had been changed and the new version was now to be found in paragraph 37 of the Final Act. He requested that the above text emanating from the informal negotiations—which at that stage had been an agreed text—should be reproduced as an additional formulation in paragraph 37 of the Final Act.

15.   Turning to paragraph 39 of the Final Act, he noted that it stated that the debt problems of both those developing countries with lower per capita income, whose debt was mainly on concessional terms and largely with official creditors, and those with higher per capita income, whose debt was mainly on market terms and largely with commercial creditors, were being addressed. He pointed out that the debt problems of those developing countries whose external debt was owed to bilateral and multilateral creditors but on non-concessional terms, and because of their limited access to private capital markets, was not being addressed. He found it difficult to associate fully with a text which clearly excluded that category of countries, which was now clearly recognized to be in need of consideration by the international community. Although he was not proposing an amendment to paragraph 39, he hoped that the problems of those developing debtor countries which relied primarily on bilateral and multilateral non-concessional flows, and with limited access to private capital markets, would be adequately addressed. For that reason, his delegation wished to propose two further amendments to the Final Act: one in subparagraph 44 (*j*) and one in subparagraph 44(*l*). The amendment to subparagraph 44 (*j*) would read as follows:

"Creditor Governments are encouraged to apply flexibility in debt restructuring operations and in providing new loans to developing debtor countries which rely primarily on official and officially guaranteed loans."

That amendment did not harm the balance of the text, in view of what was stated in subparagraph 44 (*h*), which addressed the concerns of the heavily indebted countries whose borrowings on the private capital market endangered the international financial system. Just as it was appropriate for subparagraph 44 (*h*) to be included in the Final Act, so it would be quite in order for the concerns of his delegation to be reflected.

16.   As to subparagraph 44 (*l*), which stated that in respect of the ODA debt of poorer developing countries, developed donor countries which had not yet done so should implement in full Trade and Development Board resolution 165 (S-IX) of 11 March 1978, he proposed the addition of a sentence to read:

"Consideration should be given to extending the coverage to include those developing debtor countries that rely primarily on loans from official sources and multilateral development banks."

17.   He observed that delegations from a wide cross-section had said that they understood and sympathized with the above amendments. Over the years, the Jamaican delegation had participated in the work in UNCTAD in an effort to seek better opportunities for all and not only for Jamaica. But it could not see why the pursuit of the general good should be at the expense of the national good. He had thus put forward those proposals for inclusion in the Final Act and he read the Final Act as encompassing those sections which dealt with the assessment; the policies and measures; and the orientations for the future. He wished to see his concerns reflected specifically in the Final Act and not merely accommodated in another section of the report of the Conference.

18.   The spokesman for *Group B* (Belgium) assured the representative of Jamaica that his statement would be examined with great care by the countries of Group B. The Jamaican proposals, however, referred to issues discussed during the Conference on which agreement had been difficult to reach. It would be both difficult and dangerous to reopen the discussion and it would be better not to alter a text which had been accepted by the Conference as a whole. In a concern to preserve what had been jointly accomplished, he asked the representative of Jamaica not to pursue his proposals, which Group B was not in a position to accept.

19.   The *President* noted that there seemed to be some opposition to the proposals made by the delegation of Jamaica for specific amendments to the Final Act. He noted additionally that there had been a request from the representative of Jamaica that, if such was the case, the statement should be fully reflected in the record. He sought confirmation of that.

20.   The representative of *Jamaica* said that he wished to propose that the Final Act contain in some way or other an indication that to those points had been raised. That could be done by use of an asterisk, complemented by the text of his statement in the report of the Conference.

21.   The *President* said that he did not interpret the position taken by the representative of Jamaica as being so rigid that it would hold up the proceedings of the Conference. He was sure that a suitable place would be found in the report of the Conference where the

Jamaican statement would be incorporated. A reference to it would be included in the index to observations and reservations in part I, section B, of the report.

Action by the Conference

22. At the 220th (closing) meeting, on 3 August 1987, the Conference adopted the Final Act of UNCTAD VII without dissent.[15] The draft proposals in TD/L.312, TD/L.313 and TD/L.314 were withdrawn. A further proposal on policies and measures relating to problems of the least developed countries, introduced by the representative of Bangladesh in Committee IV on behalf of the States members of the Group of 77 (TD(VII)/C.IV/L.1), was also withdrawn.

Statements made on the adoption of the Final Act

23. The spokesman for the *Group of 77* (Cuba) observed that the seventh session of the Conference had been the occasion of a major development: the decisive progress made towards the entry into force of the Agreement Establishing the Common Fund for Commodities.[16] The Group of 77 took note with deep appreciation of the action taken by Peru to deposit its instrument of ratification in Geneva and by the Union of Soviet Socialist Republics, Côte d'Ivoire and Bulgaria to sign the Agreement, and of their firm intention to ratify it very soon. The Group of 77 also took note with deep appreciation of the announcements by Madagascar that it had completed its ratification procedure and by Costa Rica, Portugal and Thailand of their intention to deposit their instruments of ratification in the very near future. The Group of 77 wished to express its gratitude to Norway and to States members of OPEC for undertaking to provide the contributions on behalf of the least developed countries.

24. Those important decisions were of high political significance. Those actions, when completed, would indeed fulfil the remaining condition for the entry into force of the Agreement. They meant that the long-awaited entry into force of the Agreement had practically become a reality. That would represent advancement towards the aims and objectives of the Integrated Programme for Commodities. It was a concrete step forward which augured well for a brighter future for international co-operation in the field of commodities.

25. The Group of 77 wished to express once again its deep appreciation to all those countries which had, before the beginning of the Conference and, for many of them, a number of years earlier, already deposited their respective instruments of ratification, acceptance or approval of the Agreement.

26. The Group of 77 reaffirmed its commitment to the Common Fund and to its principles and objectives and emphasized its importance for the developing countries. It therefore appealed to all those countries which had not yet joined the Agreement to do so as a matter of priority. It also appealed to those countries which had signed and/or ratified the Agreement to ac-

celerate the implementation of their commitment to the Fund so that it could start its operations as soon as possible.

27. When the Agreement Establishing the Common Fund came into force, the Group of 77 hoped that the Secretary-General of UNCTAD would proceed as soon as possible with the mandate given to him under paragraph 2 (*b*) of resolution 2 (IV) of 27 June 1980, adopted by the United Nations Negotiating Conference on a Common Fund under the Integrated Programme for Commodities,[17] namely to convene the first annual meeting of the Governing Council of the Fund.

28. The spokesman for *Group B* (Belgium) said that his Group welcomed the adoption of the Final Act. It appreciated the intensive efforts which had been devoted to the assessment process both before and during the Conference. The fact that those efforts had resulted in a common assessment would be widely welcomed. Naturally, each delegation had its own perceptions, and not all would agree with every word of the assessment. However, it must be recognized that that was all part of an important process leading to better understanding and co-operation in the field of development.

29. He wished to make some observations on issues to which Group B attached particular importance.

30. First, Group B would like to underscore the importance of the Uruguay Round of multilateral trade negotiations for all participants and it went without saying that the text just adopted in no way impinged on the letter or spirit of the Punta del Este Declaration.[18] The central role of the Uruguay Round in addressing the major problems in international trade had been clearly brought out during the Conference. The improvement and strengthening of the open multilateral trading system and the further liberalization of trade were objectives all shared. In that regard, Group B attached great importance to the continuation of substantive progress, achieved through the active participation of all participants, with a view to a successful and comprehensive conclusion to the negotiations within the agreed time-frame.

31. Group B welcomed the increasing recognition of the vital relationship between structural adjustment and growth and development, for all countries. In that regard, his Group fully supported the continuation of the Trade and Development Board's annual review of protectionism and structural adjustment in the agriculture, manufactures and services sectors, under its existing mandate, but with further improvement in the quality of analysis and a wider and more balanced coverage of regional groups.

32. Finally, having agreed to accept the text in section II. C, on international trade, Group B wished to express, in particular, its reservation on paragraph 105 (19) relating to UNCTAD's work on services.

33. Its concern was based on its experience with the use to which work mandated to the UNCTAD

---

[15] For the text, see part one above, section A.1.

[16] United Nations publication, Sales No. E.81.II.D.8 and corrigendum.

[17] See the report of the Negotiating Conference on its fourth session (TD/IPC/CF/CONF/26), annex.

[18] GATT, *Basic Instruments and Selected Documents, Thirty-third Supplement* (Sales No. GATT/1987-1), p. 19.

secretariat had been put, and with the extent to which that could be used either to delay or to impede the progress of negotiations on trade in services in the Uruguay Round. Group B's concerns were justified by its wish to preserve the process of negotiations in the Uruguay Round. In that context Group B encouraged all participants in the MTNs to participate actively and constructively in those negotiations.

34. Group B attached importance to the completion of the work in the existing mandate as contained in Board decision 309 (XXX) of 29 March 1985, on services, particularly the national studies.

35. Group B hoped that this message would be understood as a positive effort on its part to advance work in that area.

36. The *Legal Adviser* stated that the reservation placed on record by the representative of Belgium did not change the legal status of the text which stood adopted by the Conference. Nor did the reservation modify the legal basis for action by UNCTAD under paragraph 105 (19).

37. The *President* said that that was a common understanding.

38. The spokesman for *Group D* (Poland), speaking also on behalf of *Mongolia*, said that, in a spirit of realism, dialogue and responsibility for the future of the world economy, the Conference had been trying to find agreements and joint constructive actions or appropriate policies and measures to benefit the entire international community.

39. Group D welcomed the fact that the Conference had reached a consensus on the Final Act. It found it balanced but was of the opinion that the issue of international economic security, together with the confidence-building measures in the economic field, should remain on the agenda of UNCTAD activities.

40. The comprehensive attitude of the Group D countries on all important issues on the agenda was fully presented in TD/333 and had been expressed on various occasions during the general debate and in the Sessional Committees.

41. It was Group D's firm conviction that there existed a close relationship between disarmament and development and that all concrete steps on the way to disarmament should be linked with reallocating a portion of the resources to be released to meet the needs of economic and social progress of all countries, in particular developing ones.

42. He regretted to note that that important problem, mentioned on so many occasions during the general debate by various heads of delegation, was not adequately reflected in the operative part of the Final Act of the Conference. UNCTAD had a mandate in that field, which should be fully implemented.

43. Group D agreed that the removal of discriminatory restraints on exports was essential for liberalization. It agreed also that the export interests of developing countries should be taken into account in particular. It was his Group's understanding that that liberalization should be implemented in strict compliance with the respective principles of international

trade. With regard to the question of economic and trade sanctions, Group D's position was that they should not be imposed for non-economic reasons, except in the case of those based on General Assembly resolutions.

44. He confirmed Group D's well-known position of principle on fixed targets for ODA, Board resolution 165 (S-IX), as well as on the interpretation of the words "developed countries", and "donor countries". That position had been expressed upon the adoption by the General Assembly of the International Development Strategy for the Third United Nations Development Decade[19] and of the Substantial New Programme of Action for the 1980s for the Least Developed Countries[20] and had been reiterated on several occasions. The socialist countries of Group D would continue strengthening their trade, economic and technical cooperation with developing countries with the aim of promoting their national, social and economic development and assisting them in overcoming economic underdevelopment.

45. Concerning the orientations for the future work of UNCTAD, Group D proceeded from the understanding that UNCTAD's future activities should cover all the main fields of its work programme in accordance with its mandate as contained in General Assembly resolution 1995 (XIX).

46. The spokesman for the *Group of 77* (Cuba), referring to economic measures applied for political reasons in order to exert economic and political coercion, stated that the Group of 77 wished to reaffirm its full respect for the inalienable right of all States to ensure their economic and social development and to exercise their sovereign choice in deciding on their economic and social systems, as well as to promote the well-being of their peoples in accordance with national economic plans and policies. It was not acceptable that that right should be restricted by the arbitrary economic measures which other States imposed in order to exert economic and political coercion. They did so to achieve aims which were incompatible with the United Nations Charter and which were a violation both of bilateral and multilateral commitments entered into and of international law. In demanding the revocation of those measures of economic aggression, the Group of 77 reaffirmed its full support for, and solidarity with, the peoples victims of a policy that was directed to retarding their economic development and social welfare.

47. The representative of the *United States of America* said that his delegation considered section II.A, on debt, resources and related issues, on balance to be a constructive statement. However, there was one portion he wished to comment on. The United States believed that the international economic environment, described in paragraph 40, and as characterized elsewhere in the Conference text, had been substantially more positive than was stated in the paper. Industrial countries' growth had been sustained for five years;

[19] General Assembly resolution 35/56 of 5 December 1980, annex.

[20] *Report of the United Nations Conference on the Least Developed Countries, Paris, 1-14 September 1981* (United Nations publication, Sales No. E.82.I.8), part one, sect. A.

market access had been improved; interest rates had fallen. Those factors had been a positive and helpful influence on economic prospects of developing countries. He expressed appreciation for the constructive and co-operative efforts and leadership which resulted in the successful outcome on that item of the agenda.

48. The United States had worked hard throughout the session to reach agreement where possible on issues of substance, and where differences persisted, had sought to have those differences recorded in the text, when possible. In the area of commodities, section II.B, he recalled that the United States had voted against Conference resolution 125 (V), which commissioned a study of a new complementary financing facility, and resolution 157 (VI), which called for the establishment of an expert group. The United States did not recognize that UNCTAD had a mandate to study and make recommendations on compensatory financing and, as a result, had not and would not participate in the discussion of the expert group.

49. With respect to the conclusions reached by the Conference in section II.C, on international trade, the United States wished to express its appreciation to those who had participated constructively throughout the Conference on the important issues involved. It was because of such co-operation that the United States chose, after careful consideration, to join the consensus on that section. In so doing, the United States wished to make the following points concerning the text.

50. First, it believed that the agreement in no way compromised or reinterpreted the commitments reached in Punta del Este with trading partners on the Uruguay Round of multilateral trade negotiations, which it hoped would be concluded rapidly and with the active and constructive participation of the parties involved.

51. Secondly, with respect to paragraph 105 (19) on services, the United States fully supported the declaration made on behalf of Group B and the reservation expressed. Its decision to agree to that particular text had not been easy; none the less, it joined the consensus in order to demonstrate its constructive attitude, which it hoped was genuinely shared by all concerned. Agreement to the text should in no way be construed to extend an exclusive role to UNCTAD for the analysis of the implications for development of trade in services. The complexity of the issues involved required analysis by many interested in trade in services. It did not expect that this agreement would be used to undermine the process nor impede rapid progress in the negotiations on trade in services under way in the Uruguay Round.

52. Finally, with respect to paragraph 105 (23), regarding the international trading system, the United States maintained the position that any review or study by the Trade and Development Board should be of a general character and should not be aimed at establishing a new set of rules for international trade.

53. With respect to the least developed countries, and in particular with respect to paragraph 117 of that portion of the Final Act regarding ODA targets established in the Substantial New Programme of Action, he recalled the position of the United States on that issue which had been most recently expressed at the 1985 mid-term review of the Substantial New Programme of Action following the adoption of the report of that meeting.[21]

54. The representative of the *United Kingdom* said that his Government had throughout been working for a positive outcome to the Conference which would address the very real problems facing developing countries and contribute practically to their solution. Accordingly, it could accept the single final outcome document as a broad statement of the consensus which had been reached.

55. There was, however, a point concerning the Common Fund on which he wished to make the position of his Government clear.

56. As the Minister for Trade of the United Kingdom had said in his statement at the 214th plenary meeting of the Conference, on 28 July, the United Kingdom recognized the seriousness of the problems facing a number of developing countries whose economies were dependent upon the production of certain primary commodities. That was an area to which the United Kingdom had pledged resources both in its bilateral aid programme and through its support for activity by the international institutions. But, as the Minister had also said, the solution to the decline in commodity prices in real terms since the 1950s was not to attempt to rig the market or to distort consumer choice. It must lie in the acceptance of change and the readiness to adapt to market trends.

57. Those considerations were especially relevant, given the prospect that the Common Fund would enter into force in the foreseeable future. It was now 10 years since the negotiations establishing the Fund began. Since then there had been major changes in world commodity markets. The United Kingdom believed that it was important to reflect very carefully on the lessons learned from experience in that period. In the light of those changes States must ask themselves how far the Common Fund could still fulfil the tasks originally envisaged for it.

58. The United Kingdom believed that it was highly desirable that ways should be found in which those aspects could be examined thoroughly before steps were taken to bring the Common Fund into operation.

---

[21] See *Official Records of the Trade and Development Board, Thirty-second Session, Annexes,* agenda item 7, document TD/B/1078, paras. 220-223.

III. Other business

(Agenda item 9)

Economic situation in the occupied Palestinian territories

59. At the 220th (closing) meeting, on 3 August 1987, the *President* drew attention to a draft resolution on the economic situation in the occupied Palestinian territories, submitted by Cuba on behalf of the Group of 77 (TD/L.295).

60. The representative of *Israel* said that draft resolution TD/L.295, which was replete with falsifications, was but yet another exercise of the political and propaganda campaign waged incessantly against Israel by Arab States ever since its inception. It came on the heels of a futile attempt to challenge the credentials of his delegation and had nothing to do with the subject-matter of the Conference. It was the only political resolution, in fact the only resolution at all regarding a specific issue, which was put to the vote. Other resolutions had been adopted at Havana, but they had apparently got lost *en route*. Thus, although the United Nations was based on the principle of sovereign equality enshrined in the Charter, it appeared, again, that there was one cause which, because of the manipulation of an automatic majority, was more equal than others, namely, the singling out of Israel for blame through diplomatic pressure and economic blackmail.

61. The General Assembly might decide, upon the recommendation of the Committee of Eighteen, that unnecessary proceedings should be curtailed and the work of United Nations bodies streamlined, the Secretary-General might call for the avoidance of unnecessary confrontation, but a plethora of repetitious resolutions directed against Israel continued blithely to emanate from the Organization, at the behest of those who wished thereby to serve their terrorist purposes. Meetings of the Group of 77 and the non-aligned countries were cynically abused in order to impose these texts, as was the case with the present draft.

62. At the current session, the major problems besetting world trade and development were thus now put aside for this all-important goal of Israel's detractors to get their customary pound of political flesh. Ultimately the member States interested in the solution of these problems would be the real losers of this cynical squandering of resources, time and energy. The draft would hurt the cause of the Conference rather than that of the State of Israel. Public opinion would not fail to pay attention to this regrettable diversion, drawing its own conclusions on the validity and relevance of UNCTAD's work, as had indeed already been the case in the local press.

63. As for the real economic and commercial situation in the territories under Israeli administration, the facts were very different from the situation portrayed in the draft. Israel had submitted full data in proceedings in the General Assembly, the Economic and Social Council, Habitat, UNEP, ILO and WHO and in the Israeli statement in the general debate (216th meeting). The records were there for everybody who wished to know the true facts. The GNP in the territories under Israeli administration had increased by about 400 per cent since 1967; private and public construction had risen 900 per cent; and the value of exported goods had increased almost twelvefold, namely, from $34 million to $395 million. In this period, close to 2,500 industrial plants and workshops had been established, the industrial workforce had doubled, and the unemployment rate had dropped from 10 to 3 per cent while private consumption rose 230 per cent. All that was notwithstanding the 45 per cent increase in the population since 1967.

64. In that permanent endeavour to improve the living conditions and promote the economy of the territories, Israel more than welcomed international assistance. UNDP was carrying out a most effective programme in that respect, comprising 13 fully implemented projects and 20 projects under implementation, involving the expenditure $16.6 million.

65. It would be much more helpful for the inhabitants of the territories if international bodies like UNCTAD were called upon to do more in practice to assist in their economic growth than to host sterile debates and pass unnecessary and unwarranted resolutions. That went even more so for the wealthy Arab States, which really could finance at least the projects for which UNDP was seeking funds (see DP/1987/23).

66. Consequently, instead of belabouring a non-problem of difficulties regarding the export of goods from the territories, it would be much more appropriate to take steps to abolish import restrictions regarding those goods in various countries, partly because of illegal boycott practices. Instead of referring to a white elephant project of a commercial seaport conceived for political purposes only, it would be much more advisable to mobilize funds for a fishing port at the same location. Instead of yet another Palestinian unit at UNCTAD, in addition to an ever-growing department at Headquarters, it would be much better to spend the money involved in one of the many projects in agriculture, industry, housing, health and infrastructure in the territories, which still awaited financing.

67. It was highly incongruous to call, in a conference aiming at human betterment through the promotion of trade and development, for co-operation with those whose trade was inhuman terrorism and whose main development activity was to develop air piracy. Their production line included the preparation of explosives to be used in market places, public transportation, beaches, restaurants, schools and synagogues.

68. He called upon all member States wishing to promote the real goals of UNCTAD to reject this transparent attempt to distort and politicize the work of the Conference and to vote against the draft.

69. The observer for the *Palestine Liberation Organization*, speaking in accordance with General Assembly resolution 3237 (XXIX), said that draft resolution TD/L.295 reflected the views of the Group of 77.

He did not consider the statement by the Israeli delegation as directly related to his organization or the Arab Group but rather as an insult to the whole Group of 77. The Israeli delegation should stop preaching wisdom and pretending innocence as if it were not aware of the nature of the Conference. The draft resolution concerned UNCTAD's work, the economy of the occupied Palestinian territories and, particularly, the trade sector. He challenged the Israeli delegation to say why it had blocked the implementation of a seaport in occupied Gaza. Was not the construction of a seaport related to the question of trade? Such was the sort of assistance the Palestinian people was receiving under Israeli occupation. He also asked, with reference to the decision of the European Community agreeing to give Palestinian products access to the EEC market, on a preferential basis because the EEC was very much concerned at the deteriorating economic conditions in the occupied Palestinian territories, as were the other countries of the world, why Israel had stopped Palestinian products from being exported to the European Community? Was that an act of assistance to the Palestinian people? Was it a logical or an illogical act? International conferences had become used to false statements by the Israeli delegation, which claimed that occupation brought economic development and prosperity. Why then had the Conference spent long nights discussing the situation of the world economy? Why did not the Israeli delegation submit a resolution advising all delegations to welcome Israeli occupation in order to rid the whole world of deteriorating economic conditions? Recalling the Arabic proverb that he who has not cannot give, he said that the Israeli economy was suffering from an extremely critical crisis. It had an external debt of over $22 billion and over $23 billion of internal debt. That was in addition to inflation and a balance-of-payments deficit, and despite the aid given by the United States, which exceeded $4 billion annually.

70. That money was spent on military adventures against the Arab Nation, including the Palestinian people, and for the construction of colonial settlements in the occupied Palestinian territories. The Palestine Liberation Organization was no match for Israeli propagandists but, whatever the fine words used to conceal them, the facts spoke for themselves. There could be no economic development or growth under Israeli occupation. The Israeli delegation referred to United Nations reports. He noted, however, that such reports described the deteriorating situation. He challenged the Israeli delegation to address itself to the resolution and say why Israel did not agree to implement the EEC decision or agree to the building of a seaport. The Palestinians did not want Israel or Israeli occupation. They wanted to be free from any occupation. He noted that the President was from Zimbabwe, a country which had suffered from alien colonial occupation. He expressed confidence that the Palestinians would one day be full members of UNCTAD, despite the intentions of the Israeli delegation, which must know that the time of colonialism was long past. The time would come for Palestine and South Africa to join the ranks of the independent States.

71. He pointed out that draft resolution TD/L.295 was wholly related to trade matters and appeals for improvement of the conditions of people living under occupation and was confident that all would support it.

72. The representative of the *Syrian Arab Republic* observed that the Israeli delegation's references to happiness and prosperity, and the so-called terrestrial paradise that existed in occupied Palestinian and Syrian territories, created a certain degree of remorse and envy because the entire world had been unable to avail itself of that prosperity.

73. The Conference had been told by the Israeli delegation that it was discussing problems which did not exist and, in this connection, he recalled that Mrs. Golda Meier and Mr. Abba Eban had both asserted that the Palestinian people did not exist. Yet when the Israelis wished to kill Palestinians they knew where to find them. If the occupied Palestinian and Arab territories were such a terrestrial paradise, why had the Israeli authorities prevented the United Nations mission entrusted with investigating Israeli practices with regard to violations of human rights, and the mission enquiring into the health conditions in the occupied territories, from penetrating into those territories? Why had representatives of churches, of jurists, of legal organizations, and all those who defended and protected human rights been forbidden access to those occupied territories which, according to the Israeli delegate, enjoyed such quality of life. The situation in the occupied territories resembled only what was experienced in South Africa and Namibia at the hands of the *apartheid* régime. That was why those two régimes, the Israeli and the South African, were in sympathy, and why they collaborated, sowed discord and sought to conclude political, military and economic treaties. Those régimes, which defied the United Nations Charter and its resolutions, continued to benefit from the support of the greatest Power of the world, namely the United States.

74. The representative of the *United States of America* called for a roll-call vote on draft resolution TD/L.295.

75. The representative of the *Syrian Arab Republic* supported the request for a roll-call vote.

76. The representative of *Malta* announced that his delegation would not participate in the vote because, although it supported the attainment by the Palestinian people of their legitimate rights, his delegation considered that the seventh session of the Conference was not the proper forum in which to pursue a purpose that should rather be taken up in the Committee on the Exercise of the Inalienable Rights of the Palestinian People, at the General Assembly and in the Security Council, where Malta would continue to work for the attainment of the Palestinian rights.

77. The representative of the *Syrian Arab Republic,* speaking on a point of order, objected to the fact that, as the vote had started, the representative of Malta had no right to raise any other issue.

78. The *President* observed that the statement by the representative of the Syrian Arab Republic was very pertinent. He himself had believed that the representative of Malta intended to speak in explanation of vote, which he believed was permissible.

79.   The *Legal Adviser* stated that the representative of Malta had asked for the floor to explain his position on the draft resolution. At one point, when the process started, it should not be interrupted and all other explanations of vote or position should be made after the voting was completed and the results announced. However, to explain positions and votes before the voting had commenced was perfectly permissible.

Action by the conference

80.   At the 220th (closing) plenary meeting, on 3 August 1987, the Conference adopted draft resolution TD/L.295 by a roll-call vote of 80 to 2, with 32 abstentions.[22] The voting was as follows :

In favour: Afghanistan, Algeria, Argentina, Bahrain, Bangladesh, Benin, Bhutan, Bolivia, Botswana, Brazil, Bulgaria, Burma, Burundi, Byelorussian Soviet Socialist Republic, China, Colombia, Comoros, Cuba, Cyprus, Czechoslovakia, Democratic Kampuchea, Democratic People's Republic of Korea, Democratic Yemen, Ecuador, Egypt, Ethiopia, Gabon, German Democratic Republic, Ghana, Hungary, India, Indonesia, Iran (Islamic Republic of), Iraq, Jamaica, Jordan, Kenya, Kuwait, Lebanon, Libyan Arab Jamahiriya, Madagascar, Malaysia, Mexico, Mongolia, Morocco, Mozambique, Nepal, Nicaragua, Niger, Nigeria, Oman, Pakistan, Philippines, Poland, Qatar, Republic of Korea, Romania, Rwanda, Saudi Arabia, Senegal, Singapore, Somalia, Sri Lanka, Sudan, Syrian Arab Republic, Thailand, Togo, Trinidad and Tobago, Tunisia, Turkey, Ukrainian Soviet Socialist Republic, Union of Soviet Socialist Republics, United Arab Emirates, United Republic of Tanzania, Venezuela, Viet Nam, Yemen, Yugoslavia, Zaire, Zimbabwe.

Against: Israel, United States of America.

Abstaining: Australia, Austria, Belgium, Cameroon, Canada, Costa Rica, Côte d'Ivoire, Denmark, El Salvador, Finland, France, Germany, Federal Republic of, Greece, Guatemala, Honduras, Ireland, Italy, Japan, Liechtenstein, Luxembourg, Netherlands, New Zealand, Norway, Panama, Paraguay, Peru, Portugal, Spain, Sweden, Switzerland, United Kingdom of Great Britain and Northern Ireland, Uruguay.

81.   The representative of the *United States of America* stated that his delegation wished to register its profound dismay at the introduction and subsequent vote on draft resolution TD/L.295, and at the fact that such a resolution had found its way into a conference on trade and development. It had voted against its adoption because it dealt with a subject-matter which had absolutely no relevance to the purposes of the seventh session of the Conference. Had there been any question about that, certain of the statements made before the vote should have removed any doubts. The contribution that the seventh session of the Conference had made in finding common understandings on the fundamental issues affecting the world economy had now been flawed. UNCTAD's credibility as an ongoing forum for serious economic and development discussions, perhaps its single most precious asset, must now be called into question. All of this because a few countries could not resist using UNCTAD, a forum so potentially important to so

many developing countries, to score cheap political points. The United States delegation hesitated to speculate on the implications for the future of UNCTAD of this sorry effort to politicize the session.

82.   The representative of *Denmark*, speaking on behalf of the *European Economic Community and its member States*, stated that they had abstained in the vote on TD/L.295. It found that the resolution went beyond the agreed agenda for the session. Its vote should in no way be taken as an indication of the views of the Governments of the States members of the EEC on the substantive issue. Those views had already been fully explained in the General Assembly, where the question was regularly dealt with.

83.   The representative of *Greece* said that his delegation had joined the other States members of the European Community concerning draft resolution TD/L.295, for it found the reasons put forward in the Community statement legitimate. That, however, did not imply any change in substance of the position taken by the Greek Government on the Palestine issue in international forums as well as in the European Community, where it had been recently decided to strengthen the economic ties with the Palestinian people in the Gaza Strip and the West Bank.

84.   The representative of *Ecuador* wished to place clearly on record that, in voting in favour of draft resolution TD/L.295, his delegation did so in keeping with an unswerving principle of the international policy of Ecuador regarding the rejection of occupation and the acquisition of territory by force. The Government of Ecuador also considered that the occupation of those territories caused serious economic and social problems to the Palestinian population.

85.   The spokesman for *Group D* (Poland), speaking also on behalf of *Mongolia*, said that the delegations of his Group and Mongolia had voted in favour of draft resolution TD/L.295. They attached great importance to socio-economic aspects of the Middle East problem, which required a speedy, just, equitable and comprehensive settlement. They had strongly and consistently supported the inalienable rights of the Palestinian people to self-determination, to national independence and sovereignty and the right to establish their own independent State. It was their conviction that the path to a comprehensive settlement of the Middle East problem lay through the collective efforts of all interested parties, including the Palestine Liberation Organization, the sole authentic representative of the Palestinian people. They would in future continue to support UNCTAD activities that corresponded to those purposes in the socio-economic aspects of the Middle East situation.

86.   The representative of *Bolivia* said that his delegation had voted in favour of the draft resolution because Bolivia rejected the occupation and annexation of territories by force. At the same time, he expressed Bolivia's fervent wish for an early and permanent peace in the Middle East.

87.   The observer for the *Palestine Liberation Organization*, speaking in accordance with General Assembly resolution 3237 (XXIX), said that he would ignore completely certain remarks made after the vote

---

[22] For the text adopted, see resolution 169 (VII).

which, worthless as they were, were not worthy even of an attempt to answer them.

88. He expressed extreme gratitude to all the countries which had supported draft resolution TD/L.295. His organization understood the position of the countries which had abstained although he did not agree

with it, and hoped that they would in future be able to support such resolutions. He respected the right of Malta as a sovereign State to take any action it chose; the close relationship between the people of Palestine and the people of Malta would in no way be affected and he acknowledged the strong support of the people of Malta for the Palestinian people.

IV. Statements made at the 220th (closing) meeting of the seventh session

89. The spokesman for the *Group of 77* (Cuba) said that his Group saw in the seventh session of the Conference the continuation of a process towards achieving the aims and ideals entrusted to UNCTAD by the international community. The seventh session of the Conference could not have been more opportune, given the serious deterioration in the world economic situation witnessed during the current decade. The persistent stagnation of economic growth for developing countries, caused by the inadequacies of the international economic system, had severely retarded their social and economic progress. Their own national efforts towards achieving their development goals had thereby been seriously affected. In that connection, he recalled the following observations set forth in paragraph 7 of the Havana Declaration:

The crisis in the world economy has many dramatic manifestations. For the developing countries, these include:

(*a*) The collapse of commodity prices and deteriorating terms of trade, which have deprived them of export earnings needed to sustain their development and to service their debt;

(*b*) The intolerable debt burden which has compelled many of them to adopt, with high social and political costs, adjustment programmes constraining their development potential. The debt cannot be serviced and repaid under present conditions and without sustained economic development;

(*c*) The stagnation of official development assistance and the sharp contraction in financial flows, particularly from commercial banks;

(*d*) All the previous factors have led to a net transfer of resources from developing to developed countries;

(*e*) The proliferation of protectionist and distortive measures and policies in developed market-economy countries, which are impeding developing country exports and obstructing structural adjustments which would permit the expansion of those exports;

(*f*) The erosion of respect for the disciplines of the multilateral trading system, which exposes the developing countries to arbitrary obstacles to their trade and leaves them without redress;

(*g*) The aggravation of the structural problems of the least developed countries, especially the land-locked and island developing countries, whose unique problems and inherent disadvantages have a particularly negative impact on their development.[22]

90. He said that particular difficulties were experienced by the Palestinian people, whose living conditions had been deteriorating as a result of the Israeli occupation and who urgently needed to be liberated from their occupation to enable them to develop their national economy. The same could be said of the peoples of southern Africa and Namibia, particularly those of the front-line States, whose painstakingly developed infrastructure and legitimate development programmes were undermined by the South African régime's destabilization policy. Furthermore, the prac-

tice of imposing coercive economic measures against developing countries for purposes incompatible with the Charter of the United Nations had been an additional impediment to their economic progress. Again, the wording of paragraphs 3 and 6 of the Havana Declaration was relevant:

This situation is beset with economic, social and political tensions, within and among countries. It poses a serious threat to democracy, social stability and international peace and security. Its reversal should command the political commitment and co-operation of all nations, which must work together to build an international economic system based on the principles of equity and justice, that would contribute to the establishment of the new international economic order.

. . .

The members of the Group of 77 expect the developed countries to assume their responsibilities in the present world economic crisis, and to redesign their policies in order to contribute to an external environment more predictable and more supportive of growth and development. . . .

91. Observing that revitalizing development, growth and international trade for the benefit of all had been the main task of the Conference at the seventh session, he said that it had been a difficult and long drawn-out exercise demanding maximum effort from all participants. For more than a year the Group of 77 had seriously and tirelessly committed itself to the preparations for the Conference, through regional Ministerial Meetings in Dhaka, Addis Ababa and Costa Rica, which had culminated in the adoption of the Havana Declaration. The agenda for the Conference had singled out four interrelated and crucial areas in the international economic environment. The Group of 77 sincerely believed that more concrete and far-reaching policies and measures should have resulted from so much effort, in order to respond adequately to the gravity of the international economic situation. The Group of 77 was fully conscious of the challenge, and faced that challenge pragmatically and realistically. That was evident from the proposals drawn up by the Group and put forward in its negotiations with the other members of the international community. However, the response of some of the negotiating partners had not been commensurate with the gravity of the international economic situation.

92. Having said that, it was the sincere wish of the Group of 77 that the results of the seventh session of the Conference should herald the beginning of the reversal of the current economic situation. In particular, the Group of 77 felt that, at a time when the interdependence of nations and issues in the economic field was increasing, there was a need to take positive action to exploit the potential of international economic co-operation. That potential could best be realized through multilateral co-operation based on the recogni-

---

[23] Final document of the Sixth Ministerial Meeting of the Group of 77, held at Havana, Cuba, from 20 to 25 April 1987; reproduced in annex V below.

tion of the equality of all countries. UNCTAD remained the forum for international economic co-operation and negotiation in the field of trade, development and interrelated areas and could play a unique role in furthering that interdependence.

93. The Group of 77 was confident that all States members of UNCTAD would henceforth endeavour to work in earnest to implement the agreements reached by the Conference, that the political will would be renewed and be made more effective, that all the developed countries would assume their responsibilities in the face of the seriousness of the situation, and that multilateral co-operation for development and economic growth would become a reality.

94. The spokesman for *Group B* (Belgium) observed that the opening of the session had been marked by a certain scepticism in many capitals and even a great deal of indifference among public opinion. The results that had been achieved were due above all to those actively engaged in the work of the session. Some found those results modest. He believed that to be appreciated they should be measured not only in quantitative but also in qualitative terms as well as in the longer perspective. What had been achieved was above all the determination of common approaches to future work which would be fruitful. In the case of a problem as important as that of debt, anything that could promote a convergence of views would surely facilitate settlements in specific cases, which was currently the fundamental issue.

95. As to commodities, an area marked by frequent difficulties and confrontations, there were now grounds for hope that discussions leading to arrangements for individual commodities could take place under conditions conducive to success.

96. As to trade, it was important, if not essential, that there should be an assurance that GATT and UNCTAD could each continue to work towards results corresponding to their mandates. Then again, there were also all the measures in favour of the least developed countries which had been formulated during the session. In addition, there were the common perceptions achieved with regard to economic strategies. His feeling was that after so many years in search of a North-South dialogue, it could be said, to paraphrase Proust, that the foundations had now been laid for the rediscovery of an entente.

97. The spokesman for *Group D* (Poland), speaking also on behalf of *Mongolia,* observed that Group D countries had come to Geneva to "revitalized development, growth and international trade in a more predictable and supportive environment through multilateral co-operation". They had come prepared to negotiate in good faith in order to make things better, being deeply concerned at the current economic situation and the challenges facing every member of the international community in the process of development. In the course of the general debate and the work of the Committees, the discussion had focused on international trade and development, on the urgency of solving the debt problem, liberalizing trade, diminishing protectionism, stabilizing commodity prices, and on the least developed countries. The seventh session of the Conference had proved that UNCTAD was a unique universal international forum mandated to deal with problems of trade and development. The Group D countries had always supported its work, and that support had been manifested during the Conference. Group D was pleased that, as a result of political will on the part of all countries, the Conference had been able to reach consensus on almost all important items. That would foster revitalization of development, growth and international trade. It would also contribute to the establishment of international economic security and speed up the negotiating process within UNCTAD machinery. He expressed the hope that the results achieved at the Conference would lay good foundations for sound economic relations in the world and strengthen the role of UNCTAD. Group D was fully committed to working towards that goal.

98. The representative of *China* observed that Governments had attached great importance to the seventh session of the Conference, which had been convened at a time when the North-South dialogue had for a long time remained at a stalemate.

99. Serious discussions had been carried out on the situation of the world economy and trade as well as such other issues as financial resources for development, commodities, international trade and the least developed countries. These discussions were conducive to the promotion of mutual understanding. In the general debate, the majority of countries had expressed the wish for dialogue and co-operation and demanded the establishment of a liberalized multilateral trading system and strengthened multilateral co-operation so as to solve the economic and trade problems they confronted. The developing countries had made a positive contribution to the Conference and some developed countries had shown sympathy for their plight.

100. Thanks to the efforts of the participants, consensus had been attained on some issues and certain progress had been made which would be helpful to the continuation of constructive dialogue in the future.

101. The current international economic situation continued to be grim and the developing countries were confronted with great economic difficulties. As the economies of all States were more and more interdependent, the economic development of the developing countries would become increasingly important to the economic growth of the developed countries and to the revitalization of the world economy as a whole. The economic development of countries depended not only on their own efforts and correct policies but also on a favourable external environment and international co-operation. It would be detrimental to the developed countries if no help was offered to the developing countries to resolve their current problems and speed up their economic development. China therefore believed that the dialogue between North and South on an equal footing and the strengthening of their economic and trade co-operation would contribute not only to the prosperity of the world economy but to peace and stability as well.

102. The Conference had proved once again that UNCTAD served as an important forum within the

United Nations system for discussing and resolving issues relating to trade and development.

103. The representative of *Colombia* recalled that it had been Colombia's tradition, deeply rooted in its commitment to international peace, justice and equality, not to limit any analysis and actions in the international arena to areas of disagreement and structural discrepancies that existed in respect of so many issues, but always to persevere in the search for consensus, and for clearly defined ground rules that fostered the collective action of States in favour of international trade and development.

104. That was precisely what participants had done in the course of this important Conference, and Colombia was amply satisfied with the results achieved.

105. Geneva had once more proven fertile ground for new ideas and agreements. All had allowed their imagination and generosity to run their course, and he trusted that the seeds sown at the seventh session of the Conference would bear fruit in the not too distant future.

106. The road was now paved for UNCTAD to become, with the support of the industrialized States, a forward-looking forum of ideas as well as an effective instrument for action in favour of developing countries. The final outcome would be determined by how the international agreements subscribed to were implemented in the days ahead.

107. The work had been hard and interesting. Participants had undertaken the various tasks with integrity, dedication and shared responsibility. History would judge whether what was being proposed and had been agreed to at that session of the Conference would gradually translate into tangible results and whether today's illusions could become tomorrow's realities.

108. Developing countries, far from becoming the sort of "offensive alliance" some had anticipated, had not adopted extreme positions and, in the formulation of their policies, had taken into account the considerations and problems of the industrialized countries.

109. There were, no doubt, differing viewpoints but participants had been able to overcome such differences. There had also been—throughout the Conference—fundamental disagreements which had continuously threatened consensus. Fortunately, reason and good will had prevailed at the end, as had everyone's most sincere desire to assure the co-ordination and complementarity of various groups' efforts. All of that had resulted in the happy ending of the seventh session.

110. Those endorsing the ministerial declaration in the form of UNCTAD VII's "Final Act" had made a historic commitment. Upon signing, they pledged their word and became trustworthy keepers of the agreements reached. That ensured that the agenda Governments had agreed on would move forward and without undue delays in their respective jurisdictions.

111. Consensus had been achieved on some truly critical issues: debt, commodities, international trade and the needs of the least developed countries. On all and each of them Governments had made pledges. If they were fulfilled, the seventh session of the Confe-

rence would be remembered as a giant leap forward, and all participants would have the feeling of a job well done and the pride of having made a contribution. The Conference had supported new forms of recycling for external debt and for the transfer of financial resources; it had agreed on the basis of a dynamic and fair international trading system; it had adopted effective formulas and proposals to improve the outlook of commodities; and it had established the requirements of the least developed countries to finance the growth and development they needed to improve their people's quality of life. It could be emphatically stated that, as a result of the agreements at the current session, there was a new awakening for UNCTAD as well as the hope of a more promising future for developing countries.

112. The *Secretary-General of UNCTAD*, in a preliminary and personal political assessment of the session, observed that the atmosphere and substantive content of the discussions had been positive; they had not been confrontational; they had been constructive. They had ranged widely over the burning issues facing policy makers in all countries, in particular in developing countries, and they were not unduly constrained by narrow institutional concerns.

113. Those discussions had led to the adoption of a Final Act which was characterized by a degree of balance and moderation and which was, at the same time, realistic in content. All countries and groups of countries had worked strenuously towards an outcome to which all could rally, even though the outcome gave complete satisfaction to none.

114. The text of the assessment section of the Final Act was a case in point. Each country or group of countries would have written it differently, but all could live with it. It provided the international community with a platform for stronger international co-operation to revitalize development growth and international trade. He believed that the Conference owed a vote of thanks to the President for the skill, mastery and determination with which he had carried forward the assessment exercise and brought it to a conclusion.

115. However, delegations had come to the Conference not simply to assess economic trends and global structural change but to promote decisive action in the interests of world economic growth and development. The question thus arose: Had the Conference indeed taken decisions which would affect the course of the world economy and of international economic relations, which would benefit the welfare of the people to whom all Governments were accountable?

116. Against such a yardstick, the results of the session must be evaluated with some caution. Many, perhaps all, would have wished to have gone further. However, he believed that participants could be satisfied that the Conference had achieved constructive and significant advances in the areas addressed by its agenda. Without going into the many specifics, he had in mind, for instance, the emphasis given to the need for sustainable non-inflationary growth in the developed countries and for an environment supportive of accelerated and sustainable development; the recognition in that context of the respective responsibilities of devel-

oped and developing countries, based on the consideration that the greater the economic weight of a country, the greater the effect of its policies on other countries and on the external economic environment; the new impetus given to the evolution of a growth-oriented debt strategy; the arrangements for renewed intergovernmental co-operation in the field of commodities, for which the Common Fund will be an important instrument; the realization of the complementarity between UNCTAD and GATT in their efforts to promote world trade; fight protectionism and strengthen the international trading system; and the reaffirmation of the need for more vigorous efforts in support of the development of the least developed countries. Those might not be considered dramatic breakthroughs, but they were nevertheless important. What was more, Governments had pledged themselves in good faith to give effect to those results, nationally and internationally, in the competent forums, including UNCTAD.

117. Each participant and each delegation would evaluate the results of the session against their own yardsticks or against those suggested in his opening address. For his part, as executive head of the institution, he felt that UNCTAD had emerged strengthened from the process leading up to and including the seventh session of the Conference. He was impressed by the evolution in the attitudes of many delegations, who had come to the session in a sceptical frame of mind but who were now preparing to leave convinced that UNCTAD was an institution where they could develop common approaches to issues of international economic co-operation with their counterparts from all States and agree on effective policies which would have an impact at both the national and international levels on the problems under discussion.

118. That result was in large part due to the intensive preparatory process which had been under way for over a year. The preparations had begun with discussions on the agenda and continued through consultations on the documentation and on the issues in the different agenda areas. They were enriched by a number of sectoral meetings, by visits to and discussions at capitals, and by the contributions of the research community, the enterprise sector and non-governmental organizations. Their high points were the ministerial meetings of the various regional groups. And they ended with the initial work on assessment. Those interactions were protracted and, at the intergovernmental level, often difficult, but they were fruitful and indeed indispensable for the results now embodied in the Final Act of the Conference.

119. As to the way in which UNCTAD would evolve, he would not wish it to be said that that session of the Conference was the only basis for the future work of the institution. UNCTAD had been in existence for close to a quarter of a century, since its establishment by General Assembly resolution 1995 (XIX). It must continue to build upon all its historical experience and fulfil all the elements of its wide-ranging mandate. Moreover, the scope of that session of the Conference, although broad, had not comprehended all the issues on the UNCTAD agenda. Those issues which had not been directly treated at that session remained important and

they must continue to be given a proper place in the organization's work.

120. On that basis the secretariat would now proceed to analyse and assess the implications of the Final Act of UNCTAD VII for its programme of work for the coming years. It would do so in the light of processes of reform currently under way within the United Nations as a whole. The secretariat would come up with a package of specific work orientations for the UNCTAD of the next few years, within the context of the resolution just mentioned. That package would include activities involving research, conceptual innovation and policy analysis; information exchanges and consultations; support for intergovernmental deliberations, for negotiations and for the implementation of their outcomes; and technical co-operation. All member States would be able to shape that package through their participation in the work of the Trade and Development Board and the General Assembly.

121. Whatever the shape and content of the package, the organization had a hard road ahead. He gave an assurance that the UNCTAD secretariat would continue to exert itself to respond to the demands and interests of Governments, collectively expressed. It would also spare no effort to enhance the effectiveness of UNCTAD as an instrument of international economic co-operation, and as an agent of change in support of development.

122. In his closing statement, the *President* observed that the Conference had been an exacting event, as it was bound to be, given the nature of the agenda, a background of complex international economic problems, a withering development consensus and faltering confidence in the principles of multilateralism. He expressed deep appreciation to the heads of State and Government who had addressed the Conference and had dissipated the clouds of gloom, delivering messages of faith and hope in the future of mankind, and had underscored the importance of unity and solidarity in efforts to overcome the many problems confronting the world. Similarly, he expressed deep appreciation to the Ministers who had participated in the Conference and he emphasized that the large ministerial attendance had been a very positive omen for the final outcome. The thoroughness of the preparatory work and the outstanding quality of the documentation had made a distinct contribution to the Conference and he paid a tribute to the Secretary-General of UNCTAD and the staff of the secretariat for their unstinting support.

123. He observed that the seventh session of the Conference had in many ways been unique in the history of UNCTAD conferences. The pre-Conference preparations in the Trade and Development Board had marked a point of departure and set a precedent and standard for future conferences. The agenda of the Conference was short and well focused, discussions had been transparent and pointed and held in a non-confrontational atmosphere. The achievement of a consolidated text, the Final Act of UNCTAD VII, the product of a searching and painstaking exercise, was a milestone in the proceedings of UNCTAD and, indeed, in the conduct of the North-South dialogue. It remained to be seen whether all that would strengthen UNCTAD and

its mandate enshrined in General Assembly resolution 1995 (XIX). There was reason to believe that would be so, but nothing of that nature happened *sua sponte*. There was a need to be vigilant and to maintain the momentum.

124. It would be some time before Governments fully appreciated the results of the Conference. He himself was encouraged because expectations had been tempered by a recognition of the positive results achieved in an environment of patent international crisis as typified especially by the debt burden of developing countries, stunted growth and, of course, misalignment of macro-economic policies, particularly in the major industrialized countries, and the near collapse of multilateral economic co-operation.

125. By the same token, he was disappointed by the modest results in an environment which called for decisive action in the face of the grave international economic problems, given the potential of this forum in contributing to the formulation of joint solutions to the problems of trade and development.

126. He was persuaded to conclude, however, that the clear result of the work of the Conference had been the advancement of multilateralism and the preservation of UNCTAD itself as a unique universal forum for formulating and negotiating interlocking trade and development policy and monetary issues. UNCTAD had to be preserved and there were better times ahead.

127. A serious attempt had been made at revamping the North-South dialogue. A momentum of consensus-building had been launched which would inevitably spill over into other parallel efforts, including those of the permanent machinery of UNCTAD as well as in other forums.

128. It was encouraging that the unifying theme of "Revitalizing development, growth and international trade in a more predictable and supportive environment through multilateral co-operation" had remained a valid beacon throughout the Conference. The policies and measures adopted would provide a momentum, and indeed guidelines, which would nourish this theme in this forum and in the other forums until the objectives were achieved. The results marked a new beginning and demanded more effort and political will commensurate with the development challenges of the times.

129. In concrete terms, member States and Governments had only just begun addressing the agenda for the seventh session of the Conference: it was an agenda which would have to continue to be addressed and which all must sustain and enhance in UNCTAD as well as in other organizations. The physicist, Isaac Newton, had said that scholars, and indeed statesmen, had greater vision because they stood on the shoulders of the giants who preceded them. UNCTAD had its giants, in Governments as well as outside, and so could not fail; it must maintain their vision, sense of direction and purpose. Ideologies and ideals inspired but hard-headed management and determination were their handmaidens.

V. Reports of the Sessional Committees

A. REPORT OF SESSIONAL COMMITTEE I

1. Introduction

130. At its 205th plenary meeting, on 13 July 1987, the Conference decided to establish a sessional committee (Committee I) to consider and report on agenda item 8 (*a*): "Resources for development, including financial, and related monetary questions".

131. At the same meeting, the Conference, after deciding to waive rule 65 of its rules of procedure, elected Mr. M. Taniguchi (Japan) as Chairman of Committee I.

132. At its 1st meeting, on 14 July 1987, Committee I elected Mr. U. N. Abhyankar (India) as its Vice-Chairman and Mr. R. Saad (Egypt) as its Rapporteur.

133. At its 3rd meeting, on 15 July 1987, the Committee decided to conduct its discussions in informal meetings, which would be public.

134. In the course of the session, Committee I held four meetings and nine informal meetings from 14 to 27 July 1987.

135. At its closing meeting, the Committee adopted its draft report (TD(VII)/C.I/L.2) and authorized the Rapporteur to complete it as appropriate for submission to the Conference.

2. Consideration of agenda item 8 (*a*)

RESOURCES FOR DEVELOPMENT, INCLUDING FINANCIAL, AND RELATED MONETARY QUESTIONS

136. For its consideration of item 8 (*a*), the Committee had before it the following documents:

(*a*) TD/330 and Corr.1 and 2, "Assessment and proposals by the Group of 77 relating to the seventh session of the Conference";[24]

(*b*) TD/331, "Position paper of the People's Republic of China on issues to be considered at the seventh session of the Conference";[25]

(*c*) TD/333 and Corr.1, "Approach of the socialist countries members of Group D and Mongolia to the substantive items of the provisional agenda for the seventh session of the Conference";[26]

(*d*) TD/334, communiqué of the Council of the Organisation for Economic Co-operation and Development;[27]

---

[24] Reproduced in annex V below.

[25] Reproduced in annex VI below.

[26] *Idem.*

[27] *Idem.*

(e) TD/328/Rev.1 and Add.1, "Revitalizing development, growth and international trade: assessment and policy options: report by the secretariat to UNCTAD VII";[28]

(f) TD/328/Add.2,[29] chapter II of the report by the secretariat to UNCTAD VII;

(g) TD/329/Rev.1, "Reviving multilateral co-operation for growth and development: report by the Secretary-General of UNCTAD to UNCTAD VII";[30]

(h) TD/335, "The Havana Declaration: Final document of the Sixth Ministerial Meeting of the Group of 77";[31]

(i) TD/341, "Economic and technical assistance of the USSR to developing countries";

(j) TD/343, "Declaration by the delegation of the Socialist People's Republic of Albania;

(k) TD(VII)/Misc.2, "The role of the International Monetary Fund in adjustment with growth";

(l) UNCTAD/ST/MFD/5, "Scenarios of growth, trade, finance and debt: technical note prepared by the UNCTAD secretariat";

(m) Trade and Development Report, 1987.[32]

Reference was also made to two OECD documents which were made available to the Conference (see TD/L.288): Financing and external debt of developing countries: 1986 Survey[33] and "Resources and development in the 1980s: New realities and evolving policy responses".

137. At the 1st meeting of the Committee, on 14 July 1987, item 8 (a) was introduced by the Deputy Secretary-General of UNCTAD.

138. At the same meeting, the spokesman for the Group of 77 (Peru), on behalf of the States members of the Group of 77, introduced proposals on policies and measures regarding resources for development, including financial, and related monetary questions (TD(VII)/C.I/L.1).[34]

139. At the 2nd and 3rd meetings, general statements on the item were made by: the spokesmen for Group B (France); Denmark (on behalf of the European Economic Community and its member States) (TD(VII)/C.I/CRP.1); Japan; the Holy See; the spokesman for Group D (Czechoslovakia); China; Turkey; Finland, on behalf of the Nordic countries (Finland, Norway and Sweden) (TD(VII)/C.I/CRP.2).

140. At the 4th (closing) meeting of the Committee, on 27 July 1987, the Chairman said that, following the discussions held during the informal meetings, the Committee had decided to establish a drafting group. He had also been requested to submit texts on the basis of the group's deliberations. After a series of drafting sessions, he had been requested to revise his texts. Although significant progress had been made, it had not been possible for the drafting group to produce agreed

texts. However, as a result of the deliberations in the drafting group, he had prepared the following texts: "Introduction" (TD(VII)/C.I/CRP.3/Add.3/Rev.1); "Debt problems" (TD(VII)/C.I/CRP.3/Rev.2); "External resources for development" (TD(VII)/C.I/CRP.3/Add.1/Rev.1); "Domestic resources for development, including non-financial resources" (TD(VII)/C.I/CRP.3/Add.2/Rev.1); Related monetary questions" (TD(VII)/C.I/CRP.3/Add.4). A working text of "External resources for development", on which the final reading had not been completed, would be issued as TD(VII)/C.I/CRP.3/Add.1/Rev.2.

3. Action by Committee I

141. At its 4th (closing) meeting, the Committee agreed that the texts prepared by the Chairman be transmitted to the Contact Group of the President. It also expressed the view that those texts provided a suitable basis for further discussion and negotiation of issues before the Committee. It was further understood that all proposals and documents before the Conference which concerned the item assigned to Committee I for examination, including the proposals of the Group of 77 in TD(VII)/C.I/L.1, remained before the Committee and would therefore be before the Contact Group of the President.

Closing statements

142. The spokesman for Group B (France) said that the texts prepared by the Chairman and the Committee's informal discussions had indicated interesting possibilities of agreement on several points but had also revealed points of divergence, and much remained to be done, particularly on debt. He was not in a position to confirm his Group's agreement to a number of formulations in view of the fragmentary and preliminary nature of the texts before the Committee at the current stage. There was no doubt, however, that the texts prepared by the Chairman, as well as the statements made during their examination, would be useful to the President's Contact Group.

143. The spokesman for the Group of 77 (Peru) said that the discussions and negotiations in the drafting group had proved useful and had contributed positively to the work of the Conference. It had been possible to identify areas of disagreement, grey areas where positive agreement might be reached, and some areas of agreement which would serve as a basis for the work of the President's Contact Group. The Group of 77 had been unceasingly co-operative and flexible with a view to obtaining progress in the negotiating process. He stressed that the proposals submitted by the Group of 77 (TD(VII)/C.I/L.1) were still before the Committee and should be considered, along with the Chairman's texts, in the President's Contact Group.

144. The spokesman for Group D (Czechoslovakia) said that Group D had submitted its specific proposals to the Conference (TD/333 and Corr.1) and to the Committee. It had also accepted the proposals of the Group of 77 (TD(VII)/C.I/L.1) as a basis for the Committee's work. It noted the constructive nature of the Chairman's texts and that some positive results had

[28] Reproduced in volume III.

[29] Incorporated in TD/328/Rev.1.

[30] Reproduced in volume III.

[31] Reproduced in annex V below.

[32] United Nations publication, Sales No. E.87.II.D.7.

[33] OECD, Paris, 1987.

[34] Reproduced in annex V. B below, part II, sect. I.

been achieved. Work on item 8 (*a*) should be pursued on the basis of the Chairman's texts, with all relevant documents and texts before the Committee also being transmitted to the President. He stressed that new thinking was required by all in order to mobilize the efforts of the international community to promote development and equitable co-operation among all in monetary and financial relations. An overall and just solution to debt problems was required, as provided for, in particular, in General Assembly resolution 41/202 of 8 December 1986, and it was essential to stop the outflow of resources from developing countries and to develop such monetary and financial relations as would guarantee economic security for all. Halting the arms race, reaching agreement on nuclear disarmament and reducing military budgets would release significant resources for development in all countries, above all the developing countries. The role which UNCTAD played in efforts aimed at resolving the problems facing all countries should be enhanced.

145. The representative of *China* said that the substantive negotiations conducted in the drafting group on the basis of the Chairman's texts had produced some agreement, despite certain differences. The dialogue and negotiations on the substantive issues before the Committee should continue, with the Chairman's texts providing a basis for the consolidated text to be prepared by the President. Full account must also be taken of China's position on the issues before the Committee, as reflected in TD/331. The seventh session of the Conference should help strengthen multilateral co-operation in seeking solutions to the problems of the developing countries in the areas of trade and development and the establishment of a new international economic order.

146. The representative of *Japan* said that his country was concerned about the stagnation of financial flows to developing countries and was doing its best to improve the situation, notably through its recycling scheme. Japan called on both developed and developing countries to explore ways to increase the financial flows to the developing countries, and the Minister for Foreign Affairs of Japan had just proposed the establishment of an independent high-level wise men's group, with the support of interested countries and relevant international organizations, to examine ways and means to encourage the flow of financial resources to developing countries. It was hoped that that proposal would receive support and be reflected in the final document of the Conference.

Expression of condolences

147. At its 4th meeting, on 27 July 1987, the Committee expressed condolences to the delegation of the United States of America on the untimely death of Mr. Malcolm Baldrige, Secretary of Commerce of the United States of America.

B. REPORT OF SESSIONAL COMMITTEE II

1. Introduction

148. At its 205th plenary meeting, on 13 July 1987, the Conference decided to establish a sessional committee (Committee II) to consider and report on agenda item 8 (*b*): Commodities.

149. At the same meeting, the Conference, after deciding to waive rule 65 of its rules of procedure, elected Mr. Carlos Pérez del Castillo (Uruguay) Chairman of Committee II.

150. At its 1st meeting, on 14 July 1987, Committee II elected Mr. M. Somol (Czechoslovakia) Vice-Chairman and Mr. Alfonso Tena García (Spain) Rapporteur.

151. In the course of the session, Committee II held eight meetings, from 14 to 27 July 1987.

152. At its 8th (closing) meeting, the Committee adopted its draft report (TD(VII)/C.II/L.2) and authorized the Rapporteur to complete it as appropriate for submission to the Conference.

2. Consideration of agenda item 8 (*b*)

COMMODITIES

153. The following documents, in so far as they related to the issue of commodities, were before the Committee:[35]

(*a*) Chapter III (TD/328/Add.3 and Corr.1)[36] of the secretariat report to UNCTAD VII (TD/328/Rev.1);

(*b*) TD/329/Rev.1;

(*c*) TD/330 and Corr.1 and 2;

(*d*) TD/331;

(*e*) TD/333 and Corr.1;

(*f*) TD/334;

(*g*) TD/335;

(*h*) TD/343.

154. At its 1st meeting, on 14 July 1987, the Committee began its consideration of item 8 (*b*) with an opening statement by the Chairman of the Committee and an introductory statement by the Deputy Secretary-General of UNCTAD. The spokesman for the Group of 77 (Ethiopia) formally submitted the section relating to commodities of the proposals of the Group of 77 agreed at the Sixth Ministerial Meeting of the Group of 77, held in Havana, Cuba, from 20 to 25 April 1987 (TD(VII)/C.II/L.1).[37] A statement was also made by the representative of Albania disassociating his delegation from the views of Group D as presented in TD/333 and Corr.1 (see TD/343).

155. At the 2nd and 3rd meetings, on 15 July 1987, general statements were made by: the spokesman for Group B (Switzerland); the spokesman for Group D (Union of Soviet Socialist Republics), who referred to

---

[35] See also paragraph 136 above.

[36] See footnote 29.

[37] Reproduced in annex V. B below, part II, sect. II.

section IV of TD/333 and Corr.1 containing his Group's views on agenda item 8 (*b*); and the representative of China, who referred to the section on commodities in his country's position paper (TD/331). Statements were also made by the representative of Denmark, on behalf of the European Economic Community and its member States; the representative of Norway, on behalf of the Nordic countries (Finland, Norway and Sweden); and the representative of Japan.

156. Also at its 3rd meeting, the Committee agreed on a list of topics to be discussed (TD(VII)/C.II/CRP.2). It further agreed that discussion of these topics should be conducted within the framework of informal meetings of the Committee, without prejudice to the holding of plenary meetings to enable delegations to make general statements. The Committee held six informal meetings, from 16 to 21 July 1987.

157. At the 4th meeting, on 16 July 1987, general statements were made by the representatives of Poland and Switzerland. At its 5th meeting, on 17 July 1987, general statements were made by the representatives of the United States of America, Canada, Australia, New Zealand and Austria.

158. At the 6th meeting, on 21 July 1987, the representative of Switzerland introduced a working paper submitted on behalf of the States members of Group B (TD(VII)/C.II/CRP.3). A statement was made by the representative of the Food and Agriculture Organization of the United Nations.

159. At the 7th meeting of the Committee, on 24 July 1987, a paper was introduced by the representative of Norway on behalf of the Nordic countries (Finland, Norway and Sweden) (TD(VII)/C.II/CRP.5), and a statement was made by the representative of Japan.

160. At the 8th meeting of the Committee, on 27 July 1987, papers were introduced by the representative of Denmark, on behalf of the European Economic Community and its member States (TD(VII)/C.II/CRP.6), by the representatives of the United States of America (TD(VII)/C.II/CRP.8) and of Australia (TD(VII)/C.II/CRP.9); and a proposal was introduced by the representative of Japan (TD(VII)/C.II/CRP.7). The Chairman reported on the outcome of his informal consultations on the text on policies and measures that he had submitted in TD(VII)/C.II/CRP.4. Closing statements were made by the Chairman, the spokesmen for Group B, the Group of 77 and Group D, and by the representative of China.

3. Action by Committee II

161. At its 8th (closing) meeting, on 27 July 1987, the Committee decided to transmit to the Contact Group of the President the text submitted by the Chairman in TD(VII)/C.II/CRP.4. It further decided that the proposals submitted by the Group of 77 (TD(VII)/C.II/L.1) and the working paper submitted by Group B (TD(VII)/C.II/CRP.3) should be annexed to the report of Committee II. The Committee also decided to draw the attention of the Contact Group of the President to the views of Group D on commodities contained in TD/333 and Corr.1, and of China, as contained in TD/331. The Committee took note of the

Chairman's intention to transmit to the President of the Conference, on his own responsibility, the results of the informal consultations of the Chairman's text.

4. Appendices to the report of Committee II

APPENDIX I

Proposal on policies and measures submitted by Ethiopia on behalf of the States members of the Group of 77
[TD(VII)/C.II/L.1]

COMMODITIES

[For the text, see annex V. B below, part II, section II.]

APPENDIX II

Working paper submitted by Switzerland on behalf of the States members of Group B
[TD(VII)/C.II/CRP.3]

The task of this Committee is threefold and consists in:

(*a*) Carrying out a factual assessment of the situation prevailing on commodity markets, the causes of this situation (underlying factors), and the impact on producers and consumers, particularly on developing countries heavily dependent on commodity exports.

(*b*) Discussing, intertwined with the assessment, the appropriate policies and measures at the national, regional, international and multilateral levels to cope with the situation and its implications.

(*c*) Giving adequate orientations for further work in the framework of UNCTAD.

A. ASSESSMENT

An objective and realistic discussion on all the factors at work on the commodity markets will contribute to reaching a common assessment and to our discussion on the policy orientations. Group B shares the view expressed on several occasions by the Group of 77 that one cannot expect a complete convergence on all the elements of a comprehensive assessment, but this should not prevent the Committee from agreeing on a number of fundamentals and on their impact on commodity markets and on development.

The following elements should be taken into account in any evaluation of the present situation:

1. *Facts and trends*

Patterns of production, consumption and trade of commodities have undergone considerable changes in recent years and this evolution has a direct influence on prices.

The share of commodities in world economic output and trade has followed a declining trend. Over the past 20 years, the proportion of non-fuel primary commodities in total world exports has decreased from 30 per cent to less than 17 per cent. This is not due to falling demand in absolute terms, but essentially to faster growth of trade in other sectors. Against this background, the emergence of new producers and improved productivity overall increased competition on many saturated or protected commodity markets. For their part, developing countries now account for nearly one half of world consumption and their share in total imports of non-fuel commodities has been steadily increasing. This important trend stresses the growing importance of developing countries in world commodity trade and the prospects that may be offered by the revitalization of their development process.

Local processing of commodities in developing countries has increased over the last two decades as well as, more recently, processing of imported raw materials by a number of developing countries. Although this trend indicates an ongoing process of vertical diversification and economic development, it also partly explains the decline of trade in primary commodities.

After two decades of relative stability in dollar terms—though suffering erosion in real terms that could have been an early indicator of a secular trend—commodity prices have undergone considerable fluctuations since the early 1970s. Periods of relative buoyancy and depression were closely related to accelerated world economic cycles. This short-term instability combined with very high average prices for the whole decade of the 1970s made it difficult for economic operators to discern underlying long-term trends of commodity markets.

In the 1980s, real commodity prices have decreased despite the recent recovery of growth rates in the world economy and have fallen to levels which have not been experienced for decades. The situation in the 1980s therefore presents an inverse picture characterized by low average prices and, for certain commodities, decreasing fluctuations, slower growth in demand and excess supplies. World trade in non-fuel commodities grew only 1.1 per cent in the first half of the 1980s, compared to 3.8 per cent in the 1970s. The growth rate of world consumption followed a similar pattern. However, world production output and capacities of many commodities did not adjust correspondingly.

A more detailed examination of each individual commodity market remains necessary to complete these very general considerations. Striking differences in market situations are perceptible when looking at large groups of commodities such as metals, where lower consumption growth rates, reduced costs and excess capacities have depressed many prices; agricultural products, where structural productivity improvements, weather conditions and support measures worked together to help produce a series of bumper crops in the 1980s and contributed to considerable stock accumulation while market access remained restricted by various distortive measures; or tropical beverages, where climatic factors affecting one or a few main producers seem to remain a determinant element of price formation. The impact of exchange rate instability, interest rate levels and national pricing policies on individual markets should also be taken into account.

2. *Underlying factors*

A significant feature of commodity price behaviour in the 1980s has been the relative lack of response to periods of moderate but steady growth rates of world economy. The deterioration of the dollar exchange rate since the end of 1985 was not associated with an increase in commodity prices expressed in that currency until the latter half of 1986. The effects of lower non-dollar prices in stimulating demand were offset by increases in supply and relatively slower growth than in previous decades. All these tendencies are harmful for many producing developing countries since their productivity gains have been limited. In addition, their demographic burden has often increased considerably.

This pattern indicates that longer-term cyclical factors as well as structural changes have significantly superseded the importance of traditional short-term price fluctuations.

Among the longer-term cyclical factors at work, special mention must be made of the lagged effects of the high average prices of the 1970s that have led to considerable investments in the commodity sector, based on forecasts that did not adequately take into account some important long-term trends and therefore contributed heavily to the present situation of overcapacity, stock accumulation and oversupply. The lagged impact of this longer-term cyclical factor which coincided with cyclically weak demand has been considerably reinforced by the consequences of structural factors tending to curb the growth rate of consumption and to increase supply, such as:

(a) *On the demand side:*

The constant shift by industry to lines of production which are both less commodity intensive and less energy intensive. This evolution appreciably accelerated during the 1970s and early 1980s under the combined pressure of successive oil shocks, high prices for most commodities, and concerns about possible supply shortages and long-term depletion of natural resources. Present price and supply conditions may, in limited cases and proportions, temporarily slow down this trend but are not likely to reverse it;

Technological changes leading to increased substitution of some commodities by others or by synthetics as well as to an expansion of recycling and conservation techniques;

Increased concentration of growth within sectors not using commodities to a significant extent, such as electronics, telecommunications and services;

Lasting changes in consumer tastes and dietary habits.

Stagnation of population growth in developed countries.

(b) *On the supply side:*

Technological progress leading to increased productivity in extraction and first stages of processing of minerals and metals;

Considerable increases in agricultural output and yields and emergence of new and competitive producers and exporters.

The depressive effect on prices of the mentioned cyclical and structural factors have been exacerbated during the last decade by the impact of policies of developed and developing countries that tended to increase supply or to reduce demand. The realities of interdependence and the principle of comparative advantage have not been taken sufficiently into account by Governments: too often, decisions on measures designed to encourage or to protect national production have been taken in a narrow and short-term perspective.

Although the present situation affects all producing countries, it has particularly severe consequences for many developing countries that are, to varying degrees, dependent on their export earnings of primary or semi-processed commodities for financing their development. Weak commodity market conditions have indeed affected individual developing countries, although differently, depending on their economic situation, national policy responses and the degree of diversity in their economies. The real impact of the depressed situation of commodity markets on developing countries should be measured by the evolution of the respective purchasing power of their total incomes from their exports of manufactures, services and commodities against their total imports, including fuel.

B. POLICIES AND MEASURES

The international community as a whole has a strong interest in smoothly functioning commodity markets. This concern should be translated into increased co-operation among producers and consumers of each commodity.

The increasing interdependence among countries and among economic sectors also implies the need for sustained efforts at national and international levels to revitalize the development process, particularly of those developing countries that are heavily dependent on their exports of one or a few commodities.

In the light of those shared interests, Group B suggests that the discussions on policies be focused along two perspectives: the market perspective and the development perspective. The areas that seem more promising for fruitful co-operation are, in our view:

1. Within the market perspective:

The enhancement, strengthening or establishment, where necessary, of producer-consumer consultations, exchanges of information, improvement and/or dissemination of statistics and any other relevant data that could contribute to a greater transparency of each individual commodity market, in the light of experience gained to date;

The improvement of the functioning of commodity agreements not excluding any innovative form of co-operation that producers and consumers could deem appropriate in accordance with the needs and dynamics of each individual commodity market;

Welcoming the negotiations currently under way in the Uruguay Round and acknowledging the competence of GATT, common discussion of present problems of access to markets for producers of commodities and processed commodities: rationale for improved access conditions to existing and potential markets.

2. Within a development perspective:

The examination of the appropriate mix of policies and measures at national, regional and international levels designed to enhance research and development productivity improvements and marketing. This approach would help countries achieve development through an improved allocation of resources based upon the principles of comparative advantage and structural adjustment;

The ways and means to promote effective vertical diversification, particularly through increased local processing, where economically justified, taking into account the important role of the private sector: possible identification of new and more concrete approaches to UNCTAD's work programme in this field;

The evaluation of the appropriate policies at national, regional and international levels aiming at reducing the vulnerability of developing countries heavily dependent on export earnings of a few commodities by promoting the horizontal diversification of their economies, where economically appropriate. International co-operation in this field would be enhanced by reports from individual developing countries on their experiences. International financing institutions as well as other competent international organizations should continue to be actively involved in these matters;

Examination of the needs of developing countries, particularly the least developed countries, for more stable export earnings within a context of diversification or structural adjustment. The existing compensatory schemes and mechanisms as well as the different views on international co-operation in this area concerning the commodity-specific or the balance-of-payments focus should be taken into account.

Within an overall context, both market and development perspectives will be substantially improved by the reduction of macroeconomic imbalances and the achievement of stronger and sustained global growth. In a spirit of shared responsibilities, all member States of UNCTAD should subscribe to and encourage this aim, as has been done by the OECD countries in the Communiqué of their recent Ministerial Council meeting, and by the summit countries in the Venice Declaration.

C. WORK PROGRAMME OF UNCTAD

General orientations for future work will flow from the policy orientations sketched out above. In addition, areas or elements left open in the assessment process could, if there is a common interest, be analysed in greater depth by the secretariat of UNCTAD to allow further discussions among member States that could lead to converging perceptions to be eventually reflected in policies;

Concrete proposals on the work programme have been and will continue to be made during the Committee's discussions: they should be duly examined and decided upon.

C. REPORT OF SESSIONAL COMMITTEE III

1. Introduction

162. At its 205th meeting, on 14 July 1987, the Conference decided to establish a sessional committee (Committee III) to consider and report on agenda item 8 (c): International trade.

163. At the same meeting, the Conference, after deciding to waive rule 65 of the rules of procedure, elected Mr. Chak Mun See (Singapore) as Chairman of Committee III.

164. At its 1st meeting, on 15 July 1987, Committee III elected Mr. Lars Anell (Sweden) as its Vice-Chairman, and Mr. Stanislav Daskalov (Bulgaria) as its Rapporteur.

165. In the course of the session, Committee III held five formal meetings and a number of informal meetings, from 14 to 25 July 1987.

166. At its 5th (closing) meeting, on 25 July 1987, Committee III adopted its draft report (TD(VII)/C.III/L.2) and authorized the Rapporteur to complete it as appropriate for submission to the Conference.

2. Consideration of agenda item 8 (c)

INTERNATIONAL TRADE

167. The following proposals and documents were before the Committee for its consideration of this item:[38]

(a) Chapter IV (TD/328/Add.4)[39] of the secretariat report to UNCTAD VII (TD/328/Rev.1);

(b) The foreword by the Secretary-General of UNCTAD to TD/328/Rev.1 and the Executive Summary (TD/328/Rev.1/Add.1) of the secretariat report;

(c) TD/329/Rev.1;

(d) TD/330 and Corr.1 and 2;

(e) TD/331;

(f) TD/333 and Corr.1;

(g) TD/334;

(h) TD/335;

(i) TD/341;

(j) TD/343;

(k) TD/B/1104/Rev.1, "Objectives, guidelines and elements of a programme for further promotion of trade and economic co-operation among countries having different economic and social systems", note by the UNCTAD secretariat.

168. At its 1st meeting, on 14 July 1987, the Committee began its consideration of item 8 (c) with an opening statement by the Deputy Secretary-General of UNCTAD. The spokesman for the Group of 77 (India) introduced proposals on policies and measures for consideration by the Committee (TD(VII)/C.III/L.1 and Corr.1), based on TD/330 and Corr.1 and 2, part II, section III, on international trade.

169. At the 2nd meeting of the Committee, on 15 July 1987, the spokesmen for Group B (Federal Republic of Germany), for Group D and Mongolia (Hungary) and for the Group of 77 (India) made statements, which were submitted to the Committee as documents for the consideration of this item (TD(VII)/C.III/CRP.1, CRP.2 and CRP.3, respectively), in addition to the documents mentioned in paragraph 167 above. Statements were also made by the representatives of the European Economic Community, Turkey and China.

170. At the 3rd meeting of the Committee, on 16 July 1987, statements were made by the representatives of Japan; Albania; Poland; the Council for Mutual Economic Assistance; Sweden, on behalf of the Nordic countries (Finland, Norway and Sweden) (TD(VII)/C.III/CRP.6); and Australia.

171. Informal discussions began on 16 July 1987. In all, five informal discussion meetings were held, and 11 countries spoke, in addition to the group spokesmen, the representative of China and the representative of the European Economic Community.

172. As a result of informal consultations, the Committee agreed that its discussions would focus on the following four subject-areas:

1. Protectionism and structural adjustment, market access and policies affecting trade;
2. Systematic issues of international trade;

---

[38] See also paragraph 136 above.

[39] See footnote 29.

3. Enhancement of trade prospects for developing countries: technical assistance; and the Uruguay Round of multilateral trade negotiations;

4. Trade relations among countries having different economic and social systems.

173.   At its 4th meeting, on 17 July 1987, the Committee took up the subject of trade relations among countries with different economic and social systems. Statements were made by the representative of the Sudan on behalf of the States members of the Group of 77 (TD(VII)/C.III/CRP.4) and by the representative of Bulgaria on behalf of the States members of Group D (TD(VII)/C.III/CRP.5). A statement was also made on this issue by the representative of Jamaica. A general statement was made by the representative of Switzerland.

174.   At the 5th informal meeting, on 22 July 1987, the spokesman for Group B introduced a working paper for consideration by the Committee (TD(VII)/C.III/CRP.7).

3. Action by the Committee[40]

175.   At its 5th (closing) meeting, on 25 July 1987, the Committee decided to transmit the text submitted by the Chairman on his own responsibility to the Contact Group of the President for further consideration (TD(VII)/C.III/CRP.9 and Corr.1). The Committee understood that all documents concerning agenda item 8 (c) remained before it and would therefore be before the Contact Group of the President.

Statements made in connection with the text of the Chairman

176.   The spokesman for *Group B* (Federal Republic of Germany) said that his Group felt that a fruitful and constructive debate had taken place in the Committee. The debate and informal discussions that had followed had left open strong differences of opinion on the issues before the Committee. There were, however, some areas with promise for agreement.

177.   Although Group B had considerable difficulties with the text submitted by the Chairman in terms of structure and content, it thought that the text could serve as a basis for discussion. Group B had been ready to continue discussing the text at the Committee level, and had envisaged making specific proposals on it after all groups had given their detailed reactions so that a mutually acceptable text could have been submitted to the President of the Conference. Group B was still ready to resume the discussion. However, as others had not felt able to continue examining the text at Committee level, an agreed text could not be finalized. The Chairman's text would now be forwarded to the President of the Conference, on the Chairman's own responsibility.

178.   Group B understood that the President would make appropriate arrangements, in consultation with regional groups, for the text to be further examined, elaborated and amended. The Group requested that its own views and proposals, as contained in TD(VII)/C.III/CRP.1 and CRP.7, be remitted to the President

as attachments to the Committee's report to be taken into account in subsequent discussions.

179.   The spokesman for the *Group of 77* (India) expressed the Group's appreciation to the Chairman for the arduous efforts he had made to advance the negotiations on substantive issues. The Group would have liked to see the negotiations progress at a faster pace but the work would now have to be continued in the Contact Group of the President. The Group appreciated the contribution made by the Chairman in the form of the text submitted on his responsibility. The proposals by the Group of 77 in TD(VII)/C.III/L.1 and Corr.1 would remain before the Committee. They deserved serious negotiation and the Group looked forward to the opportunity to do so.

180.   He requested that TD(VII)/C.III/L.1 and Corr.1 and the statement he had made on behalf of the Group of 77 in TD(VII)/C.III/CRP.3 be annexed to the report of the Committee.

181.   The spokesman for *Group D* (Hungary) said that the Group considered the text which the Chairman would forward to the Contact Group on his own responsibility to be a significant contribution which would serve as a basis for further work on international trade issues. In connection with the text, Group D wished to stress again two elements: first, economic and trade sanctions that were not based on the resolutions of the General Assembly should not be imposed for political reasons; secondly, the trade régime in the textiles and clothing sector should be liberalized by the removal of discriminatory restraints on exports from all affected countries. His Group hoped that joint and co-operative efforts which took into account the interests of all participating countries would lead to a successful outcome of the work on international trade.

182.   The representative of the *Sudan*, speaking on behalf of the *Group of 77* with regard to the question of East-South trade, requested that the statement he had made, contained in TD(VII)/C.III/CRP.4 and entitled "Promotion of trade and economic co-operation among countries having different economic and social systems, with particular consideration given to the interests of developing countries", be annexed to the report of the Committee.

183.   The representative of *China* noted that, in the preceding few days, an exchange of views had taken place on a wide range of issues in the field of trade. Through numerous consultations with groups and arduous work the Chairman had prepared the text contained in TD(VII)/C.III/CRP.9 and Corr.1 for submission to the President and his Contact Group. The Chinese delegation considered that the text, on the whole, reflected the basic concerns and interests of the different parties. Although it had not proved possible to reach a successful outcome for lack of time and other reasons, the Chinese delegation believed that the deliberations in the Committee had been useful and that they would have a positive influence on the work of the President and the Contact Group in that regard. It hoped that much hard work would be done on the basis of the text submitted by the Chairman to the President so as to achieve positive results in the last stage of the Conference. The delegation also hoped that the Presi-

---

[40] See also paragraph 184 below.

dent of the Conference, in the discussions in the Contact Group, would give due consideration to the position paper of the People's Republic of China contained in TD/331[41] and the non-paper from the delegation of China entitled "Elements of action on international trade" circulated on 21 July 1987.

184. The Committee agreed that TD(VII)/C.III/ L.1 and Corr.1, and TD(VII)/C.III/CRP.1, CRP.3, CRP.4 and CRP.7 should be annexed to its report as requested.

185. The *Chairman*, summing up the work of the Committee during the preceding two weeks, noted that it had held extensive discussions on the most important issues of international trade within the framework it had established, namely (*a*) protectionism and structural adjustment, market access and policies affecting trade; (*b*) systematic issues of international trade; (*c*) enhancement of trade prospects for developing countries: technical assistance; and the Uruguay Round of multilateral trade negotiations; and (*d*) trade relations among countries having different economic and social systems. He considered that there had been some convergence of views in certain areas. In some other areas, although there had been a common perception of the problems affecting international trade, opinions differed as to their underlying causes and the policies to be followed. Positions on certain questions were very different.

186. He had found the discussions and exchanges of views in the plenary meetings, informal meetings and extended bureau meetings as well as the bilateral talks with the group spokesmen and their friends to have been very useful as they had enabled a consensus to evolve on a number of issues and led to a better understanding of each other's position on others. He hoped that the text he had prepared in the light of those discussions and exchanges would constitute a useful contribution in serving as a basis for the further work of the Conference in the area of international trade.

4. Appendices to the report of Committee III

APPENDIX I

Proposals on policies and measures submitted by India on behalf of the States members of the Group of 77
[TD(VII)/C.III/L.1]

[For the text, see annex V.B below, part II, section III.]

APPENDIX II

Statement by the representative of the Federal Republic of Germany on behalf of the States members of Group B
[TD(VII)/C.III/CRP.1]

1. The seventh session of the Conference falls at both an important and an opportune moment for the discussion of issues and problems in the area of international trade. The economic difficulties and the protectionist pressures with which we are confronted at present are heavily felt, making the need for creative, co-ordinated and effective action towards resolution of these difficulties more vital than ever. The seventh session of the Conference should provide us with the opportunity to analyse and discuss these problems and help us to reach

consensus on what the international community and individual participants in the Conference might do to help to solve these problems. Informal consultations have been a useful starting-point for the analysis of the problems. In a first stage we want to highlight again a few of the points which are important to us, in view of the discussions we have had. We shall give more precise ideas on what conclusions should be drawn and on what UNCTAD's contribution should be over the coming years, taking account of proposals of other groups.

2. Let me begin with an analysis of the international trading environment. The general economic situation which we are facing in the area of international trade contains elements of opportunity, uncertainty and risk. The economic recovery that began in 1983 is weakening, and most recent forecasts outline a slowing of this economic growth, to around 2.25 per cent. At the same time, relatively low levels of inflation continue to prevail in developed countries. As to trade, the growth in world trade in 1987 should be somewhat lower than that experienced in 1986.

3. Trade growth is influenced by both external and internal factors, as has been pointed out in chapter I of the documentation prepared by the UNCTAD secretariat. All countries rise by their own efforts, but it is clear that the world economy conditions their success. A variety of external factors affects such success. Exchange rate volatility has created uncertainties for economic operators. Misalignment of currencies both in developed and in developing countries has had a tendency to distort trade flows. Historically low levels of commodity prices have compounded the trade difficulties faced by commodity-exporting countries. Slower overall economic growth during the 1980s has negatively affected the purchasing power of many developed countries for exports of their trading partners. Debtor countries have in some cases resorted to restrictive import policies. There has been a widespread increase in protectionist pressures and measures linked to all the developments I have mentioned.

4. External factors, however, only relate a partial story. Domestic economic policies have had a major influence on economic performance, and the more economically significant the country, the greater impact such policies have had on other countries as well, both directly and indirectly. The timeliness and adequacy of domestic policy responses has governed the extent to which countries have realized their potential to adapt to the impact of such external factors in the world economy, particularly since 1973. Moreover, such policies have also in part been responsible for the incidence of these factors.

5. The growing disequilibria in world trade constitute a serious problem and will need to be tackled by the countries concerned by various means including macro-economic policy, exchange rate policy, structural reform and trade policy. There is a need for improving the international economic environment through co-ordinated policy decisions and through appropriate national measures. At the recent OECD Ministerial Meeting as well as at the Venice Summit, developed countries stated their determination to continue to carry out individually and collectively policy commitments undertaken on earlier occasions in areas such as exchange rates, structural adjustment, trade, debt and the environment, and to implement strengthened arrangements for multilateral surveillance and co-ordination of economic policies.

6. For their part, many developing countries have shown a remarkable willingness to adopt and implement growth-oriented adjustment policies at some social cost and have made great efforts at domestic resource mobilization. There have been substantial disparities in economic performance between various developing countries and regions, as described in more detail in chapter I of the documentation prepared by the UNCTAD secretariat. Even more significant have been the gaps between the growth rates achieved by individual developing countries over this period.

7. Although the situation differs considerably among developing countries and regions, many have been demonstrating an increasingly strong trade performance and have become important trade partners, both as exporters and as importers. The manufactures sector has been of key importance to trade expansion, and developing-country exports of manufactures have shown particular dynamism. Developing countries differ substantially with regard to their trade structures; there are, for example, great differences in the shares of commodities and of manufactures in total exports, as well as in the degree of product concentration of their exports. Developing countries also differ with regard to the type of economic policies they have followed, and the degree of export versus import orientation such policies have imparted to their external trade. Those developing countries that have become

---

[41] See annex VI below.

prominent exporters have also tended to be the countries that have followed outward-looking trade policies, have diversified their exports, and have allowed a greater role for the private sector and for the play of market forces.

8. Let me now turn to the main challenges in the trade field confronting all countries—both developed and developing. These challenges are: the need for appropriate structural adjustment; the need to halt and reverse protectionism and to remove distortions to trade; the need for the further liberalization and expansion of trade; and the need to reduce large external imbalances. Such imbalances carry with them the risk of intensified protectionist pressures, even though the resolution of such imbalances lies mainly in the adoption of appropriate macro-economic policies.

9. As member Governments, one of the major policy tasks we face is that of halting and reversing trade protectionism and removing distortions to trade. This is particularly important in the light of the persistent trends towards restrictive trade measures, notably of a bilateral or a discriminatory nature, outside the GATT framework and principles, and of the proliferation of protectionist pressures. Although in many cases Governments have been successful in resisting such pressures, in others protectionist actions have continued to be taken. Although the impact of such actions may differ, all countries should refrain from taking such actions and should contribute to the reduction and removal of existing barriers to trade. This problem concerns all groups of countries, both developed and developing, and from all types of economic systems.

10. In dealing with these challenges, it is vital to recognize the link which exists between trade policy and structural adjustment policy. There is a close interlinkage between the evolution of trade policy and the promotion of structural change and domestic economic adjustment, as protectionism is often the result of the refusal to adapt to structural changes. A dynamic, well-functioning domestic economy is much less prone to protectionist pressures than is an economy characterized by various internal rigidities.

11. Structural adjustment has been recognized as a major concern by Group B countries. Our aim is to reduce distortions and rigidities, which compound macro-economic problems and retard growth, through allowing a greater play of market forces. Structural adjustment has been carried out in various sensitive industrial sectors in our countries and such steps have not been without social cost at a time of high unemployment. Because structural adjustment is an ongoing process, appropriate measures continue to be necessary to ease macro-economic constraints and bring about a more efficient functioning of the price mechanism, taking into account the role of the private sector in this process. These economic concerns are relevant for all countries and groups of countries. Ministers of OECD countries recognized the importance of such policies at their meeting last May. At that time the conclusions of a major report on structural adjustment were endorsed and a recommendation made to reduce industrial subsidies, to the extent that they are a source of domestic and international distortions.

12. Structural adjustment is particularly necessary in the area of agriculture. The serious imbalances that prevail in the markets for the main agricultural products and the distortive effects of excessive support policies have been widely recognized. These problems are felt both by developed and developing countries, and the growing imbalances in the supply and demand for the main agricultural products have grave implications for all countries. Developed countries have therefore made commitments in OECD meeting and at the Venice Summit for agricultural reform. Steps are currently being taken on the national level in OECD countries to deal with the problem of agricultural reform and such efforts are being pursued and coordinated at the multilateral level as well. These reforms will be integral to the success of the negotiations taking place in the Uruguay Round, based on the Punta del Este Declaration, in which both developed and developing countries are participating. Although developed countries' domestic agricultural reforms are critical to this process, developing countries also will have to consider their own policies to ensure that this sector of their economies is more responsive to market signals. Producers and consumers must consider the implications of these developments in assessing the need for structural adjustment in their economies.

13. The service sector, which has shown dynamic growth in recent years, can be important in contributing to structural adjustment. Services, indigenous or imported as appropriate, can contribute to the development process and to growth through increased innovation and efficiency, improved employment opportunities and increased foreign exchange earnings.

14. Structural adjustment is one example of the interdependence between trade issues and other issues. It is vital that the contribution of trade policy to the adjustment process results in an expansion rather than a restriction of trade. Throughout the years a number of problems have built up in the trade field. These have been due mainly to measures taken outside GATT rules and to the lack of rules in certain fields, including new areas like services, and trade-related aspects of intellectual property rights and trade-related investment measures. Attempts to solve these problems unilaterally by appealing solely to the political will of individual contracting parties have on the whole not been successful. This is why developed and developing countries alike have come to the conclusion that only a negotiated solution in which each participant can find his own interest can reverse protectionist trends and increase the responsiveness of the GATT system to the evolving international economic environment.

15. The Uruguay Round provides the best opportunity for all participants to confront and resolve the major trade challenges for the international community, including those facing the least developed countries. The Round is the most comprehensive to date, allowing the broadest possible approach to tariffs and non-tariff measures as well as for the review and strengthening of the overall effectiveness and decision-making of GATT as an institution. It is important that the Round be supported if it is to succeed and we should not pursue proposals in UNCTAD which could in any way detract from the Uruguay Round negotiating process which developed and developing countries joined in launching. Discussions in this Committee should rather give momentum to the Uruguay Round.

16. Developed countries recognize the need for securing and enlarging market access for developing countries. This, along with the resolution of other trade problems, would have a significant positive effect on a range of other issues, including debt, which are contributing to international economic instability. The Uruguay Round offers the best vehicle for achieving these objectives and all participants can expect to benefit, just as all should contribute. Developing countries, particularly those already participating significantly in world trade, will obtain fuller benefits to the extent that they can contribute to the process through taking on greater contractual obligations and improving their observance of multilateral trade disciplines. Through their fuller participation, the trading system offers these countries the benefits of stability and predictability, transparency, non-discrimination and protection of individual country interests. Equally important, these developing countries, through their fuller integration into the international trading system, would contribute in a manner commensurate with their level of economic development to improving the functioning and viability of the system as a whole, thus helping to distribute its benefits to other, less developed countries and accelerate their rate of development. Group B also recalls in this context the specific undertaking in the Punta del Este Declaration concerning the least developed countries and the need to expand their trading opportunities.

17. South-South trade is an element which should be addressed in the Uruguay Round negotiations. Recent trends have shown that the dynamism and growing importance of this trade can contribute to an expansion of opportunities in the trading system for developing countries, including the least developed countries.

18. The Uruguay Round provides participants with the means and purpose to oppose domestic protectionist pressures through carrying out the standstill and roll-back commitments they have entered into. All countries have a stake in the successful completion of the Uruguay Round as it seeks to spread the economic benefits of trade liberalization and to increase efficiency of the patterns of production world wide.

19. Given the modest level of East-South trade, the potential for its expansion should be significant, especially when viewed from the perspective of the developing countries. This is particularly true if the proposed reforms of many of the centrally planned economies' foreign trade systems are implemented. UNCTAD is particularly well-suited to undertake a detailed examination of the evolution of East-South trade relations and Group B regrets that our attention has not in the past been focused clearly enough on this specific issue. A major difficulty facing us is the lack of detailed, reliable and accurate statistics relating to the volume, composition and origin of East-South trade flows, and this undermines our efforts to draw effective conclusions.

20. UNCTAD can make an important contribution in the areas of trade and of protectionism and structural adjustment as they affect development. Its work can provide added stimulus to policy-makers in

developed and developing countries, and promote consensus in favour of efforts to enhance development prospects. This requires serious consideration of UNCTAD's potential contribution in the trade field and of its work programme. Rigorous analysis of the relevant questions based on objective and balanced documentation prepared by the UNCTAD secretariat is an integral part of this task. As I said at the beginning, we shall come back to these questions in the light of our discussion in the Sessional Committee.

APPENDIX III

Statement by the representative of India
on behalf of the States members of the Group of 77
[TD(VII)/C.III/CRP.3]

1. The Group of 77 proposals on Conference agenda item 8 (c) (International trade) were submitted at the fifteenth special session of the Trade and Development Board, on 18 May 1987. We believe that all concerned have had the opportunity to consider them. The rationale of the proposals has already been explained in detail in part I, "Assessment", of TD/330[42] and also in the course of the informal consultations on assessment that preceded the session.

2. The proposals on international trade are contained in part II, section III, of TD/330. I take this opportunity to introduce these proposals on behalf of the Group of 77 for consideration by the Committee. The proposals cover the policies and measures in the following specific areas:

A. International trading system;
B. Protectionism and structural adjustment;
C. Market access;
D. The role of UNCTAD in connection with the Uruguay Round of multilateral trade negotiations;
E. Services;
F. Trade relations among countries having different economic and social systems.

3. We look forward to intensive and sincere negotiations on each of these proposals in the coming days so that this Committee will be in a position to submit its concrete recommendations and proposals to the President of the Conference by 24 July 1987.

4. Keeping in view this deadline for our work, I wish to submit the following proposal for the organization of work in this Committee:

(a) That 23 and 24 July be kept aside for finalization and adoption of the report;

(b) Four working days in the first week and three working days in the second week would be available for substantive work. There would be six meetings available for each of the Committees;

(c) The first meeting may be devoted to introduction of the proposals and adoption of the plan of work of the Committee;

(d) The following plan of work is proposed for adoption:

Meeting

I. Introduction.
II. (A) International trading system.
III. (B) Protectionism and structural adjustment.
IV. (C) Market access.
V. (D) and (E) The role of UNCTAD in connection with the Uruguay Round of multilateral trade negotiations and services.
VI. (F) Trade relations among countries having different economic and social systems.

APPENDIX IV

Promotion of trade and economic co-operation among countries having different economic and social systems, with particular consideration given to the interests of developing countries

*Statement by the representative of the Sudan
on behalf of the States members of the Group of 77*
[TD/VII)/C.III/CRP.4]

---
[42] See annex V below.

1. In the period between 1983 and 1986 the shares of both developing countries and of socialist countries in world trade declined. East-South trade remained stationary and the share of developing countries in socialist countries' overall trade declined in this period. This performance took place despite many efforts at bilateral, regional and international levels. The worsening international environment had its adverse effects on these relations and, as a result, the possibilities which partners could offer each other were not fully utilized.

2. During the period between the two sessions of the Conference, the composition of East-South trade remained fairly unchanged. The geographical spread of East-South trade also continued to be limited. Although some newcomers joined to enrich the network of the legal basis and institutional framework of East-South trade, the major part of this trade continued to be conducted among traditional partners. Moreover, owing to the liquidity squeeze, the period was also marked by a contraction of trade subject to hard currency and an escalation of counter-trade.

3. Although the major part of the provisions of Conference resolutions and Board decisions were implemented by considerable determination, they were insufficient to respond to the challenges of the 1980s. Therefore, the Group of 77 believes that the present session of the Conference provides an opportunity for member States to fashion joint and convergent actions aimed at enhancing trade and economic relations among countries having different economic and social systems. These relations have a considerable role to play in the process of revitalization of development and resumption of growth and the responsibility of enhancing them rests with UNCTAD as a unique international organization in which all issues pertaining to trade relations among countries having different economic and social systems could be discussed.

4. The Group of 77 is very much encouraged by the proposals formulated by the Secretary-General of UNCTAD on this subject, contained in his report, as well as those in the introductory statement by the Assistant Secretary-General in this Committee. To this end the Group of 77 reiterates its earlier position on the need for the elaboration of a concrete programme containing a set of guidelines conducive to promotion of intersystems trade and economic co-operation. Such a programme should bring about a supportive international environment in which intersystems trade could grow at a stable and reasonable rate in a predictable setting, while respecting the recognized international trade rules and principles. In fact the Board, in its decision 321 (XXXI) of 27 September 1985, invited the Secretary-General of UNCTAD to prepare proposals for further promotion of intersystems trade and economic co-operation. The revised version of these proposals, which were thoroughly discussed during the first part of the thirty-third session of the Board and further elaborated by an *Ad hoc* Group of Experts convened in January 1987, are contained in TD/B/1104/Rev.1. The Group of 77 believes that this document, together with the agreed contents of the text annexed to Conference decision 145 (VI), should constitute the basis for the elaboration of such a programme. A programme to be adopted should, however, contain the concerns of the Group of 77 as embodied in part II, section III.F, of TD/330. This includes an invitation to the socialist countries to contribute to the efforts of the developing countries to diversify and intensify their trade; to provide a growing share of their imports including manufactures from developing countries; make further improvements in the GSP schemes; improve the terms and conditions of credits to developing countries; enlarge their economic assistance; increase the share of convertible currencies in resources made available for financing developing countries' projects; and develop a flexible and efficient payment mechanism in trade operations. In all of these, account should be taken of the specific needs and requirements of the least developed countries.

5. The Group of 77 also wishes to reiterate its position on the need for the Secretary-General of UNCTAD to carry out the necessary consultations with the relevant Governments for initiating a process of negotiations leading to a further strengthening of East-South trade and economic co-operation and to report the progress made on these consultations to the Trade and Development Board at its session in March 1989.

6. The Group of 77 further wishes to reiterate the great significance of the UNCTAD technical assistance and consultative activities in this area as an important means of further promoting trade relations with the socialist countries of Eastern Europe and calls for intensification of the existing UNCTAD operational programme for the promotion of East-South trade. In this regard the Group of 77

strongly urges UNDP to provide the necessary funds for these activities.

7. The events of the past few years have proved that no single flow of trade can be treated and looked at in isolation. Any expansion or contraction in any sector of international trade influences the other sectors of international trade as well. The Group of 77 therefore wishes to support the proposal contained in paragraph 93 of the Secretary-General's report and requests that the Conference entrust the Secretary-General with the preparation of an analytical report on the interdependence of all flows of international trade, with reference, *inter alia*, to intersystems trade flows, and on the policy implications of this interdependence.

8. One encouraging element in prospects for trade and economic co-operation among countries having different economic and social systems is the process of restructuring of economic activities and reforms being contemplated in the socialist countries. The Group of 77 believes that the process should provide a new opening for the expansion of East-South trade and economic relations.

APPENDIX V

Working paper submitted by the Federal Republic of Germany on behalf of the States members of Group B
[TD(VII)/C.III/CRP.7]

The task of this Committee is threefold and consists in:

A. Carrying out a factual assessment of the situation prevailing in international trade;

B. Discussing, intertwined with the assessment, the appropriate conclusions to be drawn at the national, regional, international and multilateral levels to cope with the situation and its implications;

C. Giving adequate orientations for further work in the framework of UNCTAD.

Group B has contributed to the assessment of the situation in international trade in its introductory statement delivered in Sessional Committee III on 15 July (TD(VII)/C.III/CRP.1),[43] and subsequently through debate in informal discussions. The following is intended to: complement our earlier contributions by highlighting elements which should be taken into account in an evaluation of the present situation; propose conclusions where we believe areas of agreement might exist; and put forward a programme for future UNCTAD work.

Some of the ideas we shall bring forward are based on the OECD Ministerial Declaration of 13 May 1987, which is before you as a Conference document (TD/334).[44] While for reasons of brevity I do not wish to repeat the full text in these cases, the complete language of that Declaration remains the basis for these ideas.

I. Overall assessment

1. International trade provides, through competition, a powerful means of promoting economic efficiency and growth. Measures which impede or distort the functioning of international markets tend to impair structural adjustment, preserve outdated economic structures, damage consumer interests, weaken incentives for efficient investment and thus hinder economic growth. Therefore, it is of paramount importance to reverse recent trends towards restrictive trade measures, notably of a bilateral or a discriminatory nature, and to act with determination to strengthen and extend the open multilateral trading system.

2. There is a need to adopt a consistent approach in tackling the challenges faced by all countries in the trade field. These challenges include: the need for further liberalization and expansion of trade to facilitate economic growth and development; the need to halt and reverse protectionism and to remove distortions to trade; the need for appropriate structural adjustment; and the need to promote the fuller participation of developing countries in the multilateral trading system.

3. The Uruguay Round provides the best opportunity for all participants to confront and resolve the major trade challenges facing the international community, and presents a unique opportunity to create an improved framework for trade in the 1990s and beyond. The Round is the most comprehensive to date, allowing the broadest possible approach to tariffs and non-tariff measures as well as for the review and strengthening of the overall effectiveness and decision-making of GATT as an institution.

4. In recent years, there has been a growing recognition of the interrelationship between trade and the wider economic environment and between trade policy and other domestic economic policies. At the national level, insufficient attention has been given by Governments in the past to the interface between macro-economic and micro-economic policies for promoting positive structural adjustment. Macro-economic strategies need to be co-ordinated with micro-economic measures that are taken to reduce adjustment pressures on sectors or firms. Policy-makers have to break out of the vicious circle of macro-economic instability and micro-economic rigidity, which maintains the *status quo* through protectionist policy measures that will, in any case, prove counter-productive in the long run. For all countries the challenge is to develop the capacity to respond quickly and effectively to technological change and take advantage of new and expanding opportunities in the trading system. A greater role for the private sector and for the play of market forces can enhance this capacity.

5. Structural adjustment is by definition a continuous process which is occurring in all countries. Although the respective roles of government and economic operators may vary from country to country, appropriate domestic policy choices, giving consideration to various national concerns, are central to the facilitation of structural adjustment. It is broadly recognized that the timeliness and adequacy of domestic policy responses have governed the extent to which countries have realized their potential to adapt to the impact of such external factors in the world economy. The responses of individual countries to the international environment differ for a variety of reasons. However, the adoption of outward-oriented approaches responsive to international economic change has clearly contributed to economic growth and expansion of trading opportunities.

II. Conclusions

6. We recognize the critical role of the Uruguay Round of multilateral trade negotiations, which includes the commitment by all participants to halt and reverse protectionism by implementing standstill and roll-back and to work for greater liberalization of trade and the strengthening and improvement of the open multilateral trading system. The active participation of the Governments involved in the negotiations will be necessary to achieve rapid, sustained and substantive progress towards a balanced global result which will benefit both developing and developed countries.

7. Developing countries have a recognized need for a more secure and enlarged access for their exports. Developing countries, particularly those already participating significantly in world trade, will obtain fuller benefits to the extent that they take on greater contractual obligations and improve their observance of multilateral trade disciplines.

8. The growing differences of economic growth and development among different developing countries cause both hope and concern. The situation of the least developed countries requires particular attention. Efforts should be made by all other countries to facilitate the trade of the least developed countries so as to enhance their development prospects.

9. Promotion of structural change and adjustment has a crucial role to play in revitalizing world production and trade. There is a need for improving the international economic environment through co-ordinated policy decisions and through appropriate national measures. A reasonably stable international economic environment is of great importance for the maintenance of the open multilateral trading system and also for timely adjustment to structural change in line with evolving patterns of comparative advantage.

10. The serious imbalances that prevail in the markets for the main agricultural products and the distortive effects of excessive support policies underline the urgent need for concerted reform in the area of agriculture to be implemented in a balanced and progressive manner. Agricultural policy reforms which allow a greater role for market signals will be integral to the success of the negotiations taking place in the Uruguay Round, which aim at the improvement of market access, the improvement of the competitive environment by increasing discipline, and the reduction of trade barriers in agriculture.

---

[43] Appendix II to the report of Committee III.

[44] See annex VI below.

11. There is scope for improving the manner in which measures which affect the pattern of production and trade are evaluated by national authorities. Government action in all countries should be subject to greater transparency in this area. Measures affecting trade should be clearly defined and should be implemented in a transparent and predictable manner.

12. Many countries attach importance to the continuation of GSP schemes. The contribution of these schemes to development is recognized.

13. The growing importance of South-South trade can also contribute to an expansion of opportunities for developing countries in the framework of the multilateral trading system.

14. There is a need to foster an environment conducive to private investment and industrial co-operation, with a view to enhancing the export potential of developing countries. There is also a need for more effective promotion of the trade of developing countries through improved bilateral or multilateral programmes, *inter alia*, through the International Trade Centre UNCTAD/GATT.

15. UNCTAD could make a significant contribution to improving the understanding and expertise of Governments and to promoting consensus in favour of efforts to enhance development prospects through its programmes on technical assistance and its analytical work.

III. UNCTAD work programme

16. UNCTAD should continue its work on protectionism and structural adjustment in the agriculture, manufactures and services sectors, under its existing mandate, but with further improvement in quality of analysis, and broader and more equal coverage of regional groups.

17. In fulfilling its work on protectionism and structural adjustment, UNCTAD should undertake analysis of the principal elements and effects of structural adjustment policies, including trade policies, paying particular attention to the role of:

An efficiently functioning price and market mechanism in fostering sound productive structures among a range of developing countries;

The private sector in heightening economic efficiency and increasing output;

A favourable investment climate;

Technological change.

18. UNCTAD should carry out specific analysis of domestic trade policy issues facing developing countries, also in the context of structural change and development, taking into account the increasing diversity of their situations, interests and performance in recent years, and the importance of simplifying and rendering more transparent national trade legislation.

19. UNCTAD should continue work under its existing mandate to further its consideration of the role of services in the development process.

20. UNCTAD should carry out further analytical work on developments in East-South trade, in particular as concerns its product structure as well as an analysis of the differing roles played in this trade by various developing countries.

21. UNCTAD should do further work on the data base on non-tariff measures with a view to its improvement and in order to:

Resolve methodological and definitional problems and increase the country and regional coverage of the identified measures;

Improve and expand data on East-South trade flows, with greater product coverage of individual socialist Eastern European countries;

Work towards the convening of a second meeting of the Intergovernmental Group of Experts on the UNCTAD Data Base on Trade Measures, upon improved background work by the secretariat and appropriate preparation for such a meeting;

Make it available to member Governments.

22. The UNCTAD secretariat should continue and further develop its technical assistance efforts to developing countries, with particular reference to the needs of the least developed, in the following areas:

(i) In connection with the Uruguay Round, the UNCTAD secretariat, in consultation with other international organizations, should provide analytical and technical assistance to developing countries, upon request, on the technical aspects of the negotiations in order to assist them to participate more effectively in the Round;

(ii) In the context of the GSP, the UNCTAD secretariat should continue its technical assistance project and prepare a brochure describing such activities for the benefit of member States;

(iii) In the context of the Global System of Trade Preferences, the UNCTAD secretariat should continue to provide further assistance to developing countries in preparing and carrying out the GSTP negotiations;

(iv) In connection with restrictive business practices, the UNCTAD secretariat should continue its help to developing countries in elaborating their national legislation in this area;

(v) In connection with East-South trade, the UNCTAD secretariat should continue its technical assistance efforts by means of voluntary contributions from socialist countries;

(vi) In connection with services, the UNCTAD secretariat should continue to provide technical assistance for the carrying out of national studies on services in developing countries upon request, which should be made available to all UNCTAD members upon their completion.

23. The UNCTAD secretariat should keep member States informed on the progress and activities of the technical assistance projects and should be required to report in detail on them annually to the spring session of the Trade and Development Board. This report would promote transparency, help member Governments set priorities and ensure an adequate geographic distribution of such projects.

D. REPORT OF SESSIONAL COMMITTEE IV

1. Introduction

187. At its 205th plenary meeting, on 13 July 1987, the Conference decided to establish a sessional committee (Committee IV) to consider and report on agenda item 8 (*d*): Problems of the least developed countries, bearing in mind the Substantial New Programme of Action for the 1980s for the Least Developed Countries.

188. At the same meeting, the Conference, after deciding to waive rule 65 of its rules of procedure, elected Mr. M. Huslid (Norway) as Chairman of Committee IV.

189. At its 1st meeting, on 15 July 1987, Committee IV elected Mr. M. W. Namfua (United Republic of Tanzania) as its Vice-Chairman and Mr. Wang Baoliu (China) as its Rapporteur.

190. In the course of the session, Committee IV held four meetings, from 15 to 27 July 1987, as well as several informal meetings.

191. At its 4th (closing) meeting, on 27 July 1987, the Committee adopted its draft report (TD(VII)/C.IV/L.2) and authorized the Rapporteur to complete it as appropriate for submission to the Conference.

2. Consideration of agenda item 8 (*d*)

PROBLEMS OF THE LEAST DEVELOPED COUNTRIES, BEARING IN MIND THE SUBSTANTIAL NEW PROGRAMME OF ACTION FOR THE 1980s FOR THE LEAST DEVELOPED COUNTRIES

192. The following documents, in so far as they related to item 8 (*d*) were before the Committee:[45]

(*a*) TD/328/Rev.1;

(*b*) Chapter V (TD/328/Add.5 and Corr.1)[46] of the secretariat report to UNCTAD VII (TD/328/Rev.1);

(*c*) TD/329/Rev.1;

(*d*) TD/330 and Corr.1 and 2;

(*e*) TD/331;

(*f*) TD/333 and Corr.1;

(*g*) TD/334;

(*h*) TD/335;

(*i*) TD/343;

(*j*) TD(VII)/Misc.1, resolution adopted by ESCAP at its forty-third session (April 1987).

193. At its 1st meeting, on 15 July 1987, the Committee began its consideration of item 8 (*d*) with an opening statement by the *Chairman* of the Committee. The *Deputy Secretary-General of UNCTAD* made an introductory statement. General statements on this item were made by: the *Minister for Development Co-operation of Norway*; the spokesmen for the *Group of 77* (Bangladesh); *Group B* (Netherlands); *Group D* (German Democratic Republic); the representative of *China*; and the representative of Denmark, speaking on behalf of the *European Economic Community and its member States* (TD(VII)/C.IV/CRP.5). In particular, the spokesman for the Group of 77 referred to his Group's proposals contained in TD/330.[47] The spokesman for Group B referred to his Group's proposals contained in TD/334.[48] The spokesman for Group D referred to his Group's proposals contained in TD/333.[49] The representative of China referred to the proposals made by his country contained in TD/331.[50]

194. At the 2nd meeting, on 16 July 1987, general statements on this item were made by the representatives of the *Congo, Finland, Israel, Italy, Japan, Sweden, Switzerland, Turkey*, the *Union of Soviet Socialist Republics*, and the *United Republic of Tanzania*. The representative of the *United Nations Development Programme* also made a statement.

195. At the same meeting, the Committee decided to establish a Contact Group of the Chairman to undertake a detailed consideration of agenda item 8 (*d*).

196. At the 3rd meeting, on 17 July 1987, general statements on this item were made by the representatives

of *Bulgaria, Canada, Nepal, Portugal, Spain* and the *United States of America*.

197. At the same meeting the spokesman for the *Group of 77* (Bangladesh) introduced the document entitled "Proposal on policies and measures, submitted by Bangladesh on behalf of the States members of the Group of 77" (TD(VII)/C.IV/L.1), as well as a document entitled "Statement by the representative of Bangladesh on behalf of the States members of the Group of 77" (TD(VII)/C.IV/CRP.1).

198. The spokesman for *Group D* introduced a document entitled "Statement by the representative of the German Democratic Republic on behalf of the States members of Group D" (TD(VII)/C.IV/CRP.2/Rev.1).

199. The spokesman for *Group B* introduced a document entitled "Statement by the representative of the Netherlands on behalf of the States members of Group B" (TD(VII)/C.IV/CRP.3).

200. The representative of *China* drew attention to section IV of the "Position paper of the People's Republic of China on issues to be considered at the seventh session of the Conference" (TD/331), which contained his country's views and proposals on the agenda item. He also expressed his delegation's support, in principle, for the proposals submitted by the Group of 77 (TD(VII)/C.IV/L.1), which would be a good basis for the work of the Committee.

201. In the course of the session, the Nordic countries submitted a document entitled "Views of the Nordic countries (Finland, Norway and Sweden)" (TD(VII)/C.IV/CRP.6).

202. At the 4th (closing) meeting, on 27 July 1987, the spokesman for *Group B* introduced the proposal by the Netherlands on behalf of the States members of Group B and described the main outlines of that proposal. The Group B proposal was subsequently circulated in TD(VII)/C.IV/CRP.9.

3. Action by Committee IV

203. At the request of the Committee, the Chairman, on 23 July 1987, submitted for consideration a draft report contained in TD(VII)/C.IV/CRP.7 and Add.1.

204. Subsequently, the Committee, in the form of a Contact Group, held five meetings, discussing some of the elements contained in the Chairman's draft. Owing to time constraints, the Committee did not manage to complete these discussions.

205. Against this background, the Committee, at its 4th (closing) meeting, on 27 July 1987, decided to transmit the Chairman's draft to the President's Contact Group. In addition, the Committee decided that that draft and proposals and documents prepared by the various regional groups should be annexed to the Committee's report.

---

[45] See also paragraph 136 above.

[46] See footnote 29.

[47] See annex V below.

[48] See annex VI below.

[49] *Idem.*

[50] *Idem.*

4. Appendices to the report of Committee IV

APPENDIX I

Report by sessional Committee IV to the President's Contact Group: Chairman's draft

[TD(VII)/C.IV/CRP.7 and Add.1]

Introduction

Some basic features of the general economic situation and trends in relation to least developed countries

1. The LDCs constitute the group of the 40 poorest countries in the world. Their average GDP per capita is slightly higher than $200, which is less than one quarter of the developing countries as a whole and only about 3 per cent of that of the developed countries. A high proportion of the LDCs' population lives in conditions of mere subsistence.

2. The LDCs have for a long time been lagging behind in growth and development compared with other countries and many of them seem to have come into a vicious circle of constraints, poverty and population explosion with stagnation or even backsliding as a result.

3. Since the adoption of the Substantial New Programme of Action in 1981, the situation of the LDCs has deteriorated further. Despite a modest improvement in 1985, GDP per capita declined from $220 in 1980 to slightly more than $200 in 1985. The share of LDCs in world economy and trade has been declining. The trends for the coming years, according to present assumptions, are also unfavourable.

4. Structural handicaps make the LDCs particularly vulnerable to the external economic environment. On the whole this environment has been unfavourable to the LDCs over the last years. Of particular concern has been the historically low level of commodity prices, the mounting debt problem and stagnating external financial flows. Adverse weather conditions and natural calamities have in some cases further contributed to reducing output and already very low living standards.

5. In the light of this general background, the Committee formulated the following conclusions aiming at an improvement of the economic and social conditions in the LDCs:

I. National efforts

6. It was reaffirmed that the LDCs will continue to have primary responsibility for their overall development.

7. It was generally acknowledged that many LDCs have undertaken comprehensive policy reforms and implemented adjustment programmes. They have made efforts to improve the effectiveness of domestic resource mobilization and use, by strengthening economic and financial management. These efforts should be actively pursued.

8. In particular it appears imperative, taking due account of individual characteristics of each LDC:

To accelerate agricultural development and enhance food security;

To design structural adjustment and diversification programmes suited to each country's particular social and economic condition;

To endeavour to mobilize fully human resources through education and training in required skills;

To strengthen the role of women in the development process.

II. International efforts

A. FINANCIAL AND TECHNICAL ASSISTANCE

9. In addition to national efforts, international programmes of financial and technical assistance as well as other supportive measures from all groups of donors are fundamental.

10. For aid to make a sustained contribution to development, it has to be geared to the support of overall policy objectives of growth-oriented programmes. At the same time, policies which create a receptive environment in LDCs will greatly enhance aid effectiveness.

11. The Substantial New Programme of Action should be fully and effectively implemented. For this purpose a substantially enlarged volume of financial assistance to the LDCs on terms which correspond to their immediate and long-term development needs will be required.

The volume and forms of aid must be commensurate with the growing requirements of policy reform programmes and broader development efforts.

12. ODA will continue to play a decisive role in LDC's external financing. Within the context of the Substantial New Programme of Action, donor countries which have not yet done so should make best efforts to attain 0.15 per cent of their GNP as ODA to the LDCs as soon as possible and not later than 1990.

13. The multilateral assistance to the LDCs through such channels as IDA, IFAD, regional development banks and their funds, UNDP, the Special Measures Fund for the Least Developed Countries, UNCDF, UNVP, etc., should be significantly increased to meet the increased needs of the LDCs, and donors should channel a substantial part of their aid through these institutions and agencies.

14. The Structural Adjustment Facility of IMF should be tripled as requested by the Managing Director.

15. Relevant international institutions should continue their concerted efforts to increase the share of concessional assistance to LDCs.

16. IMF should be invited to undertake a review of the principles on which its conditionality rests in such a way as to reflect the peculiar social, economic and political priorities of the LDCs.

17. The international community should support the efforts of LDCs to increase their per capita food production and, in view of the energy problems, provide financial and technical assistance for research, exploration and development of energy resources; and should assist in maximizing capacity utilization of their productive economic units.

18. Donors should endeavour to provide emergency assistance and financing of costs involved in the management and relief operations in African and other LDCs affected by food shortages and other emergencies.

B. AID MODALITIES

19. LDCs and donors alike should take all necessary steps to improve the quality and effectiveness of aid.

20. Concerned donors should provide timely assistance on appropriate terms to mitigate the adverse effects of adjustment programmes and should support the efforts of the LDCs in implementing the required policy changes.

21. Immediate steps should be taken to provide bilateral ODA to the LDCs essentially in the form of grants and to provide loans without discrimination on highly concessional terms, at least as concessional as those provided by IDA.

22. Urgent steps should be taken by donor countries with a view to providing ODA loans and grants to LDCs on an untied basis.

23. Donors and LDCs should make efforts to eliminate the time-lag between aid commitment and disbursement. In this regard, a mechanism that would ensure automaticity and predictability of disbursement should be considered.

24. Advance payments should be made, as appropriate, by the donors concerned against their commitment in order to minimize delays in disbursement and improve the effectiveness of assistance.

25. Donor countries should take steps for increased local-cost as well as recurrent-cost financing.

26. Concerned donors should provide increased balance-of-payments support as well as commodity aid, programme aid, including sector assistance and general import financing, and their terms should be flexible enough to facilitate their effective use.

27. Assistance should be provided to strengthen LDCs, capacities to establish and implement their own policies and programmes, including programmes for strengthening the role of the private sector and increasing the efficiency of the public sector.

28. Efforts should be made to harmonize and simplify existing aid procedures. Country review mechanisms should facilitate such efforts.

C. COUNTRY REVIEW MECHANISM

29. The country review meetings, which are the mechanisms for the periodic review and implementation of the Substantial New Programme of Action, should be further strengthened and improved to

măke them more effective. UNDP and the World Bank, as the lead agencies, should expand their technical assistance to the LDCs to enable them to prepare efficiently for these meetings. Donor countries should be represented at an adequately high level. The meetings should facilitate an increased and improved flow of assistance through a better understanding and dialogue between LDCs and their development partners.

D. LAND-LOCKED AND ISLAND DEVELOPING COUNTRIES AMONG THE LEAST DEVELOPED COUNTRIES

30. In accordance with the United Nations Convention on the Law of the Sea of 1982, Conference resolutions 137 (VI) and 138 (VI), Trade and Development Board resolution 319 (XXXI), and other relevant resolutions of the United Nations as adopted on the specific needs and problems of land-locked and island countries among the LDCs and the extremely acute nature of the problems:

(*a*) Transit countries should intensify co-operation with the land-locked countries among the LDCs to alleviate the transit problems;

(*b*) Concerned donors, while providing technical and financial assistance to land-locked and island countries among LDCs, should particularly focus on capital input in infrastructural development;

(*c*) International bodies, in particular UNDP and the United Nations regional commissions, should continue to support those LDCs with measures required to alleviate their specific transit-transport and communications problems.

E. COMMODITIES/INTERNATIONAL TRADE

31. The LDCs have greatly suffered from vulnerability to declines in the prices of their basic commodity exports. It is in the LDCs that the impact of the commodity price situation has been the most severe.

32. In this context, depending on the nature and intensity of specific country and commodity circumstances, the LDCs should, as appropriate, endeavour to diversify their economic structures. The international community should support these efforts through improved co-operation in the commodities sector aiming at better market transparency, increased market access and reduced market distortions as envisaged by the Uruguay Round. Sustained efforts should be made to provide carefully considered aid for structural measures; and technical assistance in support of improved management capacity and infrastructure.

33. The importance of the Integrated Programme for Commodities for the LDCs was again underlined, both in respect of stabilization and development measures.

1. *Compensatory financing*

34. Special measures should be taken to strengthen the commodity markets and enhance export receipts of the LDCs from their commodities.

35. The international community should consider the possibility of providing full compensation to LDCs for all shortfalls in commodity export earnings. For this purpose the existing Compensatory Financing Facility of IMF should be improved, with provision for special treatment for the LDCs ensuring better coverage of their export earnings shortfalls, subsidization of their interest payments on outstanding drawings and a longer repayment and grace period than hitherto. The enlargement of Stabex and Compex should be considered. Developed countries which have not yet done so should consider adopting special measures in order to compensate fully the export earnings shortfalls of the LDCs. In the event that a complementary facility for compensating the commodity export earnings shortfalls of the developing countries is established, it should ensure special provisions for the LDCs.

2. *Access to markets*

36. Steps should be taken by developed countries to further improve GSP or MFN treatment for products from the LDCs with the objective of providing duty-free access to such products, and to eliminate quantitative restrictions and other non-tariff measures affecting exports of LDCs. Special schemes should be prepared by each of them to realize these objectives. Flexible rules of origin should also be applied in favour of LDCs to facilitate expansion of their export trade. A simple duty- and quota-free system of imports of hand-made products from the LDCs should be established promptly by developed countries.

37. As agreed in the Ministerial Declaration, adopted at the special session of GATT at Punta del Este, Uruguay, in September 1986, the contracting parties of GATT should ensure that the Uruguay Round of multilateral trade negotiations results, *inter alia*, in positive measures to facilitate the expansion of the LDCs' trading opportunities. Furthermore, appropriate attention should be given by member States to the expeditious implementation of the relevant provisions of the 1982 Ministerial Declaration concerning the LDCs.

38. Increased technical assistance should be given to the LDCs, *inter alia*, through the International Trade Centre UNCTAD/GATT and UNCTAD for promotion of trade and expansion of production facilities for export and to help improve their capacity to benefit from existing preferential arrangements in favour of developing countries. In particular, developed countries and international organizations should also assist the LDCs to create industries for on-the-spot processing of raw materials and food products, and the development of integrated projects for the expansion of exports and to provide adequate resources to overcome supply bottle-necks.

39. The developed countries should assist the LDCs in entering into long-term arrangements for exports, as called for in the Substantial New Programme of Action.

F. GLOBAL REVIEW AND APPRAISAL OF THE IMPLEMENTATION OF THE SUBSTANTIAL NEW PROGRAMME OF ACTION

40. In line with General Assembly resolution 40/205, the Conference recommends that a United Nations conference on the least developed countries should be convened in 1990 to appraise and review the implementation of the Substantial New Programme of Action for the 1980s for the Least Developed Countries and to launch a Programme of Action for the 1990s.

41. It further recommends that the General Assembly accept the generous offer made by France to host the Conference.

Debt problems of the least developed countries

42. The debt situation of the LDCs has considerably worsened in past years. The ratios of debt to GDP and debt service to exports have increased in the case of many LDCs to unmanageable levels. A major cause resides in depressed export earnings, which have impaired further the debt-servicing capacity of the LDCs. Their debt burden now constitutes for many of them a major hindrance to their development process.

43. The critical debt situation of the LDCs calls for a programme for immediate relief. Developed countries which have not yet done so, should fully implement Trade and Development Board resolution 165 (S-IX) expeditiously and cancel all outstanding bilateral ODA loans of all the LDCs without exception. The developing countries which have provided concessional loans to LDCs should consider extending similar debt relief measures to these countries.

44. Creditors of other official or officially guaranteed loans to LDCs should lower interest rates of LDCs' existing debts to concessional levels on IDA terms. When appropriate, outright cancellations of such debts should also be considered.

45. Creditors should provide substantial and multi-year scheduling of private debts on favourable terms.

46. In order to alleviate the burden of debt service due to multilateral institutions, suitable arrangements such as interest-subsidy schemes and refinancing schemes should be considered. The establishment of a special facility for debt relief for the LDCs within the framework of an existing financial institution should also be actively considered.

47. Substantially increased concessional finance, essentially in grant form, is required to enable LDCs to resume growth so as to cope with their debt problems in the long run. This task should be pursued both bilaterally and by international financial institutions.

48. Given the interrelationship of issues, the measures to alleviate the debt burden for the LDCs should be supplemented and strengthened by technical assistance, as appropriate, as well as by measures in other fields such as trade, commodities, etc.

APPENDIX II

Proposal on policies and measures submitted by Bangladesh on behalf on the States members of the Group of 77
[TD(VII)/C.IV/L.1]

PROBLEMS OF THE LEAST DEVELOPED COUNTRIES, BEARING IN MIND THE SUBSTANTIAL NEW PROGRAMME OF ACTION FOR THE 1980s FOR THE LEAST DEVELOPED COUNTRIES

[For the text, see annex V.B below, part II, section IV.]

APPENDIX III

Statement by the representative of Bangladesh on behalf of the States members of the Group of 77
[TD(VII)/C.IV/CRP.1]

1. The Group of 77 proposals on sub-items (*a*) through (*d*) of Conference agenda item 8 —namely: Resources for development, including financial, and related monetary questions; Commodities; International trade; and Problems of the least developed countries, bearing in mind the Substantial New Programme of Action for the 1980s for the Least Developed Countries were submitted at the fifteenth special session of the Trade and Development Board, on 18 May 1987. We believe that all concerned have had the opportunity to consider them. The rationale of the proposals has already been explained in detail in part I, "Assessment", of TD/330[51] and also in the course of the informal consultations on assessment that preceded the Conference.

2. The proposals on problems of the LDCs, bearing in mind the Substantial New Programme of Action for the 1980s for the Least Developed Countries, are contained in part II, section IV, of TD/330. I take this opportunity to introduce these proposals on behalf of the Group of 77 for consideration by the Committee. These proposals cover the following specific areas:

A. Specific policy measures suggested for adoption;

B. Financial and technical assistance;

C. Compensatory financing;

D. Aid modalities;

E. Debt problems of the least developed countries;

F. Access to markets;

G. Land-locked and island developing countries;

H. Country review mechanism;

I. Equitable benefits of assistance.

We look forward to intensive and sincere negotiations on each of these proposals in the coming days so that this Committee will be in a position to submit its concrete recommendations and proposals to the President of the Conference by 24 July 1987.

3. Keeping in view this deadline for our work, I wish to submit the following proposal for the organization of work in this Committee:

(*a*) 23 and 24 July be kept aside for finalization and adoption of the report;

(*b*) Three working days in the first week and three working days in the second week would be available for substantive work. There will, therefore, be six sessions available for substantive work of this Committee;

(*c*) The first session may be devoted to introduction of the proposals and adoption of the plan of work of the Committee;

(*d*) The following plan of work is proposed for adoption:

First session—Introduction of proposals and adoption of the plan of work of the Committee.

Second session—Consideration of items A and B, i.e. specific policy measures suggested for adoption and financial and technical assistance.

Third session—Consideration of items C and D, namely, compensatory financing and aid modalities.

Fourth session—Consideration of items E and F, i.e, debt problems of the least developed countries and access to markets.

Fifth session—Consideration of items G, H and I, i.e. land-locked and island developing countries, country review mechanism, and equitable benefits of assistance.

---

[51] Reproduced in annex V below.

APPENDIX IV

Statement by the representative of the German Democratic Republic on behalf of the States members of Group D
[TD(VII)/C.IV/CRP.2/Rev.1]

1. Mr. Chairman, let me first congratulate you on your election. I wish to express our conviction that your skilful guidance will contribute to the successful outcome of our deliberations. I may assure you that my Group will support you in that respect.

2. The socialist countries regard the acceleration of the social and economic development of LDCs as one of the acute problems in the world economy of today. The solution of that problem would allow the LDCs to satisfy the basic needs of their peoples and create, to an ever-growing extent, the prerequisites to develop in the economic field in a self-sustained and self-reliant manner.

3. Socialist countries consider the Substantial New Programme of Action for the 1980s for the Least Developed Countries, which is closely linked with the Declaration on the Establishment of a New International Economic Order and the Charter of Economic Rights and Duties of States, to be one of the basic United Nations documents on social and economic matters.

4. The 1985 mid-term review of the Substantial New Programme of Action showed the generally unsatisfactory progress towards its implementation. Since the adoption of that programme in 1981, the social and economic situation in the majority of LDCs has deteriorated considerably. Crisis phenomena, growing protectionism and discrimination, worsening terms of trade for the LDCs, increasing foreign indebtedness of LDCs, the negative impact of TNCs' activities as well as natural calamities hampered the LDCs' social and economic development.

5. The situation of the LDCs, which preoccupies the whole of mankind, reflects in a concentrated manner the unsound, dangerous and intolerable state of international relations. The arms race, which leads to the development of ever more destructive weapons, not only threatens the very existence of mankind, but also undermines the possibilities for shaping a fruitful international co-operation and swallows up huge material, financial and intellectual resources which could otherwise be earmarked for the solution of burning social and economic problems of countries, including the LDCs, in particular to help eliminate hunger, poverty and illness.

6. Socialist countries are convinced that any step towards disarmament will be conducive to the improvement of the international political climate and to the establishment of a reliable system of international economic security for all States. Socialist countries hold that all concrete steps on the way to disarmament should be linked with rechannelling a portion of the resources to be released to meet the needs of economic and social progress of developing nations, including the LDCs.

7. In their support for LDCs, socialist countries are guided by a comprehensive understanding of the factors hampering prompt social and economic development. Structural imbalances and the slow pace of socio-economic development in many LDCs result, among other reasons, from their colonial past, the unjust and disadvantageous position of developing countries within the framework of the international division of labour, foreign indebtedness, the negative impact of TNCs' activities and today's strained monetary and financial relations. Some problems are also due to the fact that socio-economic reforms were not implemented consistently and that some government measures and concepts have not always been effective in some LDCs. The tremendous difficulties of many LDCs emanate from the cumulative impact of those factors. The pressure exerted by certain quarters on developing countries to the effect that they should overcome the current complicated economic situation by restraining the role of the State in the economy and by exclusively employing market forces may, in the long run, only aggravate existing difficulties and jeopardize those countries' independence.

8. Socialist countries consider that it is the right of each nation to determine its economic policy in a sovereign manner. They believe that the strengthening of the role of the State and the development of the public sector as well as the attainment of higher effectiveness in State management and planning are important elements which can help strengthen political independence and speed up LDCs' social and economic development. At the same time, the employment of market mechanisms in accordance with each country's national characteristics may contribute to economic development.

9.   It is a basic principle of the socialist countries' foreign policy to support developing countries effectively, including the LDCs, in their just struggle for social and economic progress, against neo-colonialism and for independence. Economic co-operation between socialist and developing countries represents a new type of international relations which is based, *inter alia*, on the principles of equality, mutual advantage, and non-interference in internal affairs—exploitation being alien to it. According to that type of economic co-operation, socialist countries employ *vis-à-vis* LDCs a number of flexible instruments which have proved their effectiveness and reliability: e.g. bilateral intergovernmental agreements, joint trade and economic commissions which elaborate the long-term targets of co-operation and co-ordinate their fulfilment. That co-operation is a comprehensive and effective one. The various requirements and interests of LDCs are widely taken into account. Within the framework of such co-operation, socialist countries provide assistance in the development of different economic sectors, in the field of vocational training, in science and technology as well as in the establishment of effective management and planning systems. Socialist countries will continue to pay due attention to the expansion of co-operation with LDCs. They will take into account the LDCs' suggestions and proposals with a view to further developing co-operation on the basis of mutual interests. They are prepared to expand already existing relations with LDCs and to establish new ones with those interested. They will impact to the LDCs interested their experience in social development, in economic management and planning.

10.   Socialist countries hold that international economic security, which equally protects each State from discrimination, sanctions and other economic coercive measures prompted by political reasons, will be conducive to the development of LDCs as well.

APPENDIX V

Statement by the representative of the Netherlands on behalf of the States members of Group B
[TD(VII)/C.IV/CRP.3]

1.   On behalf of Group B, I extend to you, Mr. Chairman, the Vice-Chairman and the Rapporteur our congratulations on your election. I assure you that our Group has a positive interest in the work of this Committee and is ready to co-operate fully with you on matters related to the special problems of the LDCs. We approach our deliberations in a positive spirit and we appreciate the opportunity to promote common perceptions and effective policies on issues before us in this Committee. I will now turn to some general observations.

2.   I should like to recall that the international community adopted the Substantial New Programme of Action for the 1980s for the Least Developed Countries in 1981 in order to give concerted international support to national measures undertaken by individual least developed countries. The Substantial New Programme of Action is now in place and all commitments made to it by members of Group B are valid as stated in individual interventions at the time of the adoption of the Substantial New Programme of Action and at the subsequent review conference in 1985. The implementation of the Substantial New Programme of Action will be reviewed when the programme expires in 1990. In the mean time, an ongoing review process is taking place as provided for in the Substantial New Programme of Action through existing mechanisms such as the World Bank Consultative Groups, the UNDP Round Tables and the Club du Sahel, and Group B members are actively participating in this work. Against this background, this Committee should focus on special problems of the LDCs in the fields of resources, international trade and commodities.

3.   The challenges of economic and social progress in the LDCs—where despite much improvement in nutrition, health and education, many millions of people remain without the conditions of a decent life—are an important concern for the Governments of my Group and for the people they represent.

4.   We note with satisfaction the economic progress of some LDCs, especially in the last few years. None the less, we remain concerned about the steady downward trend in the average income level and serious debt-servicing problems of many of the LDCs. This downward trend can be mainly attributed to three broad sources:

(i)   On the one hand, they have suffered from extreme vulnerability to declines in the prices of their basic commodity exports. It is in the LDCs that the full impact of the commodity price situation can be seen.

(ii)   On the other hand, serious weaknesses in the institutions that formulate and implement economic policy as well as a weak infrastructure led to inappropriate economic performance in many of these countries: large fiscal deficits, overvalued exchange rates and a general erosion of incentives on domestic product and factor markets, especially in the agricultural sector.

(iii)   Finally, these countries have suffered from environmental problems, adverse weather conditons and socio-political constraints such as high population growth.

5.   There are no easy solutions. A continuous adaptation of our perceptions is necessary if we are to confront together the urgent development tasks in the LDCs.

6.   Group B believes that the reorientation of development policies and the diversification of economic structures—reflecting the nature and intensity of specific country and commodity circumstances—are emerging as priorities. To support this effort, the members of my Group see scope for joint, international action in the following areas: improved co-operation in the commodities sector such as better market transparency; increased market access and reduced market distortions as envisaged by the Uruguay Round; sustained efforts to provide carefully considered aid for structural measures; and technical assistance in support of improved management capacity and infrastructure in the LDCs.

7.   There is now widespread agreement among donors and recipients that for aid to make a sustained contribution to development, it has to be geared to the support of overall policy objectives of growth-oriented structural adjustment and that adjustment and growth are mutually supportive. Indeed, many LDCs have undertaken courageous adjustment policies. Although the specific contents will inevitably vary among countries, efforts to redress the situation in the LDCs need:

To improve the effectiveness of domestic resource mobilization and use by strengthening economic and financial management, including the capacity to co-ordinate external assistance;

To increase the productivity of the agricultural sector, especially in food production;

To adopt market-oriented incentive systems, including appropriate exchange rates;

To strengthen investment in human resources, notably in areas such as education and training;

To increase the efficiency of the public sector;

To enhance the conditions required for the development of a strong private sector.

8.   In other words, my Group believes that determined domestic action is required if development is to be put on new, solid and durable foundations. The success of such action depends to a great extent upon public acceptance of their necessity and effectiveness. We believe, therefore, that the Governments of the LDCs should continue to take an active part in the formulation and implementation of their own structural adjustment programmes, explain their purpose and content, and implement them with resolve. This way, the prospects for success would be greatly enhanced. At the same time, we fully recognize that social and political conditions as well as traditional values and local customs of each individual country must be taken into consideration when development programmes are elaborated and implemented.

9.   In addition to national efforts international programmes of financial and technical assistance as well as other supportive measures from all groups of donors are also fundamental in addressing the basic structural rigidities of these economies. Group B countries' record in this respect is already substantial but we expect aid from all sources to be further improved. The volume and forms of aid must be commensurate with the growing requirements of policy reform programmes and broader development efforts, taking into account the recommendation of the Substantial New Programme of Action as adopted in 1981 and Conference resolution 142 (VI) as adopted pertaining to substantive resources to be channelled to the LDCs. However, external financial resources made available in support of domestic policy reform undertaken by the LDCs have in many cases not been adequate to support policy reform and to generate substantially increased growth. Also, it would favour the development process if adjustment programmes, to a greater extent, could cover a time period long enough to achieve sustained growth at a level above the rate of population growth.

10. Multilateral development institutions also have an important role to play. The dialogue that takes place in UNDP Round Tables and World Bank Consultative Groups has provided for better policy dialogue and aid co-ordination and has allowed least developed countries to review, and sometimes reorient, their development policies and also allowed donors to improve their support efforts. In particular, we note with satisfaction the contribution made by the Eighth Replenishment of IDA, the IMF Structural Adjustment Facility and the joint policy framework process. The IMF, the World Bank and UNDP may wish to comment on the various aspects of this evolving situation. Moreover, we look forward to the forthcoming negotiations on the Third Replenishment of IFAD in early 1988.

11. Before concluding my statement, may I reiterate my Group's intention to engage in constructive discussions on the special problems of the LDCs. Finally, may I add that my statement will be supplemented later by members of my Group.

APPENDIX VI

Schedule for the second week, 20-24 July 1987, submitted by the Chairman
[TD(VII)/C.IV/CRP.4]

Monday, 20 July (morning)

Aid and other flows: financial and technical assistance; aid modalities; country review mechanism

Land-locked and island countries among the LDCs

Commodities/compensatory financing

Tuesday, 21 July (morning)

Commodities/compensatory financing (*continued*)

Trade/access to markets

Wednesday, 22 July (afternoon)

Debt problems of the LDCs.

Structure of draft elements to be circulated

Thursday, 23 July (morning and afternoon)

First reading of draft elements; revised version to be made available

Friday, 24 July (afternoon)

Second and final reading of revised draft

Final plenary meeting of Committee IV.

APPENDIX VII

Statement by the representative of Denmark on behalf of the European Economic Community and its member States
[TD(VII)/C.IV/CRP.5]

1. The European Community and its member States have been committed for many years to assisting, as a special priority, the LDCs in their development efforts. As the LDCs' principal trading partner and their main source of external assistance, the Community and its member States gave their full support to the preparation of the Substantial New Programme of Action for the 1980s for the Least Developed Countries and remain committed to achieving its objectives.

2. The present situation of the LDCs is characterized by stagnating or falling GNP per capita, high population growth and inadequate infrastructures generally, often aggravated by severe geographical and climatological constraints such as isolation, drought and desertification and a high incidence of other natural disasters. It is further compounded by a combination of debt-servicing burdens, reduced flows of non-concessional financial resources and worsening terms of trade which put a severe strain on their efforts to sustain the development process. We are deeply concerned about the negative effects of the current world economic situation which in particular affects LDCs. Given the work done at the mid-term review of the Substantial New Programme of Action we are hopeful that the seventh session of the Conference will make it possible through an appropriate assessment process, to understand better and help to resolve their underlying problems.

3. The European Community and its member States are aware of the special difficulties of the LDCs. We recognize the primary importance of LDCs' own development efforts. We also regard the development of South-South trade as of special significance for the LDCs. During the first half of the 1980s the volume of yearly assistance on concessional terms (both bilateral and multilateral) by Community donor countries has risen steadily; indeed several of them have already exceeded the target of the Substantial New Programme of Action as adopted. We reaffirm the importance of the objectives and content of the Substantial New Programme of Action as adopted, which provides for both quantitative increases in aid flows, and for qualitative improvements in the terms of aid. However, as concluded in the mid-term review in 1985, further efforts are needed:

To attain the objective of allocating 0.15 per cent of GNP to the LDCs according to the Substantial New Programme of Action as adopted;

To use more flexible and faster-disbursing forms of intervention, taking into account recurrent costs and import requirements to support structural adjustment;

To improve co-ordination between LDC Governments and donors at all levels, including World Bank Consultative Groups and UNDP Round Tables;

To provide technical assistance and other support to LDCs seeking to mobilize their own human and capital resources and strengthen the role of the private sector in the development process and increase the efficiency of the public sector.

As regards the Sub-Saharan African LDCs and their critical economic situation, the General Assembly, at its special session in May 1986, adopted the United Nations Programme of Action for African Economic Recovery and Development 1986-1990. That programme includes many of the priorities identified and the recommendations made in the Substantial New Programme of Action. Its implementation will contribute significantly to the implementation of the Substantial New Programme of Action in so far as LDCs in Africa are concerned.

4. The Community and its member States consider it essential that all industrialized countries, including those with centrally planned economies, should enhance market access for the products of the LDCs through more favourable rules of origin, through special treatment for LDCs within an improved GSP and through positive and flexible use of the fourth Multifibre Arrangement. Moreover, we call on all industrialized countries to help stabilize the export earnings of LDCs. In this respect the Stabex and Compex systems of the European Community have granted particularly favourable treatment to exports originating from LDCs. At the same time appropriate financial ODA contributions should be directed on a case-by-case basis towards the LDCs for whom the fall of commodity prices has had a significant medium-term impact on their development so as to support structural adjustment programmes aimed at greater diversification.

5. Donors from both industrialized and developing countries should carefully examine the evolution of financial flows to the LDCs. Since the Paris Conference these flows have varied considerably, while at the same time the LDCs have faced falling prices for their exported raw materials and have had to implement structural adjustment programmes. It is necessary to ensure that the international financial institutions, including the regional development banks, IFAD and IDA, have the resources and instruments needed to accomplish their tasks. Furthermore, we welcome the consideration given towards a significant increase in the resources of the IMF's Structural Adjustment Facility.

6. Moreover, we call on those countries which have not done so to apply Trade and Development Board resolution 165 (S-IX). In the spirit of the Venice Summit and in the context of the Paris Club renegotiations, extended grace and repayment periods should be agreed for the most heavily indebted among the poorest countries which are making adjustment efforts. Furthermore, a lowering of interest rates for these countries' existing debt should be considered.

APPENDIX VIII

Views of the Nordic countries (Finland, Norway and Sweden)
[TD(VII)/C.IV/CRP.6]

1. Differentiation among developing countries has been further increasing during the 1980s. For the LDCs the average socio-economic situation has been deteriorating. Taking note of the different economic performance also among the LDCs, the following elements appear dominant: the average economic growth, especially the agricultural production, has been declining on a per capita basis. The aggregate debt is approximately 50 per cent of the LDCs' GDP.

Declining commodity export earnings, stagnating financial inflows including ODA and decreasing remittances from nationals working abroad have all had a depressive effect on the foreign-exchange reserves of the LDCs.

2. Many LDCs have undertaken major policy reforms and structural adjustment programmes aiming at recovery, sustained economic growth and development. The implementation of these policy reforms must continue. To foster this process it is of paramount importance to increase the support from the international community, particularly in the fields of resources, debt relief, commodities and trade promotion. Complementarity between all measures at the national and international levels is particularly strong in LDCs. Various measures can be successful only if they are all directed in an orchestrated manner to mutually accepted objectives.

MEASURES AT THE NATIONAL LEVEL BY LDCs

3. LDCs should continue their efforts to implement national measures, especially policy reforms and structural adjustment in order to mobilize domestic resources, both economic and human, and create an economic and social environment which is conducive to development and to the successful implementation of the international support measures. The policy reforms should be designed and implemented so that the basic living conditions of the poor, and the social services in the fields of education and health, are not adversely affected. The ecological carrying capacity in the LDCs should also be taken duly into consideration.

INTERNATIONAL SUPPORT MEASURES

1. *Resources*

4. In the coming years the LDCs will continue to rely mainly on ODA for their external financing. ODA flows could play a catalytic role in obtaining other external financing for development. The target to channel to the LDCs an aid equivalent of 0.15 per cent of GNP or to double the aid volume level should be achieved by all donors as soon as possible.

2. *Quality and aid modalities*

5. Aid should be given as grant or at least on IDA terms in order not to increase debt burden. Aid modalities should be simplified and harmonized. Predictability of aid (multi-year allocations) should be improved to enable proper planning and co-ordination by recipients. Increased aid should, according to the needs, be directed to quickly disbursed import support, sectoral and programme support, local and recurrent costs and to rehabilitation and maintenance.

3. *Co-ordination*

6. Coherent utilization of all available resources is a crucial task in LDCs where external aid and other support measures play an exceptionally important role in the development process, including the implementation of policy reforms. Consultative groups and round tables should be used more efficiently for co-ordination on policy level and for allocation of aid. Local co-ordination on sectoral level should also be improved in order to ensure an adequate overall co-ordination process.

4. *Debt*

7. The debt burden of the LDCs should be relieved through the cancellation of official debts in accordance with Trade and Development Board resolution 165 (S-IX). In the Paris Club both the extension of the rescheduling periods and the lowering of interest rates should be considered. Additional measures in other appropriate forums should be developed to alleviate other debt-service obligations.

5. *Trade promotion*

8. The principle of more favourable treatment of the LDCs should be elaborated so as to achieve further well-defined advantages for these countries, such as:

Improving the GSP through introduction of duty-free treatment for export products of interest to the LDCs;

Supporting efforts to grant exceptional treatment to the LDCs in the field of non-tariff measures;

Giving priority to the LDCs in the provision of technical assistance with regard to quality, technical standards and sanitary requirements;

Increasing technical assistance to enable better utilization of the GSP systems.

9. The International Trade Centre UNCTAD/GATT has an important role to play in providing technical assistance to the LDCs and this work should be strengthened.

6. *Commodities*

10. A range of international support measures is needed in the area of commodities. This is also the case for the commodity problems in the LDCs, highly dependent on one or two commodities for their entire export earnings. Among the various measures needed, commodity development measures and diversification of the LDCs' economies are particularly important. There is a critical need for stable and continuous financial mechanisms, *inter alia*, the Second Account of the Common Fund.

11. The work on the compensatory financing scheme linked to structural adjustment should also be pursued further with the aim of securing necessary finance to enable the poorest and most commodity-dependent LDCs to diversify away from excessive dependency on commodity production with a bleak future.

REVIEW OF THE SUBSTANTIAL NEW PROGRAMME OF ACTION IN 1990

12. The Nordic countries confirm their support for a high-level meeting to review the Substantial New Programme of Action in 1990. It is important that in the review meeting the experiences of the 1980s be clearly presented and consequent measures for the future be agreed upon.

APPENDIX IX

Amendments proposed by the representative of China to TD(VII)/C.IV/CRP.7 and Add.1[52]

[TD(VII)/C.IV/CPR.8]

A. AMENDMENTS PROPOSED TO TD(VII)/C.IV/CRP.7

Paragraph 12

In line 3, to replace the words "make best efforts" with "fulfil their commitments".

Paragraph 21

In line 1, after the word "taken" insert "by developed countries".

Paragraph 25

In the first line, change the word "Donor" to the words "Developed donor".

Paragraph 27

Replace the paragraph with the following: "Assistance should be provided to strengthen LDCs' capacities to establish and implement their own policies and programmes, including programmes for strengthening the role of the private and public sectors as well as increasing their efficiency."

Paragraph 33

Replace the paragraph with the following: "In the implementation of the Integrated Programme for Commodities, the special needs of the LDCs should be taken into full account."

Paragraph 35

In the first line, after the word "community", insert the following: "and, in particular, the developed countries".

B. AMENDMENT PROPOSED TO TD(VII)/C.IV/CRP.7/Add.1

Paragraph 2 [new paragraph 43 of appendix I above]

Replace the paragraph with the following:

"Developed countries should fully implement Trade and Development Board resolution 165 (S-IX) expeditiously and convert all outstanding bilateral ODA loans of all the LDCs into grants, without discrimination."

---

[52] Appendix I to the report of Committee IV.

APPENDIX X

**Proposal by the Netherlands on behalf of the
States members of Group B**

[TD(VII)/C.IV/CRP.9]

Introduction

*Some basic features of the general economic situation and trends in
relation to least developed countries*

1. The LDCs are the poorest countries in the world. In spite of
some significant growth in some LDCs, their average GDP per capita
is slightly higher than $200, which is less than one quarter of that of
the developing countries as a whole and only about 3 per cent of that
of the developed countries. A high proportion of the LDCs' population lives in conditions of mere, and often below, subsistence.

2. At the 1985 mid-term review of the Substantial New Programme of Action for the 1980s for the Least Developed Countries it
was noted with serious concern that since the adoption of the Substantial New Programme of Action in 1981 there has been a significant
deterioration in the overall socio-economic situation of the LDCs, the
causes of which were external, domestic and environmental. GDP per
capita declined from $220 in 1980 to slightly more than $200 in 1985.
The share of LDCs in world economy and trade has been declining.
The trends for the coming years, according to present assumptions,
are also generally unfavourable. The continuous monitoring of the
implementation of the Substantial New Programme of Action to date
shows that, despite certain improvements in the situation of some
LDCs since 1985, negative economic and other factors have persisted.

3. Although LDCs face widely differing circumstances and needs,
they generally have for a long time been lagging behind in growth and
development compared with other countries and many of them seem
to have come into a vicious circle of constraints, poverty and population explosion, with stagnation or even backsliding as a result.

4. Structural handicaps make the LDCs particularly vulnerable to
the external economic environment. On the whole this environment
has been unfavourable to the LDCs over the last few years. Of particular concern have been the historically low level of commodity
prices which, *inter alia*, increased the debt-servicing problems of
LDCs, and insufficient external financial flows. Adverse weather conditions and natural calamities have in some cases further contributed
to reducing output and already very low living standards. Many of
these countries initiated structural adjustment programmes and some
engaged in reforms designed to make their economies more efficient in
a manner consistent with their own national conditions and priorities.
These adjustment measures have begun to have positive effects in
some of these countries. Complementary international support for
these efforts, in the form of both multilateral and bilateral ODA, has
on the whole resumed a rising trend but there is a continuing need for
additional efforts. Those developed countries which have not fully
participated in efforts to assist the LDCs should do so.

5. There was a consensus on the need for full and expeditious implementation of the Substantial New Programme of Action and of the
recommendations of the mid-term review as adopted; some problems
facing the LDCs call for further study. In the light of this general
background and of its own fruitful discussion, the Committee formulated the following conclusions aiming at an improvement of the
economic and social conditions in the LDCs.

I. National efforts

6. It was reaffirmed that the LDCs will continue to have primary
responsibility for their overall development.

7. It was generally acknowledged that many LDCs have undertaken comprehensive policy reforms and implemented adjustment
programmes. In order to attain sustainable, non-inflationary growth,
they should adopt and pursue economic development policies designed to improve the effectiveness of domestic resource mobilization
and use, to strengthen economic and financial management and to ra-
tionalize public expenditure and the role of government in production
activities. These efforts should be actively pursued.

8. In particular it appears imperative, taking due account of individual characteristics of each LDC:

(*a*) To accelerate agricultural development and enhance food
security;

(*b*) To design structural adjustment and diversification programmes suited to each country's particular social and economic condition;

(*c*) To endeavour to mobilize fully human resources through education and training in required skills;

(*d*) To strengthen the role of women in the development process;

(*e*) To strengthen the domestic environment for public and private
flows;

(*f*) To adopt market-oriented incentive systems;

(*g*) To increase the efficiency of the public sector;

(*h*) To enhance the conditions required for the development of a
strong private sector;

(*i*) To give priority to the advancement of the poorest in the
development policy and adopt measures to protect the most
vulnerable parts of the population during the adjustment;

(*j*) To take account of environmental issues.

II. International efforts

A. FINANCIAL AND TECHNICAL ASSISTANCE

9. In order to complement national efforts, international programmes of financial and technical assistance as well as other supportive measures from all donors are fundamental.

10. For aid to make a sustained contribution to development, it
has to be geared to the support of overall policy objectives of growth-
oriented programmes. At the same time, policies which create a receptive environment for public and private flows in LDCs will greatly
enhance aid effectiveness.

11. Donors are urged to intensify efforts to enhance the volume of
financial assistance to the LDCs on terms which correspond to their
immediate and long-term development needs. The volume and forms
of aid should be supportive of, and commensurate with, the growing
requirements of policy reform programmes and broader development
efforts. Developed countries should effectively mobilize additional
resources for the poorest countries, especially for Africa in accordance with the commitments undertaken in the context of the United
Nations Programme of Action for African Economic Recovery and
Development 1986-1990.

12. ODA will continue to play an important role especially for
poorer countries. In compliance with the recommendations of the
Development Committee's Task Force on Concessional Flows,
developed countries should pursue their efforts to achieve, as soon as
possible, the internationally agreed targets of 0.7 per cent of GNP for
total ODA and of 0.15 per cent of GNP for ODA, or doubling their
ODA, to LDCs as adopted in the Substantial New Programme of Action and the mid-term review.

13. Some donors are not ready to endorse aid targets but they
review the needs of individual countries on a continuing basis and
determine how they can best respond to these needs.

14. Multilateral development institutions should be strengthened
by endowing them with adequate resources and instruments to fulfil
their tasks. Members of the World Bank are invited to support an
early general increase of its capital as needed to support quality
lending. Donors should meet expeditiously their commitments to the
Eighth Replenishment of IDA. Regional development banks and
funds also need to be strengthened, and the adequacy of their capital
and lending programmes should be kept under review.

15. The distribution as well as the overall volume of multilateral
assistance to the LDCs, through such channels as IDA, IFAD,
regional development banks and their funds, UNDP, the Special
Measures Fund for the Least Developed Countries, UNCDF, UNVP,
etc., should be adequate to meet the increased development needs of
the LDCs. All donors, especially those who have not to date participated in these institutions, should channel a substantial part of
their aid through these institutions and agencies.

16. The proposal by the Managing Director of IMF for a significant increase in the resources of the Structural Adjustment Facility
over the three years from 1 January 1988 is welcomed. Discussions on
this proposal ought to be concluded within this year. In this respect,
we also welcome closer co-operation between the World Bank and
IMF and increasing bilateral co-financing with the World Bank.

B. AID MODALITIES

17. Donor and recipient countries should together seek to ensure that aid is fully supportive of development efforts and that aid effectiveness is strengthened, *inter alia*, through improved co-ordination. In this regard, central responsibility for aid co-ordination lies with each recipient Government.

18. International financial institutions should continue to take into account, among other things, the need to achieve the necessary adjustment with adequate rates of growth and to protect the poor segments of the population, as well as the period required for adjustment with growth. The increasing co-operation between IMF, the World Bank and other multilateral financial institutions is welcomed and should not lead to cross-conditionality.

19. Further steps should be taken by all donors who have not yet done so to provide bilateral ODA to the LDCs essentially in the form of grants and to provide loans on highly concessional terms.

20. Technical assistance should be provided to strengthen LDCs' capacities to establish and implement their own policies and programmes and to address the basic structural rigidities of their economies. Special attention should be given to support programmes for strengthening the role of the private sector and increasing the efficiency of the public sector. There is scope for joint international action in the area of technical assistance in support of improved management capacity and infrastructures.

21. The valuable work carried out by non-governmental organizations both in the field of development and emergency assistance in the LDCs, and in raising the public consciousness of the development process, is appreciated. The Committee urged increasing participation by the population, both women and men, in the work of non-governmental organizations. It called upon LDCs and non-governmental organizations to further increase the co-operation in implementing effective development programmes, consistent both with LDCs' own policies and priorities and with the autonomous character of non-governmental organizations. It also called on donors to continue co-operating closely with non-governmental organizations in implementing effective development programmes.

C. COUNTRY REVIEW MECHANISM

22. The Committee welcomed the ongoing improvements of the country review meetings which are the mechanisms for the periodic review and implementation of the Substantial New Programme of Action. Nevertheless, the need for further strengthening and improvement was recognized. In this context the primary responsibility of the LDCs, among other things, to convene on a regular basis and prepare such meetings was emphasized. UNDP and the World Bank, as the lead agencies, should expand their technical assistance to the LDCs to enable them to prepare appropriately for these meetings. Donor countries should be represented at an adequately high level. The meetings should facilitate an improved flow and effectiveness of assistance through a better dialogue and co-ordination between LDCs and their development partners.

D. COMMODITIES/INTERNATIONAL TRADE

23. The LDCs have greatly suffered from vulnerability to declines in the prices of their basic commodity exports. It is in the commodity-dependent LDCs that the impact of the commodity price situation has been the most severe.

24. In this context, depending on the nature and intensity of specific country and commodity circumstances, the LDCs should endeavour to promote economically sound diversification of their economic structures, both vertically and horizontally. The international community should support these efforts through improved co-operation in the commodities sector aiming at better market transparency, increased market access and reduced trade distortions. Continued efforts should be made to provide carefully considered aid for structural and development measures as well as technical assistance in support of improved management capacity and infrastructures.

25. Producers and consumers have already considered a number of developmental programmes which could be financed under the Second Window of the Common Fund. The entry into force of the Common Fund could lead to specific concrete actions in the framework of the respective international commodity bodies.

1. *Compensatory financing*

26. It was recognized that commodity-related shortfalls in export earnings of LDCs were an important obstacle to their development efforts.

27. The needs of developing countries, particularly the LDCs, for more stable export earnings within a context of diversification or structural adjustment should be examined. In this context, the existing compensatory schemes and mechanisms as well as the different views on international co-operation in this area concerning the commodity-specific or the balance-of-payments focus should be taken into account. The role of the EEC Stabex and Compex was recognized.

2. *Access to markets*

28. It is recognized that benefical action is already undertaken by developed countries to provide market access for the products of LDCs in the context of their GSP schemes. All other countries, developed and developing, which have not yet done so should make similar efforts. Steps should be taken further to improve GSP or MFN treatment for products of particular export interest to LDCs and to eliminate or reduce non-tariff measures affecting such products.

29. LDCs are invited to utilize fully the opportunities which are already available in the field of market access, in particular under GSP schemes.

30. As mentioned in the GATT Ministerial Declaration, adopted at the special session of GATT at Punta del Este, Uruguay, in September 1986,

"Special attention shall be given to the particular situation and problems of the least developed countries and to the need to encourage positive measures to facilitate expansion of their trading opportunities. Expeditious implementation of the relevant provisions of the 1982 Ministerial Declaration concerning the least developed countries shall also be given appropriate attention."[53]

31. Increased technical assistance should be given for trade promotion of the LDCs, *inter alia*, through the International Trade Centre UNCTAD/GATT and UNCTAD.

32. Moreover, in the framework of the multilateral trading system the promotion of South-South trade through the GSTP particularly for the benefit of the LDCs and through regional integration could make an important contribution to the expansion of trading opportunities and greater multilateralism. Progress towards promotion of subregional trade should be enhanced. East-South trade should also be further developed.

E. DEBT PROBLEMS OF LEAST DEVELOPED COUNTRIES

33. The debt-servicing situation of the LDCs has remained serious and in many cases worsened in past years. The ratios of debt to GDP and of debt service to exports have increased in the case of some LDCs to unmanageable levels. Major causes include the depressed export earnings, which have impaired the debt-servicing capacity of the LDCs, in particular for those which are heavily dependent on commodities. Their debt-servicing burden constitutes for many of them a hindrance to their development process. Problems of the LDCs' debt to the multilateral financial institutions were also recognized.

34. The critical debt situation of the LDCs calls for programmes for immediate relief. Interested developed countries which have not yet done so are firmly invited to implement fully commitments undertaken in pursuance of Trade and Development Board resolution 165 (S-IX). The developing countries which have provided concessional loans to LDCs should consider extending similar debt relief measures to these countries.

35. The Committee welcomes measures taken by the Paris Club on larger repayment and grace periods to ease the debt-service burden of the most heavily indebted among the poorest countries which are undertaking adjustment efforts. For those countries, the possibility of applying lower interest rates to their existing debt could be considered.

36. The overall trends towards innovative and more flexible approaches on the financing side, both official and private, should also be examined in relation to making debt burdens of LDCs more manageable and restoring capital flows to these countries.

---

[53] GATT, *Basic Instruments and Selected Documents, Thirty-third Supplement* (Sales No. GATT/1987-1), p. 21, sect. B, para. (vii).

37. Measures should be taken, particularly by debtor countries to facilitate non-debt-creating capital flows, especially direct investment to LDCs.

38. Measures to alleviate the debt-servicing burden for the LDCs should be supplemented and strengthened by technical assistance, as appropriate.

F. GLOBAL REVIEW AND APPRAISAL OF THE IMPLEMENTATION OF THE SUBSTANTIAL NEW PROGRAMME OF ACTION IN 1990

39. In line with General Assembly resolution 40/205, the Committee took note of the generous offer made by France to host the Conference.

III. Future work

40. Against this background, UNCTAD should, while taking into account the work of other competent international bodies and within existing and available resources, endeavour:

(*a*) To analyse the nature and causes of similarities and differences in economic performances of LDCs, taking into account the work of other competent international institutions;

(*b*) To continue to examine the complementarity between domestic and international environments in order to develop better understanding of the problems of mobilizing external public and private resources as a complement to the effective use of domestic resources of LDCs;

(*c*) To study the short-, medium- and long-term effects of national structural adjustment policies on economic performance and growth;

(*d*) To examine ways to improve the awareness of technical assistance for strengthening manpower and administrative capacity that is available to LDCs on a multilateral and bilateral basis;

(*e*) To prepare the global review of the Substantial New Programme of Action in 1990;

(*f*) To study and propose measures for assisting LDCs to promote the role of the enterprises sector in their economies based on the recommendations of the UNCTAD Enterprises Symposium;

(*g*) To give due consideration in the other fields of interest (resources, trade, commodities) to the case of the LDCs.

Part Three

ORGANIZATIONAL AND PROCEDURAL MATTERS

A. Opening of the Conference
(*Agenda item 1*)

1. The seventh session of the United Nations Conference on Trade and Development was held at the Palais des Nations, Geneva. The session was opened on Thursday, 9 July 1987, under the temporary presidency of Mr. Lazar Mojsov, President of the Presidency of the Socialist Federal Republic of Yugoslavia, and President of the sixth session of the Conference.

B. Election of the President
(*Agenda item 2*)

2. At its 201st (opening) meeting, on 9 July 1987, the Conference elected by acclamation as its President the Honourable Bernard T. G. Chidzero, Minister of Finance, Economic Planning and Development of Zimbabwe. On assuming office, the President of the Conference made a statement (TD/B/L.284).[1]

C. Report of the Pre-Conference Meeting

3. At its 205th meeting, on 13 July 1987, the Conference took note of an oral report on the Pre-Conference Meeting of Senior Officials, held at Geneva from 7 to 13 July 1987, by Mr. Saad Alfarargi (Egypt), President of the Trade and Development Board, in his capacity as Chairman and endorsed the proposals of the Pre-Conference Meeting regarding the work of the seventh session (TD/336).

D. Election of Vice-Presidents and the Rapporteur
(*Agenda item 4*)

4. At its 205th meeting, on 13 July 1987, the Conference elected Mr. Andrei Ozadovski (Ukrainian Soviet Socialist Republic) as its Rapporteur.

5. At the same meeting, the Conference elected the representatives of the following 29 States as Vice-Presidents: Argentina, Austria, Bangladesh, Cameroon, Canada, China, Colombia, Denmark, Dominican Republic, Egypt, Germany, Federal Republic of, Hungary, Jamaica, Jordan, Kuwait, Madagascar, Mexico, Netherlands, Nicaragua, Nigeria, Pakistan, Philippines, Poland, Senegal, Spain, Union of Soviet Socialist Republics, United Kingdom of Great Britain and Northern Ireland, United Republic of Tanzania, Yugoslavia.

E. Adoption of the agenda
(*Agenda item 6*)

6. At its 201st meeting, on 9 July 1987, the Conference decided, in view of the fact that the Pre-Conference Meeting of Senior Officials had not yet completed its work, to waive rule 8 of its rules of procedure and proceed with the adoption of the provisional agenda, together with the related understandings, in TD/327. In this connection the President referred to Board decision 341 (XXXIII) of 3 October 1986 and to the report of the Trade and Development Board on the first part of its thirty-third session,[2] section III, paragraphs 4 to 7, which reflected the positions taken at the Board at the time of the adoption of the provisional agenda. The Conference adopted the provisional agenda together with the related understandings on that same basis.[3]

F. Credentials of representatives to the Conference
(*Agenda item 5*)

1. APPOINTMENT OF THE CREDENTIALS COMMITTEE

7. At its 205th meeting, on 13 July 1987, the Conference decided that the Credentials Committee might be composed of the same nine States as had been members of the Credentials Committee of the General Assembly at its forty-first session, namely: Bahamas, China, Fiji, Ghana, Netherlands, Rwanda, Union of Soviet Socialist Republics, United States of America, Venezuela. The Committee would be chaired by Venezuela, which had chaired the Credentials Committee of the General Assembly at its forty-first session.

8. At its 210th meeting, on 24 July 1987, the Conference, having noted that Bahamas and Fiji were not represented at the session, appointed Barbados and Burma to replace them.

2. REPORT OF THE CREDENTIALS COMMITTEE

9. At the 220th (closing) meeting, on 3 August 1987, the *President* drew attention to the report of the Credentials Committee (TD/346).[4] He announced that the Islamic Republic of Iran wished to be associated with the letter dated 9 July 1987 addressed to the Secretary-General of UNCTAD from the delegations of the Arab

---

[1] See volume II.

[2] *Official Records of the General Assembly, Forty-first Session, Supplement No. 15* (A/41/15).

[3] For the agenda as adopted, the related understandings and the statements of position on the adoption of the provisional agenda, see annex I below.

[4] See annex VII below.

Group (TD/342). In that connection he further drew attention to communications addressed to the Secretary-General of UNCTAD from the head of the delegation of the Yemen Arab Republic (TD/349) and the Permanent Representative of Israel (TD/348).

10. The representative of *Pakistan* associated his delegation with paragraph 7 of the report of the Credentials Committee for the reasons already stated by the delegation of Pakistan at the forty-first session of the General Assembly.

11. The representative of Yemen, speaking on behalf of the *Arab Group* and as co-ordinator of the members of the League of Arab States, recalled that for 40 years Arab and other delegations had been consistently expressing reservations concerning the credentials of the Israeli delegation to the United Nations and other international conferences, and had explained the basic reasons for those reservations in letters. At the beginning of the current session, they had sent a letter to the Secretary-General of UNCTAD expressing reservations concerning the credentials of the Israeli delegation to the seventh session of the Conference, explaining the reasons. The letter had been circulated under the symbol TD/342.

12. It had been expected that the Credentials Committee would feel duty-bound to pay a certain amount of attention to those reservations, particularly since they were expressed by one seventh of the total number of delegations to the Conference. However, the Committee's report, when recording its discussion of reservations concerning the credentials of some delegations and the reservations of some members concerning the reservations expressed by other members, made only a passing reference, in paragraph 4, to TD/342.

13. Accordingly, he had cabled the Secretary-General of UNCTAD and the Chairman of the Credentials Committee expressing the great astonishment and profound indignation of the Arab delegations at the manner in which their letter had been disregarded. He had drawn attention to the fact of Israel's violations of the Charter of the United Nations, of the principles of international law, of the rights of the people of Palestine and of the status of the Holy City of Jerusalem. The Arab delegations had then contacted the Chairman of the Credentials Committee, as well as a number of its members and members of the Conference, to inform them that they found the text of the Committee's report totally unacceptable in view of its lack of objectivity and its disregard of the tenor of the reservations expressed by the Arab Group in its letter.

14. That was the position of the Arab Group with regard to the report of the Credentials Committee and the credentials of the Israeli delegation. It was based on a desire to ensure the success of the Conference, to the work of which the Arab Group had made a substantial contribution. He asked that that reservation be entered in the record.

15. The representative of the *Syrian Arab Republic* pointed out that the end of paragraph 4 of TD/346 read "The Committee also had before it TD/342", without any explanation of the content of that document. It did not mention the names of the Arab delegations that had sent the letter to explain their reservations with regard to the credentials of the Israeli delegation for the reasons appearing in that communication (TD/342) and the authors thus avoided mentioning Israel or exposing it to criticism. Dozens of delegations participating in the Conference would not recall the content of the document if it was referred to simply by its symbol. The sentence in question should therefore specify the purpose of the letter and should not be vague and anodyne. He had asked the Chairman and some members of the Committee what the reasons were for that vagueness. He had been told that the matter was one of form, that the letter had been addressed not to the Credentials Committee but to the Secretary-General of UNCTAD and that the Committee had learned of it upon its publication as a Conference document. The reply of the Arab delegations to those verbal excuses was unambiguous; the message was within the competence of the Committee and, as it had become aware of it, the Committee had two options—either to mention the letter in its report, specifying its purpose and stating to whom it had been addressed, or to omit it entirely if it chose to ignore it altogether, provided the Committee stated the formal reasons why the message was not included in the report. The procedure actually followed had been ambiguous and inappropriate. To say that the principle of consensus should apply in the drafting of the report was neither valid nor convincing. Any decision that the letter did not require a value judgement by the party to whom it was addressed should have been left to the delegations concerned by the matter. What had happened, however, was that one of the delegations on the Committee had insisted that there should be no mention either of Israel or of the Arab delegations which had reservations with regard to Israel's credentials. He did not wish to say that the Chairman was responsible, yet the fact that the Committee had maintained that unsatisfactory text in paragraph 4, because of threat of a boycott or the withdrawal of the delegation concerned, had created a situation about which it was impossible to remain silent. He had accordingly sent a cable on 27 July to the Chairman and the Secretary-General of UNCTAD expressing astonishment at the text of the report, adding that he would be taking the matter up at the appropriate time. On 28 July the Co-ordinator of the Arab Group had also sent a cable to the Chairman of the Committee.

16. Finally, he observed that what had happened could create a regrettable precedent in the proceedings of international conferences, particularly those involving the countries of the third world, for he had noticed during the current session that when a group of delegations sought to raise vital issues and delicate matters, they were told that they were politicizing the Conference and that the appropriate forum was elsewhere. When the same delegations raised economic problems and expressed concern at the prices of commodities and debt, they were reminded of the head of the United States delegation's advice to those delegations to take advantage of their presence in Geneva to walk by the lake and leave those matters to others since that was preferable for all concerned.

17. The representative of *Afghanistan* said that the ritual observations of the representatives of China and the United States with regard to his delegation were

reflected in paragraphs 7 and 9 of the Committee's report. In that connection, and in respect of the ill-intentioned remarks by the representative of Pakistan, he emphasised that the delegation of the Democratic Republic of Afghanistan also reiterated the position of its Government as set forth during the most recent session of the General Assembly.

18. The representative of *Indonesia* recalled his delegation's position with regard to the representation of Israel as expressed during the forty-first session of the General Assembly and associated his delegation with the position of the signatories of TD/342.

19. The representative of *Saudi Arabia* supported the statement by the representative of Yemen with regard to the credentials of Israel. In addition, with regard to the participation of Afghanistan at the seventh session of the Conference, he affirmed Saudi Arabia's position as recorded in the report of the Credentials Committee of the General Assembly at its forty-first session.

20. The representative of *Malaysia* associated his delegation with the statement by the representative of Yemen with regard to the credentials of Israel.

Action by the Conference

21. At its 220th (closing) meeting, on 3 August 1987, the Conference adopted the report of the Credentials Committee,[5] together with the resolution contained therein.[6]

22. The representative of *Israel* expressed regret that the seventh session of the Conference should have been exploited for unnecessary, unwarranted and unseemly confrontation under item 5. There was no need to respond further to the slanderous attacks against his delegation's credentials beyond what was stated in his delegation's letter of 29 July 1987 (TD/348), and that the more so in the light of the action just taken by the Conference without objection.

G. Constitution of sessional bodies
(*Agenda item 3*)

23. At its 205th meeting, on 13 July 1987, the Conference established four Sessional Committees to consider and report on agenda item 8 as follows:

Committee I
Resources for development, including financial, and related monetary questions (sub-item 8 (*a*)).

Committee II
Commodities (sub-item 8 (*b*)).

Committee III
International trade (sub-item 8 (*c*)).

Committee IV
Problems of the least developed countries, bearing in mind the Substantial New Programme of Action for the 1980s for the Least Developed Countries (sub-item 8 (*d*)).

The Conference further decided that all other items would be considered in plenary meeting. It was understood that the Sessional Committees would not establish sub-committees, that no more than three Sessional Committees would meet in parallel and that they would be open to participation by all members of the Conference.

H. Bureau of the Conference

24. In accordance with rule 22 of the rules of procedure, the Bureau of the Conference consisted of the following 35 members: the President and the 29 Vice-Presidents of the Conference, the Chairmen of the Sessional Committees and the Rapporteur of the Conference.

25. At its 205th meeting, on 13 July 1987, the Conference decided that the Chairmen of other sessional bodies and the co-ordinators of regional groups would be fully associated with the work of the Bureau.

I. Appointment of "Friends of the Rapporteur"

26. At its 205th meeting, on 13 July 1987, the Conference agreed that the Rapporteur of the Conference should be assisted in the preparation of his draft report by a group of "Friends of the Rapporteur", composed of two members each from the African, Asian and Latin American Groups, two members each from Group B and Group D, and one member from China. The members subsequently designated were: China, Czechoslovakia, German Democratic Republic, Indonesia, Jamaica, Malta, Morocco, Sweden, United Kingdom of Great Britain and Northern Ireland, Venezuela, Zambia.

J. Establishment of a High-Level Contact Group of the President of the Conference

27. At its 213th plenary meeting, on 13 July 1987, the Conference established a High-Level Contact Group of the President which, on the basis of past practice, was composed of nine members from the Group of 77 (three from Africa, three from Asia, three from Latin America), six members from Group B, three members from Group D, and China. It was understood that, in conformity with the usual practice, the Contact Group would be open-ended.

28. In addition, the Conference agreed that the seven regional group co-ordinators (Group of 77, African Group, Asian Group, Latin American Group, Group B, Group D and China) and the sectoral co-ordinators would participate in the work of the Contact Group. Pursuant to paragraph 2 of General Assembly resolution 41/169, all Ministers of member States present during the final stage of negotiations would also be invited to participate fully in the work of the Contact Group.

K. Membership and attendance

29. The following 141 members of UNCTAD were represented at the seventh session of the Conference:

---

[5] *Idem.*

[6] For the text, see resolution 168 (VII).

Afghanistan, Albania, Algeria, Angola, Argentina, Australia, Austria, Bahrain, Bangladesh, Barbados, Belgium, Benin, Bhutan, Bolivia, Botswana, Brazil, Brunei Darussalam, Bulgaria, Burkina Faso, Burma, Burundi, Byelorussian Soviet Socialist Republic, Cameroon, Canada, Cape Verde, Chile, China, Colombia, Comoros, Congo, Costa Rica, Côte d'Ivoire, Cuba, Cyprus, Czechoslovakia, Democratic Kampuchea, Democratic People's Republic of Korea, Democratic Yemen, Denmark, Djibouti, Dominican Republic, Ecuador, Egypt, El Salvador, Ethiopia, Finland, France, Gabon, Gambia, German Democratic Republic, Germany, Federal Republic of, Ghana, Greece, Guatemala, Guinea, Haiti, Holy See, Honduras, Hungary, India, Indonesia, Iran (Islamic Republic of), Iraq, Ireland, Israel, Italy, Jamaica, Japan, Jordan, Kenya, Kuwait, Lao People's Democratic Republic, Lebanon, Lesotho, Liberia, Libyan Arab Jamahiriya, Liechtenstein, Luxembourg, Madagascar, Malaysia, Maldives, Malta, Mauritania, Mauritius, Mexico, Mongolia, Morocco, Mozambique, Namibia, Nepal, Netherlands, New Zealand, Nicaragua, Niger, Nigeria, Norway, Oman, Pakistan, Panama, Papua New Guinea, Paraguay, Peru, Philippines, Poland, Portugal, Qatar, Republic of Korea, Romania, Rwanda, Sao Tome and Principe, Saudi Arabia, Senegal, Singapore, Somalia, Spain, Sri Lanka, Sudan, Swaziland, Sweden, Switzerland, Syrian Arab Republic, Thailand, Togo, Trinidad and Tobago, Tunisia, Turkey, Uganda, Ukrainian Soviet Socialist Republic, Union of Soviet Socialist Republics, United Arab Emirates, United Kingdom of Great Britain and Northern Ireland, United Republic of Tanzania, United States of America, Uruguay, Venezuela, Viet Nam, Yemen, Yugoslavia, Zaire, Zambia, Zimbabwe.

30. The Office of the Director-General for Development and International Economic Co-operation and the Department of International Economic and Social Affairs were represented.

31. The Economic Commission for Europe, the Economic and Social Commission for Asia and the Pacific, the Economic Commission for Latin America and the Caribbean, the Economic Commission for Africa, the Economic and Social Commission for Western Asia, the Office of the United Nations High Commissioner for Refugees, the United Nations Children's Fund, the United Nations Development Programme, the United Nations Environment Programme, the United Nations Institute for Training and Research, the United Nations Fund for Population Activities, the United Nations University—World Institute for Development Economics Research and the World Food Council were represented. The International Trade Centre UNCTAD/GATT was also represented.

32. The following specialized agencies were represented: International Labour Organisation, Food and Agriculture Organization of the United Nations, United Nations Educational, Scientific and Cultural Organization, World Health Organization, World Bank, International Monetary Fund, International Telecommunications Union, World Intellectual Property Organization, International Fund for Agricultural Development, and United Nations Industrial Develop-

ment Organization. The International Atomic Energy Agency and the General Agreement on Tariffs and Trade were also represented.

33. The following intergovernmental bodies were represented: African, Caribbean and Pacific Group of States, African Development Bank, Arab Federation of Shipping, Arab Monetary Fund, Asian-African Legal Consultative Committee, Association of Iron Ore Exporting Countries, Caribbean Community, Commonwealth Secretariat, Council for Mutual Economic Assistance, Economic Community of West African States, Economic Co-operation Organization, European Economic Community, European Free Trade Association, Inter-American Development Bank, Intergovernmental Committee for Migration, International Center for Public Enterprises in Developing Countries, International Cocoa Organization, International Jute Organization, International Natural Rubber Organization, International Sugar Organization, International Textiles and Clothing Bureau, International Tropical Timber Organization, International Wheat Council, Islamic Development Bank, Latin American Economic System, League of Arab States, OPEC Fund for International Development, Organisation for Economic Co-operation and Development, Organization of African Unity, Organization of the Islamic Conference, Organization of the Petroleum Exporting Countries, Permanent Secretariat of the General Treaty on Central American Economic Integration.

34. The following non-governmental organizations in the general category were represented: Afro-Asian Peoples' Solidarity Organization, Europe-Third World Center, Commission of the Churches on International Affairs of the World Council of Churches, Friends World Committee for Consultation (Quakers), International Alliance of Women, International Association of Agricultural Economists, International Association of State Trading Organizations of Developing Countries, International Bar Association, International Chamber of Commerce, International Christian Union of Business Executives, International Coalition for Development Action, International Confederation of Free Trade Unions, International Co-operation for Development and Solidarity, International Co-operative Alliance, International Council of Voluntary Agencies, International Council of Women, International Foundation for Development Alternatives, Inter-Parliamentary Union, Lutheran World Federation, Society for International Development, United Towns Organization, Women's International League for Peace and Freedom, World Assembly of Small and Medium Enterprises, World Association of Former United Nations Internes and Fellows, Inc., World Confederation of Labour, World Federation of Trade Unions, World Peace Council and World Veterans Federation; and in the special category: International Air Transport Association, International Association of Islamic Banks, International Ocean Institute, and International Organization of Consumers Unions.

35. The Palestine Liberation Organization was represented pursuant to General Assembly resolution 3237 (XXIX) of 22 November 1974.

36. The African National Congress of South Africa and the Pan Africanist Congress of Azania were

represented pursuant to General Assembly resolution 3280 (XXIX) of 10 December 1974.

37.   The South West Africa People's Organization was represented pursuant to General Assembly resolution 31/152 of 20 December 1976.

L.   Other business
(*Agenda item 9*)

1.   PERIODIC REVIEW BY THE CONFERENCE OF THE LISTS OF STATES CONTAINED IN THE ANNEX TO GENERAL ASSEMBLY RESOLUTION 1995 (XIX)[7]

38.   At its 201st meeting, on 9 July 1987, the Conference, in conformity with paragraph 6 of General Assembly resolution 1995 (XIX), reviewed the list of States contained in the annex to that resolution, as amended. The Conference approved the inclusion, in the appropriate lists, of the following States which had become members of UNCTAD since the sixth session of the Conference:

List A: Brunei Darussalam;

List C: Saint Kitts and Nevis.

2.   DESIGNATION OF INTERGOVERNMENTAL BODIES FOR THE PURPOSES OF RULE 80 OF THE RULES OF PROCEDURE OF THE CONFERENCE[8]

39.   At its 201st meeting, on 9 July 1987, the Conference decided that the International Tropical Timber Organization (ITTO), and the International Textiles and Clothing Bureau (ITCB), which had applied for designation under rule 80 of the rules of procedure of the Conference, should be so designated. Information on these organizations is contained in TD/L.273 and TD/L.274, respectively.

3.   REVIEW OF THE CALENDAR OF MEETINGS[9]
(*Agenda item 9* (d))

40.   At its 220th (closing) meeting, on 3 August 1987, the Conference adopted the calendar of meetings for the remainder of 1987 (TD/INF.24 and Corr.1).

4.   FINANCIAL IMPLICATIONS OF THE ACTIONS OF THE CONFERENCE
(*Agenda item 9* (e))

41.   At its 220th (closing) meeting, on 3 August 1987, the Conference took note of a statement by the Secretary-General of UNCTAD that the various actions taken by the Conference, including the adoption of the Final Act under item 8, contained programme indications for the work of the UNCTAD secretariat. These indications would be taken fully into account by the Secretary-General of UNCTAD in drawing up in final form, immediately after the Conference, the UNCTAD submission for the 1988-1989 programme budget. It would be the task of the Working Party on the Medium-term Plan and the Programme Budget and of the Trade and Development Board in discussing this submission to assess the way in which the indications given by the Conference had been translated by the Secretary-General into the programme terms and to review their implications for UNCTAD's work programme *in toto*.

5.   REPORT OF THE TRADE AND DEVELOPMENT BOARD
(*Agenda item 9* (b))

42.   At its 220th (closing) meeting, on 3 August 1987, the Conference took note of the report of the Trade and Development Board, which consisted of the reports of the Board on its twenty-seventh session, twenty-eighth session, thirteenth special session, twenty-ninth session, the first and second parts of its thirtieth session, its fourteenth special session, its thirty-first session, the first and second parts of its thirty-second session, the first and second parts of its thirty-third session and its fifteenth special session. The reports were brought to the attention of the Conference in a note by the secretariat (TD/332).

M.   Adoption of the report of the Conference to the General Assembly
(*Agenda item 10*)

43.   At its 220th (closing) meeting, on 3 August 1987, the Conference adopted the draft report on its seventh session (TD/L.300), and authorized the Rapporteur to complete it as appropriate and to introduce editorial adjustments and corrections, as necessary, in consultation with those concerned.

N.   Closure of the seventh session of the Conference

44.   After statements by the spokesmen for the regional groups, the representatives of Colombia and China, the Secretary-General of UNCTAD and the President,[10] at the 220th meeting, on 3 August 1987, the President declared the seventh session closed.

---

[7] See part one above, section A.4, "Decisions": (*a*).

[8] *Ibid.*, (*b*).

[9] *Ibid.*, (*c*).

[10] See volume II.

ANNEXES

Annex I

AGENDA FOR THE SEVENTH SESSION OF THE UNITED NATIONS CONFERENCE ON TRADE AND DEVELOPMENT

as adopted by the Conference at its 201st plenary meeting, on 9 July 1987

1. Opening of the Conference.
2. Election of the President.
3. Constitution of sessional bodies.
4. Election of Vice-Presidents and the Rapporteur.
5. Credentials of representatives to the Conference:
   (a) Appointment of the Credentials Committee;
   (b) Report of the Credentials Committee.
6. Adoption of the agenda.
7. General debate.
8. Revitalizing development, growth and international trade, in a more predictable and supportive environment, through multilateral co-operation: assessment of relevant economic trends and of global structural change, and appropriate formulation of policies and measures, addressing key issues in the following interrelated areas:
   (a) Ressources for development, including financial, and related monetary questions;
   (b) Commodities;
   (c) International trade;
   (d) Problems of the least developed countries, bearing in mind the Substantial New Programme of Action for the 1980s for the Least Developed Countries.
9. Other business.
10. Adoption of the report of the Conference to the General Assembly.

Understandings

I. In the assessent of relevant economic trends, due attention should be paid to the role of the private sector in development.

II. The formulation relating to "a more predictable and supportive environment" is intended to subsume the interest expressed in referring to the need for security, dependability and confidence-building in the world economic environment, as well as for equity and justice in international economic relations.

III. Monetary questions will be considered in the context of the mandate of UNCTAD and without prejudice to the competence of the International Monetary Fund and other international financial institutions.

IV. Sub-item 8 (c)—"international trade"—includes issues arising in trade relations among countries having different economic and social systems.

Positions taken on the adoption of the provisional agenda for the Conference during the thirty-third session of the Trade and Development Board as recorded in the report of the Board to the General Assembly on the first part of its thirty-third session[a]

4. At its 702nd meeting, on 3 October 1986, the Board, acting on a proposal of the President, adopted draft decision TD/B/L.815 (see decision 341 (XXXIII)). The President directed that the position of the United States delegation . . . be duly recorded in the report of the Board. Draft decision TD/B/L.812 was withdrawn by its sponsors.

---

[a] *Official Records of the General Assembly, Forty-first Session, Supplement No. 15* (A/41/15), section III.A.

5. The representative of the *United States of America* said that after long and careful review by the United States authorities, his delegation had found it necessary to call for a vote on TD/B/L.815 and to cast a no vote.

6. The United States had participated in a long and hard effort to develop an agenda that would have held out the expectation that the seventh session of the Conference would seriously tackle the problems of development—an agenda that would have reflected the realities of today's world. His Government was of the view that the document before the Board failed to do this.

7. He wished there to be no mistake concerning the United States action at the current meeting. It was meant to convey its disagreement over the document before the Board. It in no way indicated an abandonment of United States efforts to work with UNCTAD and its members to change positively the course that the organization had followed for the past 20 years. The United States would continue to seek positive change. It would continue to work closely with the secretariat and other delegations to see to it that UNCTAD was not buried under the avalanche of economic change overtaking the contemporary world. It would continue to work for an UNCTAD that was current, credible and conscientious.

Annex II

LIST OF HEADS OF STATE OR GOVERNMENT, HEADS OF INTER-GOVERNMENTAL BODIES, AND OTHER REPRESENTATIVES AND OBSERVERS WHO ADDRESSED THE CONFERENCE DURING THE GENERAL DEBATE

A. Heads of State or Government and other speakers above ministerial rank

		Date	Plenary meeting number
France	Mr. François Mitterrand	10.7.1987	202
Egypt	Mr. Mohammed Hosny Mubarak	10.7.1987	202
Norway	Mrs. Gro Harlem Brundtland	10.7.1987	203
Congo	Colonel Denis Sassou Nguesso	10.7.1987	203
Pontifical Commission	His Eminence Cardinal Roger Etchegaray	10.7.1987	203
China	Mr. Tian Jiyun	13.7.1987	204
Zimbabwe	Mr. Robert G. Mugabe	14.7.1987	207
Jordan	H.R.H. Crown Prince Hassan Bin Talal	27.7.1987	212

B. Countries

Afghanistan	Mr. Mohammad Khan Jalallar	29.7.1987	216
Albania	Mr. Kostandin Hoxha	13.7.1987	206
Algeria	Mr. Mohamed Aberkane	14.7.1987	208
Argentina	Mr. Bernardo Grinspun	28.7.1987	214
Australia	Mr. Alan Robert Oxley	27.7.1987	213
Austria	Mr. Heinrich Neisser	14.7.1987	208
Bahrain	Mr. Karim Al-Shakar	14.7.1987	208
Bangladesh	Mr. A. Munim	14.7.1987	208
Barbados	Mr. E. Evelyn Greaves	28.7.1987	215
Belgium	Mr. H. de Croo	27.7.1987	212
Benin	Mr. Girigissou Gado	24.7.1987	211
Bhutan	Mr. Tobgye S. Dorji	13.7.1987	209
Bolivia	Mr. Raúl España-Smith	29.7.1987	216
Brazil	Mr. Roberto Costa de Abreu Sodre	29.7.1987	217
Brunei Darussalam	Dato Paduka Haji Selamat Bin Haji Munap	30.7.1987	218
Bulgaria	Mr. Hristo Hristov	10.7.1987	203
Burkina Faso	Mr. Mohamadou Touré	24.7.1987	211
Burma	U Tin Tun	30.7.1987	218
Byelorussian Soviet Socialist Republic	Mr. Vassili I. Peshkov	29.7.1987	216
Cameroon	Mr. Michael Elangwe Namaya	24.7.1987	210
Canada	Mrs. Monique Landry	15.7.1987	209
Chile	Mr. Luis Escobar Cerda	27.7.1987	212
Colombia	Mr. Samuel Alberto Yohai	24.7.1987	211
Comoros	Mr. Said Kafe	24.7.1987	210

		Date	Plenary meeting number
Costa Rica	Mrs. Muni Figueres de Jiménez	28.7.1987	215
Côte d'Ivoire	Mr. Nicolas Kouandi Angba	14.7.1987	207
Cuba	Mr. Ricardo Cabrisas Ruiz	10.7.1987	202[a]
Cyprus	Mr. Michael Michaelides	29.7.1987	216
Czechoslovakia	Mr. Bohumil Urban	14.7.1987	207
Democratic People's Republic of Korea	Mr. Choi Jong Gun	13.7.1987	205
Democratic Yemen	Mr. Abdullah Saleh Al-Ashtal	27.7.1987	213
Denmark (on behalf of EEC)	Mr. Uffe Ellemann-Jensen[b]	10.7.1987	202
Dominican Republic	Mr. F. Daniel Suazo	14.7.1987	208
Ecuador	Mr. Galo Leoro Franco	24.7.1987	211
Egypt	Mr. Yousri Mustafa	28.7.1987	214
Ethiopia	Mr. Gebre Kidan Tadesse	14.7.1987	207
Finland	Mr. Pertti Salolainen	28.7.1987	215
France	Mr. Georges Chavanes	29.7.1987	217
German Democratic Republic	Mr. Gerhard Beil	13.7.1987	205
Germany, Federal Republic of	Mr. Martin Bangemann	29.7.1987	217
Ghana	Mr. Kofi Djin	27.7.1987	212
Greece	Mr. Yannos Papantoniou	29.7.1987	216
Guatemala	Mr. Antonio Pallares-Buonafina	30.7.1987	218
Guinea	Mr. Kory Kondiano	14.7.1987	208
Haiti	Mr. Gervais Charles	14.7.1987	208
Holy See	Mgr. Justo Mullor García	30.7.1987	219
Hungary	Mr. Tibor Melega	13.7.1987	205
India	Mr. P. Shiv Shanker	10.7.1987	202
Indonesia	Mr. Ali Wardhana	27.7.1987	213
Iran (Islamic Republic of)	Mr. Ali Akbar Velayati	27.7.1987	212
Iraq	Mr. Qubais Saied Abdul Fatah	29.7.1987	217
Ireland	Mr. Sean Calleary	28.7.1987	215
Israel	Mr. Itzhak Minerbi	29.7.1987	216
Italy	Mr. Francesco Cattanei	27.7.1987	212
Jamaica	Mr. K. G. Anthony Hill	10.7.1987	203
Japan	Mr. Tadashi Kuranari	27.7.1987	212
Kenya	Mr. Jonathan Ng'Eno	13.7.1987	206
Kuwait	Mr. Salem Jaber Al-Ahmad Al-Sabah	27.7.1987	213
Lao People's Democratic Republic	Mr. Maligna Saignavongs	13.7.1987	206
Lebanon	Mr. Salim Naffah	30.7.1987	219
Lesotho	Mr. Moletsane Mokoroane	30.7.1987	218
Libyan Arab Jamahiriya	Mr. Farhat Salah Sharnanh	28.7.1987	214
Luxembourg	Mr. Robert Goebbels	27.7.1987	213
Malaysia	Mr. Kok Wee Kiat	13.7.1987	205
Maldives	Mr. Abdul Sattar Moosa Didi	30.7.1987	219
Malta	Mr. Victor J. Gauci	27.7.1987	213
Mexico	Mr. Héctor Hernández Cervantes	28.7.1987	214
Mongolia	Mr. J. Dulmaa	13.7.1987	204
Morocco	Mr. Abdellah Azmani	13.7.1987	204
Mozambique	Mr. Daniel G. Tembe	29.7.1987	217
Namibia (represented by the United Nations Council for Namibia)	Mr. Nihat Akyol	28.7.1987	214
Nepal	Mr. Prakash Bijaya Thebe	28.7.1987	215
Netherlands	Mrs. Yvonne van Rooy	13.7.1987	204
Nicaragua	Mr. Alejandro E. Martínez Cuenca	10.7.1987	203
Niger	Mr. Nouhou Amadou	29.7.1987	216
Nigeria	Mr. Alhaji Samaila Mamman	14.7.1987	207
Norway	Mr. Thorvald Stoltenberg	28.7.1987	214
Oman	Mr. Ahmed bin Abdul Nabi Macki	27.7.1987	212
Pakistan	Mr. Mahbub Ul-Haq	10.7.1987	202

[a] Speaking as representative of the Head of State of the Republic of Cuba, to present the results of the Sixth Ministerial Meeting of the Group of 77.

[b] Speaking also on behalf of the European Economic Community and its member States.

		Date	Plenary meeting number
Panama	Mr. Marcos A. Villarreal	30.7.1987	218
Papua New Guinea	Mr. Samuel Abal	30.7.1987	218
Peru	Mr. José Ley-Elias	29.7.1987	216
Philippines	Mr. José D. Ingles	15.7.1987	209
Poland	Mr. Andrzej Wojcik	10.7.1987	203
Portugal	Mr. Fernando A. Santos Martins	28.7.1987	215
Republic of Korea	Mr. Kwang Soo Choi	24.7.1987	210
Romania	Mr. Ilie Vaduva	14.7.1987	208
Saudi Arabia	Mr. Soleiman El Saleem	28.7.1987	215
Senegal	Mr. Abdourahmane Touré	13.7.1987	205
Somalia	Mr. Mohamud Said Mohamed	15.7.1987	209
Spain	Mr. Miguel Angel Fernández Ordóñez	13.7.1987	205
Sri Lanka	Mr. M. S. Amarasiri	24.7.1987	211
Sudan	Mr. Abdel Magied Ali Hassan	29.7.1987	217
Sweden	Ms. Anita Gradin	27.7.1987	212
Switzerland	Mr. Jean-Pascal Delamuraz	14.7.1987	208
Thailand	Mr. Montree Pongpanit	24.7.1987	211
Trinidad and Tobago	Mr. Basdeo Panday	14.7.1987	207
Tunisia	Mr. Habib Kaabachi	29.7.1987	216
Turkey	Mr. Ali Bozer	28.7.1987	215
Uganda	Mr. Israel Kayonde	30.7.1987	218
Ukrainian Soviet Socialist Republic	Mr. Andrei A. Ozadovski	30.7.1987	219
Union of Soviet Socialist Republics	Mr. Boris Aristov	13.7.1987	204
United Arab Emirates	Mr. Saif Ali Al Jarwan	13.7.1987	205
United Kingdom of Great Britain and Northern Ireland	Mr. Alan Clark	28.7.1987	214
United Republic of Tanzania	Mr. Daudi N. Mwakawago	27.7.1987	213
United States of America	Mr. Dennis G. Goodman	29.7.1987	217
Uruguay	Mr. Enrique V. Iglesias	13.7.1987	205
Venezuela	Mr. Héctor Meneses	10.7.1987	202
Viet Nam	Mr. Dy Nien Nguyen	13.7.1987	206
Yugoslavia	Mr. Ibrahim Tabakovič	14.7.1987	208
Zaire	Mr. Kasereka Kasai	15.7.1987	209
Zambia	Mr. J. K. M. Kalaluka	14.7.1987	207

C. United Nations Secretariat

Secretary-General of the United Nations	Mr. Javier Pérez de Cuéllar	9.7.1987	201
Secretary-General of UNCTAD	Mr. Kenneth K. S. Dadzie	9.7.1987	201
United Nations Centre on Transnational Corporations	Mr. Peter Hansen	14.7.1987	208
United Nations Children's Fund	Mr. Richard Jolly	28.7.1987	215
United Nations Development Programme	Mr. William H. Draper III	10.7.1987	203
United Nations Environment Programme	Mr. Mostafa K. Tolba	15.7.1987	209
United Nations University (World Institute for Development Economics Research)	Mr. Lal E. Jayawardena	24.7.1987	211
Economic Commission for Europe	Mr. G. Hinteregger	29.7.1987	217
Economic and Social Commission for Asia and the Pacific	Mr. K. Gunaratnam	29.7.1987	217
World Food Council	Mr. Gerald Ion Trant	24.7.1987	210

*

*   *

Mr. Gamani Corea	Former Secretary-General of UNCTAD	15.7.1987	209

D. Specialized agencies, GATT, International Trade Centre UNCTAD/GATT

		Date	Plenary meeting number
International Labour Organisation	Mr. Francis Blanchard	27.7.1987	213
Food and Agriculture Organization of the United Nations	Mr. Edouard Saouma	13.7.1987	205
United Nations Educational, Scientific and Cultural Organization	Mr. Amadou-Mahtar M'Bow	30.7.1987	218
World Bank	Mr. Barber B. Conable Jr.	10.7.1987	202
International Monetary Fund	Mr. Michel Camdessus	27.7.1987	212
International Telecommunication Union	Mr. Richard E. Butler	24.7.1987	211
International Fund for Agricultural Development	Mr. Idriss Jazairy	14.7.1987	208
United Nations Industrial Development Organization	Mr. Domingo L. Siazon Jr.	10.7.1987	203
GATT	Mr. Arthur Dunkel	28.7.1987	214

* * *

International Trade Centre UNCTAD/GATT	Mr. Göran Engblom	13.7.1987	206

E. Other intergovernmental bodies

Arab Monetary Fund	Mr. Faris Bingaradi	30.7.1987	218
Asian-African Legal Consultative Committee	Mr. Akira Nagasaka	29.7.1987	217
Commission of the European Communities	Mr. Claude Cheysson	13.7.1987	205
Commonwealth Secretariat	Mr. Shridath S. Ramphal	27.7.1987	213
Council for Mutual Economic Assistance	Mr. M. Marinov	13.7.1987	206
Economic Co-operation Organization	Mr. Behçet Türemen	24.7.1987	211
International Center for Public Enterprises in Developing Countries	Mr. Ziga Vodusek	28.7.1987	215
International Cocoa Organization	Mr. Kobena G. Erbynn	24.7.1987	210
International Jute Organization	Mr. Harbans Singh	24.7.1987	210
International Natural Rubber Organization	Mr. P. Soeparto	24.7.1987	210

		Date	Plenary meeting number
International Sugar Organization	Mr. Alfredo A. Ricart	24.7.1987	210
International Tropical Timber Organization	Mr. B. C. Y. Freezailah	24.7.1987	210
International Wheat Council	Mr. Jean Parotte	24.7.1987	210
Organisation for Economic Co-operation and Development	Mr. Jean-Claude Paye	28.7.1987	214
Organization of the Islamic Conference	Mr. Driss Alaoui Mdaghri	27.7.1987	213

F. Non-governmental organizations

General category

Afro-Asian People's Solidarity Organization	Mr. Julien Randriamasivelo	30.7.1987	218
Commission of the Churches on International Affairs (World Council of Churches)	Ms. Agnes Chepkwony	14.7.1987	208
International Chamber of Commerce	Mr. Hans Koenig	14.7.1987	208
International Coalition for Development Action	Mrs. Georgina Ashworth	30.7.1987	218
International Confederation of Free Trade Unions	Mr. Edouard Laurijssen	30.7.1987	219
World Assembly of Small and Medium Enterprises	Mr. Hulas C. Golchha	13.7.1987	206
World Confederation of Labour	Mr. Blaise Roble	30.7.1987	219
World Federation of Trade Unions	Mr. Ivan Mitiaiev	30.7.1987	218
World Peace Council	Mr. Jacques Le Dauphin	30.7.1987	219

G. Other organizations

African National Congress of South Africa[c]	Mr. Patrick Magapatona	29.7.1987	217
Palestine Liberation Organization[d]	Mr. Ahmad Suleiman Abu-Alaa	27.7.1987	213
Pan Africanist Congress of Azania[e]	Mr. Elliot Mfaxa	30.7.1987	219
South West Africa People's Organization[f]	Mr. Ben Amathila	30.7.1987	219

---

c Pursuant to General Assembly resolution 3280 (XXIX).
d Pursuant to General Assembly resolution 3237 (XXIX).
e Pursuant to General Assembly resolution 3280 (XXIX).
f Pursuant to General Assembly resolution 31/152.

Annex III

ADDRESSES DELIVERED AT THE INAUGURAL CEREMONY ON 9 JULY 1987

A. *Statement by Mr. Javier Pérez de Cuéllar, Secretary-General of the United Nations* *

It is a very great pleasure for me to address you on the occasion of this seventh session of the United Nations Conference on Trade and Development. It is particularly satisfying that the session should be presided over by an eminent African personality, Mr. Bernard Chidzero, who is well known to the whole international community for his contribution to the work of the Conference and, more generally, to the cause of international economic co-operation. I am convinced that we shall all derive great benefit from the wisdom of his counsels and from his authority.

The first session of the United Nations Conference on Trade and Development was held at Geneva in 1964. The fact that we are meeting here again reminds us of the immense hopes and high aspirations of the founders of UNCTAD as well as of the importance of its achievements and its capacity to do even greater work. In this connection, I wish to pay a tribute to two former Secretaries-General of the Conference, Raúl Prebisch and Manuel Pérez Guerrero, both of whom have passed away since the sixth session. Their contribution to the work of the Conference and to the overall process of international co-operation for development is a precious legacy which will continue to guide our efforts to provide a more favourable framework for development. The work which they had begun has, fortunately, been continued by personalities as competent as Mr. Gamani Corea, who is with us for this session of the Conference, and Mr. Kenneth Dadzie, the present Secretary-General.

Let me also once again welcome the presence here of Mr. Pierre Aubert, President of the Swiss Confederation, whom I must thank, together with the Swiss people for the courteous and efficient hospitality that they continue to offer the United Nations family.

The sixth session of the United Nations Conference on Trade and Development took place in very different circumstances. The world economy was barely recovering from a serious recession; the extent of the debt problem and of other imbalances in the world economy was becoming more clearly evident; the events of the 1970s and the early 1980s had shaken the confidence of Governments in the machinery of international co-operation to solve the economic problems; and more and more Governments were seeking bilateral and case-by-case solutions to external economic problems.

The work of the sixth session of the Conference and its results had been essentially marked by awareness of the need, for all countries, to concentrate their efforts on strengthening the recovery of the world economy and promoting an accelerated development of the developing countries. It had, moreover, been accepted that adjustment programmes would achieve their ends more readily if they were supported by a stronger world economy. Nevertheless, these concerted efforts have not yet been successful. In the major market-economy countries, inflation has been curbed and the nominal rates of interest have fallen, results which are far from being negligible. However, serious imbalances have appeared in the economic relations of the industrialized countries, creating uncertainty with regard to exchange rates, interest rates and the prices of the main commodities.

Protectionist pressures have increased, the result being a distinct slow-down of investment and growth. In fact, this year, forecasts of growth rates have been regularly revised downwards. In short, the world economy has not experienced the sustained growth which would make it possible satisfactorily and rapidly to resolve the serious economic and social problems which we have to face.

Recently, under the combined effect of weak world growth and the persistence of uncertainties, the support needed for the accelerated development of the developing countries has not materialized to any significant extent. Many countries, particularly in Latin America and Africa, which are making painful adjustment efforts, have been severely affected thereby. In the case of a large number of these countries, their per capita income is still decreasing. The fall in commodity prices, the stagnation of official development assistance and the ever-increasing debt-servicing burden have, in recent years, nullified the efforts made by many developing countries to produce a surplus of national income for investment and growth. The fall in oil prices has also hit many developing countries hard. In 1986, the economic results of some large developing countries, particularly in Asia, continued to improve. This improvement has not, however, been sufficiently widespread and, in the light of the current economic situation, is unlikely to continue.

---

* Initially circulated as TD/L.290.

In such an unfavourable international situation, the social consequences of adjustment efforts give rise to grave concern, since it is the vulnerable groups who pay the heaviest price as has been amply demonstrated, with documentary support, by various United Nations bodies. There are far too many developing countries in which social progress has slowed down, if not receded. This has not only had the effect of heightening political tension in the immediate future: the long-term development prospects are themselves endangered, albeit in a less obvious way.

It cannot be said, however, that there are no energetic forces capable of revitalizing the international economy. What is needed is for a number of countries to take more systematic steps and combine their efforts to stimulate and direct these forces.

Countries have adopted some positive measures in a number of critical areas. In particular, the need for co-operation to resolve international economic difficulties is better understood. More specifically, the industrialized countries have reaffirmed their intent to co-ordinate their macro-economic policies, most recently at the Venice Economic Summit. With regard to multilateral trade negotiations, those which have just begun in Uruguay make it possible to hope for a liberalization of international trade and a reversal of the protectionist trends which have a particular impact on the developing countries. As for the acute debt problem of the developing countries, it is agreed that adjustment must be accompanied by growth and some specific programmes have been prepared to that end. The Paris Club and other forums have made it possible to reschedule debt on a longer-term basis. The General Assembly has adopted the United Nations Programme of Action for African Economic Recovery and Development 1986-1990,[a] which embodies the commitments entered into by both the African countries and the international community.

These are facts which cannot but be welcomed and which open the way to new joint initiatives with a view to strengthening international economic co-operation. They are still, however, inadequate. The commitments entered into must be respected. The strategies adopted must be applied. The preparation of joint strategies and decisions must be followed by practical measures. It is thus essential to act very quickly and vigorously to prevent the world economy from being sucked into a nosedive whose effects would be detrimental to all countries. Accelerated development of the developing countries could make an essential contribution to the health of the world economy. I am convinced that the seventh session of the Conference offers a noteworthy opportunity to change the course of events by joint efforts in the search for more effective ways of reactivating world growth and development.

These joint efforts are, in fact, in keeping with the exceptional mission of UNCTAD which is to promote dialogue on the global scale and promote concerted initiatives to overcome the difficulties which are affecting the world economy and influencing the development process. It is important therefore, as evidenced by the very agenda of this seventh session, that these joint efforts should concentrate on certain key sectors and certain critical problems.

Since its establishment, UNCTAD has had the basic task of settling commodity questions. Almost all recent statements, whether emanating from industrialized countries or developing countries, have unequivocally recognized the seriousness of the present situation, attributable to the constant weakness of the prices of these products. For instance, the losses suffered by the developing countries in 1986 because of the deterioration in the terms of trade had been estimated at about \$100 billion.

The situation in this area is a complex one and reflects the peculiar features of each commodity as well as those of the producer countries. Nevertheless, there is general agreement that, in the long term, the developing countries must diversify their productive structures and that that will require additional financial support. It is also essential that progress be made as regards the treatment, processing and marketing of foodstuffs and commodities. This will be a slow evolution, however, because it forms part of the very process of development. In the immediate future, it is imperative that steps be taken to improve the operation of the markets and to stabilize earnings. The same applies to the opening of the developed countries' markets to manufactures and semi-manufactures.

As for trade, the coming years will be focused on the Uruguay Round of negotiations. The protectionist danger has not disappeared and, in many cases, has even become worse. To a considerable extent, international trade is taking place today outside the framework of the rules adopted at the international level.

Your deliberations can help to create rapidly a spirit of consensus that will be useful to the trade negotiations, with due regard for the need to secure as quickly as possible advantages for the developing countries in the areas of special importance to them. UNCTAD has a specific role to play as an international forum in which the problems of the international trading system as a whole are discussed. It is important not to forget the particular problems of the developing countries when discussing services, the transfer of technology and trade in agricultural products. The commitments recently entered into regarding standstill and roll-back must be respected and their application must be monitored.

The seventh session of the Conference also provides an opportunity for considering measures to strengthen the potential for trade between the developing countries and the socialist countries of Eastern Europe. It is essential that all groups of countries should work together to strengthen economic relations between countries having different systems.

The question of resources for development is also to be found among the principal items of the agenda for the seventh session. Financial flows have halted, in some cases they have even been reversed. In conjunction with the worsening of the debt burden, this has given rise in some cases to net transfers of resources from the developing to the developed countries. It is important that this movement should be reversed.

---

[a] General Assembly resolution S-13/2 of 1 June 1986.

The total amount of the debt is now the chief obstacle to the revitalization of the development of the heavily indebted countries and this is particularly true in the case of those whose economies depend on commodity exports. A number of factors are emerging which, I am convinced, could together supply ways and means of alleviating the debt burden. One positive factor of note is the increased awareness of the shared responsibility of the private and public sectors. Moreover, steps are being taken to replenish the resources of the multilateral finance institutions.

Some countries are showing a growing interest in recycling a portion of their surpluses towards the developing countries. The provisions adopted by the Paris Club with a view to rescheduling public debt on more favourable conditions are equally welcome.

All of these are positive elements, but they are still inadequate either to lighten the debt burden or to promote the establishment of new external flows to remedy the serious difficulties of the countries concerned. In the absence of any far-reaching new efforts to make progress on this front, there is a real danger that the desperate adjustment efforts that have been undertaken in the recent past may fail to achieve their objective, which is to reactivate the development of the countries concerned, and this would give rise to serious risks of frustrations at the social and political levels.

A crucial point is that of channelling increased financial resources to the heavily indebted countries. It would be particularly useful if the resources of the World Bank and of the regional development institutions were increased. Such measures would encourage the recycling of the surpluses of the major industrialized countries.

At this stage, it would be altogether well-advised to provide additional assistance to the low income countries. If their development efforts are to be strengthened, they must be able to increase their imports. I welcome the reference in the Venice Summit communiqué to the target set for the level of official development assistance. Other financial flows, including trade and multilateral flows, are also of crucial importance.

This point is particularly important for the least developed countries, within the context of the Substantial New Programme of Action for the 1980s for the Least Developed Countries. Their economic situation has deteriorated. Corrective measures, particularly of a financial nature, are needed now. The target set for the level of official development assistance to those countries and the other measures decided upon in the Substantial New Programme of Action must be put into practical effect as a matter of great urgency. I welcome, therefore, the recent decision to replenish the resources of the International Development Association. This decision must now be put into effect as quickly as possible.

In view of my responsibilities for the implementation of the United Nations Programme of Action for African Economic Recovery and Development 1986-1990, I have asked a group of experts to give me advice on the problem of the flow of the resources to Africa and on the debt problem. Governments and multilateral institutions have an important part to play in solving this problem. I am still concerned about the implementation of the Programme because, to date, the international community had not provided the desired support, particularly financial support, for the structural adjustment efforts of the African countries. This concern has not been dispelled by the International Conference on Africa: the challenge of economic recovery and accelerated development, which was held at Abuja, Nigeria, in June.

Our programme of action would not be complete if we remained silent concerning the policies of the developing countries themselves. There is a growing awareness of the contribution that they can make to strengthening their own growth and their own development. They must increase their savings, invest in projects with a high rate of yield, achieve greater economic viability in the public sector, encourage effective mobilization of their material and human resources, be competitive at the international level and co-operate with one another, as they have already done in the past. Continuation of efforts in that direction should create the conditions needed for the return of capital to the developing countries. The untapped energies of their populations, whose standard of education and information is constantly growing, are still their greatest source of hope and of economic potential. Governments should intervene more energetically to encourage the maximum deployment of the dynamism, spirit of enterprise and initiative of their peoples. The United Nations system of technical co-operation must give its full support to such efforts.

In short, it is not enough to seek adjustment without guaranteeing growth. On the other hand, it is difficult to conceive of growth without appropriate adjustment. Such is the factual situation which must underpin the discussions at this session.

These questions are of great complexity. There will, perhaps, be a consensus on the nature of the major problems to be solved, but it will be difficult to reconcile all the interests at stake within the framework of joint action. This being said, even if such a consensus cannot be achieved in the immediate future, a timetable should be set for examining the problems that have still to be solved. Goodwill and compromise are the very essence of all co-operation. Time is not on our side. We must seize every opportunity that offers itself to make headway.

The central theme of this session—"revitalizing development, growth and international trade"—covers an important political stake. Several recent phenomena—such as the disappearance of certain jobs in the industrialized countries as a result of the reduction in imports from the developing countries, to cite but one example—have clearly demonstrated that the solution to the serious social and economic problems of our era must go beyond the framework of national frontiers. The Brundtland Commission[b] recently recalled this fact in the course of its search for a pragmatic model for durable growth and development.

_____
[b] World Commission on Environment and Development, under the chairmanship of Gro Harlem Brundtland (Norway). For the report of the Commission, see Our Common Future (Oxford, Oxford University Press, 1987).

As I have already said, I am encouraged by the fact that perceptions are evolving and that the usefulness of international co-operation for a wider and wider range of human problems is being recognized.

Political power is becoming more diffuse throughout the world but the governing forces still have a crucial role to play. A greater degree of collective decision-making will be needed in view of the increasing interdependence of countries and of economic activities.

Steps will have to be taken that are commensurate with the extent of the problems to be solved and that attempt to respond to the needs of all countries. I have given some specific examples. In their efforts to speed up their own growth, the industrialized countries should make full use of the positive contribution that can be made by a new upturn in the developing countries. If one side wishes to speed up its growth, it must as a counterpart speed up the development of the other. If it is important that the industrialized countries should correct their own imbalances, it is just as important that

they should simultaneously endeavour to support the efforts of the developing countries. The global dimensions of the debt problem should be better recognized, with the due regard also for the international financial and commercial context, even if a separate solution is sought for each country.

I am confident that this seventh session will mark a decisive turning-point in the attitudes, priorities and actions of the international community. UNCTAD was established to encourage growth and equity in trade and development and is universal in its representativeness. In addition, it supplies an opportunity for some hard and authoritative thinking which should make an objective contribution to one of the most important dialogues of our era. UNCTAD has done some lasting work—as has United Nations as a whole—whenever the political will existed. We are here in Geneva to act. To come up to the expectations of the founders of UNCTAD, I trust that we shall be able to agree on fundamental measures calculated to revitalize trade and development and create a more reliable economic environment for all.

B. *Welcoming address by Mr. Pierre Aubert, Federal Councillor, President of the Swiss Confederation**

Satisfaction, gravity and confidence. It is in this spirit that I welcome today, on behalf of the Swiss Federal Council, and the Canton and Commune of Geneva, participants in the seventh session of the United Nations Conference on Trade and Development.

Satisfaction, first of all, at being able to welcome you. We have long known that a welcoming environment contributes to the success of the work of a major international conference. Switzerland, and Geneva in particular, will do everything in their power to ensure that you are able to enjoy such an environment.

Satisfaction, too, at being able to demonstrate once again the importance attached by Switzerland to multilateral co-operation, its readiness to host organizations and conferences which are the embodiment of such co-operation and its desire to maintain close links with the United Nations. Those elements, and I wish to emphasize this, are fundamental to Swiss foreign policy, conducted as it is in accordance with the principles guiding its relations with the United Nations.

Multilateral co-operation, regardless of the difficulties which it may encounter, is today an indissociable and essential part of the international political scene, serving the interests of States and individuals. For this reason, I wish to pay a tribute here to the outstanding services rendered by the Secretary-General of the United Nations to multilateral co-operation. Switzerland, for its part, will endeavour to continue to contribute within the limits of its resources to the strengthening and further intensification of such co-operation.

Development and the economic dimension of international relations have become an essential component of

the work of the United Nations. UNCTAD plays an important role in this respect, a role which is of particular importance now when—let us not deceive ourselves, indeed you have already raised the point, Mr. Secretary-General—the developing countries find themselves in a very difficult situation.

This is why I also welcome you with gravity. Admittedly, since the creation of UNCTAD in 1964, indisputable progress has been made in such fundamental areas as health and education, industrialization, agriculture and participation in international trade.

Yet that progress has not benefited all countries or all strata of their populations to the same extent; far from it. In addition, progress is hampered by the serious obstacles of very high population growth, the urban explosion and damage to the environment.

Added to this are the radical charges in the world economy, stemming from the upheavals brought about by technological progress, changes in the demand for oil and raw materials, and the emergence of new influential forces in international economic relations.

It should also be borne in mind:

The revival of economic growth in recent years has contributed less to the developing countries as a whole than to the industrialized countries;

The welcome drop in inflation has been accompanied by a noticeable rise in real interest rates;

The debt burden has grown heavier;

Access to foreign markets has become more difficult;

Too many countries, developed and developing alike, have responded to these challenges with policies which are economically inadequate.

The reasons for opening this Conference with "gravity" are therefore clear.

---

* Initially circulated as TD/L.292.

The Secretary-General of UNCTAD recently noted that our objective must be to reconcile economic efficiency with social justice. I think that formula sums up aptly what the targets of our co-operation should be, not only at this Conference, but also over the coming years, namely, poverty, hunger, destitution, the excessive debt burden and inadequate access to foreign markets, all of which threaten to widen the gap between rich and poor to an intolerable extent. How can one fail to feel deep concern at the idea of a world increasingly divided between the deprived and the privileged and the grave consequences which could ensue?

Nevertheless, I am also moved by a feeling of confidence, based on the numerous examples in recent years of the determination of many developing countries to address the underlying causes of their economic problems. It is based on the resoluteness with which a number of Governments have rectified their economic policies and the support provided by the international community. It also stems from our determination to ensure the success of the new multilateral trade negotiations, which are decisive for the future of international trade. Finally, it is based on the conviction that the in-dustrialized countries will become increasingly aware of the need to substantially increase their support for the efforts of the developing countries. In short, I owe this confidence to the tangible evidence of our common will to assume our collective responsibilities.

Community of interests, community of action: These represent the thread of Ariadne which will, I hope, guide you in your work. UNCTAD has, on other occasions, been able to find a meeting point for the interests of all member States. This has led to solutions which have benefited the international community as a whole, not the least being the decision to erase the debt of the poorest countries to the developed countries.

The present situation demands more than ever that we should continue together the search for realistic and equitable solutions. I therefore make an appeal: that all the intelligence, energy, imagination and, I hope, sympathy and understanding for the most deprived which you will deploy over the next few weeks will serve to bring the points of view of our countries closer together. May your deliberations help to place co-operation among all countries firmly on the path to understanding and solidarity, which is the mission of UNCTAD.

C. Address by Mr. Lazar Mojsov, President of the Presidency of the Socialist Federal Republic of Yugoslavia*

It is a great honour for me, on behalf of the Socialist Federal Republic of Yugoslavia, the host country of the sixth session of the Conference in Belgrade, to address this inaugural ceremony of the seventh session of the United Nations Conference on Trade and Development.

I should like to greet all the eminent guests and delegates present here, and at the same time to express our common wish for the successful work and positive outcome of the seventh session.

In view of the significance of this Conference and the negotiating process which is being initiated today, it is only natural that we should be imbued not only with a feeling of responsibility and concern, but also with the hope that the creative quest for a way out of the numerous economic difficulties currently confronting the whole world will bear fresh fruit and open up new prospects.

In the next three weeks the Conference will have a complex and responsible task to perform. In this process, the world will in a sense once again be taking a test of collective conscience, political wisdom and maturity in facing up to its own realities.

The issues which will be deliberated on in the next three weeks in the Palais des Nations have to do with the progress, vital prospects, welfare, and often even the bare survival of millions of people—not only those who are grappling with the difficulties of our day, but future generations as well. I am convinced, however, that a feeling of confidence and a common political will to ensure the successful work and outcome of the seventh session will prevail at this Conference. The stakes are immense.

This beautiful and hospitable city in which we are meeting today has been the venue of many important international gatherings. For understandable reasons, one of them holds this very day a special place in our memory. The first United Nations Conference on Trade and Development was held in Geneva nearly a quarter of century ago. That gathering, which was convened on the initiative of the developing countries after the Conferences in Belgrade and Cairo, was without doubt a milestone in the whole history of contemporary international economic relations. That event gave the young generation of that time reason to believe in the power of solidarity; it awakened new hopes in the accessibility of peace and prosperity for peoples on all the continents, and triggered off a wide range of scientific and negotiating initiatives, aimed at accelerated economic development and the establishment of a more equitable international economic order. The conviction prevailed at that time that mankind was ready to take a firm hold of its destiny, that peace and prosperity were not only for the select few and that history does not have to be an unforeseeable and endless series of ups and downs, wars and armistices, despair and fragile hopes. Was all that no more than wishful thinking?

World circumstances have been changing during the quarter of a century that has elapsed since that historic first Conference, but many key problems remain unsolved, while others have even deteriorated further. Many of them have been addressed by UNCTAD, which has become a centre and catalyst of new economic thought, and in spite of certain

* Initially circulated as TD/L.286.

breakthroughs, many hopes and expectations have been betrayed. We proceeded from the belief that everyone is entitled to the right to development and to peace, while today we are faced with wars and interventions, with poverty and with a growing gap between the rich and the poor. International relations have rarely been as complex as they are today, characterized by processes reflecting profound contradictions, differences and divisions in the world.

Multilateral economic negotiations within the United Nations system, in which UNCTAD has assumed a central place, have produced initiatives, elaborations and the adoption of not only general principles, but also specific instruments of international economic co-operation, the adoption and signing of codes, conventions, programmes, as well as a series of operative decisions. In addition, UNCTAD was the framework within which many prominent world statesmen and economists have launched new, reasonable and logical ideas and concepts, emanating from a new, different, democratic political consciousness. During the 1960s and 1970s the international community did indeed take a big step forward in paving the way to the future.

What do the results of world economic development in this ninth decade testify to? The developing countries have once again become the net suppliers of resources to the developed world. The world economy is increasingly exposed to the disruptions caused by *ad hoc* short-range measures, with devastating effects on the economies of the developing world. But not only the developing world. I am afraid that if a new awareness of mutuality and interdependence is not created, the highly developed world will also soon be confronted with new critical challenges.

The world economy and international economic relations in general are once more in the throes of a crisis. The standstill in the development of the developing countries has been the longest since the Second World War.

It is beyond comprehension that this should be happening at a time when the economies of the developed countries are experiencing major technological advances, a new industrial revolution with structural changes which signify the beginning of a post-industrial era. On one side of the globe there is an abundance of means, knowledge, possibilities, development resources, creative potentials, and on the other frustrated opportunities, stagnation, the inability to stimulate one's own creative forces. The communication and technical revolution is coinciding with the loss of an integral concept of the paths of progress for the whole of mankind. Where is it heading, towards which new divisions and conflicts, on the threshold of the twenty-first century? There are no firm bridges between the North and the South across the ever wider economic gap between them.

The awareness voiced recently by the developing countries in the Havana Declaration that the 1980s are a decade lost for development is alarming. Numerous and undeniable facts and analyses speak for themselves. Since the end of the last decade the real GNP per capita of more than half of the developing countries has either been stagnating or declining.

Behind these facts—and what we tend to forget at times—is that there are millions of jobless people, with a minimum degree of social security, millions of young people without a future, hungry and underfed children whose health has been impaired in the very first years of their life. Behind these figures is the frail social stability in countries in which not even numerous economic sacrifices nor the utmost internal austerity can compensate for the resources which, owing to the distorted international trade and monetary systems, are being drained from the developing into the developed countries, as a result of the drastic fall in commodity prices, the general deterioration of the terms of trade for the developing countries, external indebtedness and high interest rates. These indicators imply potential new hotbeds of crises in the world, foci of instability which are a source of drastic injustices and inequalities.

The international community should and can embark upon a different road. The growth of the developing countries can no longer be postponed. Without their economic growth and the strengthening of their all-round economic potentials, there is no way out of the crisis. In brief, without growth and development there can be no solution to the other economic problems of the world.

What are the impending implications? Which roads are we to follow in the years ahead in international economic relations, as well as in the vital field of safeguarding security and peace in a world oversupplied with suicidal, annihilating weapons?

I do not wish to repeat the well-known facts on the vast funds being spent on armaments in the world. It is easy to imagine—after all, precise calculations are available—what the release of such material, technological and creative potentials would mean for the development of the developing countries, I would say for the development of all, for the resolution of so many accumulated economic and social problems throughout the world, in the countries of the North and the South, in the countries of the West and the East.

More realistic indications of favourable changes in the field of disarmament point to the possibility of these vast potentials and material means being put to a different use.

It goes without saying that we welcome the efforts exerted by the big Powers to achieve an agreement in the near future, more than 40 years after the first use of nuclear weapons and their constant advancement and stockpiling since then. This will mark the beginning of their reduction and elimination and create both a new climate and a concrete basis for the necessary confidence, as well as more favourable prospects for addressing other equally important problems. I have in mind above all the exceptionally grave problems of economic relations in the world, the problems with which all of us in this hall are so much concerned.

A new mentality is required in the consideration of all crucial issues faced by the contemporary world. It is necessary integrally to perceive the survival and the further development of world civilization. Concurrently with the elimination of the threats of nuclear annihilation, existing hotbeds of war, as well as of economic and social conflicts and crises, should begin to be eliminated as soon as possible. This leads to the inevitable conclusion that the problems of development of the vast majority of mankind, which is lagging behind owing to historical reasons, should become the priority of the entire international community. This is surely the initial and the most important step before tackling other world economic problems. This does not imply the redistribution of the world's wealth, with which individual centres of economic and financial power are frequently intimidating both themselves and others. It is only a logical, reasonable goal with manifold benefits for the world economy as a whole.

Development assistance is not charity, but an indispensable, although partial compensation for the unequal position of the developing countries in the world economy and their losses due to inequitable exchange. The fulfilment of obligations undertaken by the developed countries in respect of public development assistance is only one way of enabling the poor, and particularly the African and least developed countries to become independent and equitable partners in international trade, which is also in the interest of the developed countries.

Only within the context of interdependence of development—of the developed and developing countries—is it possible to realize the necessary structural changes, ensure the transfer of technology, expand market possibilities, secure employment and the corresponding development of all sectors of the economy in all countries of the world, in the North and the South alike. This is also the pre-condition for and the road towards the optimum development of the world economy.

Yugoslavia, like other developing countries, considers the seventh session of the Conference to be a unique opportunity to provide for conducting an open dialogue directed towards constructive and action-oriented negotiations for the achievement of general agreements and frameworks, as well as for adopting concrete policies and measures in all four fields which are on the Conference agenda.

In its document on policies and measures, the Group of 77 submitted numerous, very specific proposals which will be the subject of concrete and, we hope, successful negotiations in the next few days. I would like to emphasize just a few issues which are, in my opinion, of crucial importance and significance.

The initiation of a political dialogue between debtors and creditors with a view to co-ordinating global frameworks for defining a lasting and development-oriented solution to the debt problems of the developing countries represents the right way out of the present debt crisis which is the gravest impediment to the development of the majority of developing countries, and consequently to the overall growth of world production and trade. The responsibility and burden of the debt crisis should be equally shared by the debtors and creditors alike. A number of statesmen and economists from highly developed countries have already given their views and suggestions to that effect. It is necessary to examine how realistic and feasible the suggested formulas are. In that respect one of the possible ways of resolving this crisis is through the reallocation of debts

to development projects, linking repayments to the volume of exports or to GNP, the lowering of interest rates, significant extension of repayment periods, and in the case of the least developed countries, the writing-off of debts.

Parallel with the resolution of the debt crisis the present trend of the outflow of financial resources from the developing to developed countries should be reversed by means of public assistance and bank and private capital flows.

In the sphere of international trade, simultaneously with the Uruguay Round of multilateral trade negotiations in GATT, it is indispensable that through UNCTAD, the principally agreed programmes directed towards the reduction of protectionism and discrimination in general, and protectionism and discrimination against the developing countries in particular, as well as the establishment of a universal multilateral trade system, should be further developed and realized.

The implementation of the earlier agreements and identification of new forms of international co-operation for the resolution of the grave difficulties facing the developing countries—commodity exporters—should be in the focus of attention of this Conference. The implementation of the objectives of the Integrated Programme for Commodities, adopted at the fourth session of the Conference, and particularly the coming into force of the Agreement Establishing the Common Fund, represent an essential pre-condition for the establishment of stable foundations for the development and diversification of production and exports of the developing countries whose economy primarily depends on commodities.

I am convinced that there is general agreement that the problems of the least developed countries, particularly those in the sub-Saharan region, are the greatest and the most urgent. We fully commend all those countries which are contributing to the overcoming of these problems. That is why I believe that the agreed programmes for the resolution of these priorities will be supported by this Conference.

The developing countries have always stressed that they themselves are primarily responsible for their own development. Experience has taught them that in directing and formulating their national economic policies, they have to rely to the greatest extent possible on their own natural, material, financial and human resources. But, in addition to such efforts, aimed at accelerated development and more equitable integration in the international division of labour, it is necessary to co-operate and to transfer funds and modern technology, from the developed to developing countries, instead of the developed countries' practice of imposing their own terms and concepts, thereby creating even greater possibilities for interference in the internal affairs of individual countries and the creation of new conflicts.

It is indispensable that the new thrusts and achievements in technology should be accessible to all countries and that they be allowed to apply this technology in an undisturbed manner which would bring prosperity to all. Technology by its inherent nature and according to the laws of its dissemination and application, does not recognize borders, either those between the developed and developing countries, or those dividing the world into different blocs. Technology should not be put at the service of their rivalry, nor should it be used to widen the already deep and dangerous gap in the levels and possibilities of development.

This brings to mind the contradictions inherent in the process of integration of all present economic efforts. This is a natural process which should lead to the rational mobilization and integration of resources, labour and knowledge in the interest of general progress. However, this legitimate process, which should not recognize any borders and which is intrinsically universal as a confirmation of the close ties and interdependence of the world, should not be carried out within closed groupings and particularly not under the influence of military-political considerations, which would benefit the progress of some and neglect the interest of others.

Understanding, confidence, mutual benefit and cooperation which proceed from the equality of all, but also from their mutual linkage, is the only option. The international community must therefore spare no efforts to urgently restore developmental consensus in order to encourage concerted action of all countries, and particularly more responsible and far-sighted behaviour on the part of those who after all have the greatest influence on world economic developments today.

The present political situation in the world holds somewhat greater promise today than in the past concerning the possibilities for the renewal of this consensus. Political developments in the world today are entering a stage which is without precedent in recent history. A vast concentration of military, economic and financial power unknown till now in world history has been created within a relatively narrow circle of countries, causing planetary imbalance. This high concentration of enormous military might has made it clear to all that planetary explosion is possible. The appeals for disarmament which have been voiced for many years now

raise more realistic hopes as to their effect, in spite of all the existing disagreements, which should not be underestimated. The protagonists of the arms race have, undoubtedly, come to the conclusion that there cannot be, nor should there be, any retreat from the fundamentally agreed objective that only negotiations and dialogue are in the mutual interest.

This already constitutes a new political climate which can create possibilities for a substantial relaxation of tension in the world. Détente as such should set off a chain reaction which will also encompass the resolution of global economic issues.

UNCTAD provides a concrete framework and opportunity, forum and instrument for this purpose. It is true that in recent years negotiations within UNCTAD have rarely contributed towards real progress. Most of the decisions of the sixth session of the Conference have not been carried out. It goes without saying that the forum is not to be blamed for this, but rather the inconsistency of policies of member countries' Governments. This organization, I am sure, could play a more important role in the contemporary trends in the world economy in the context of existing international relations only with the active and constructive participation of all its members with the aim of jointly affirming the negotiating function and action orientation of UNCTAD. Your presence here provides assurance that there is broad-based readiness to engage in the negotiating process in a responsible manner and with full awareness of its far-reaching implications.

In conclusion, I would like to point out once again that Yugoslavia remains deeply committed to the irreplaceable mission of UNCTAD. We shall continue to support all efforts aimed at strengthening this universal, democratic international economic organization, guided by a spirit of openness and solidarity, so that it should join in the universal process of resolving the accumulated world problems. This is a wish we believe is shared by the majority of member States and by all of you, distinguished delegates.

Annex IV

MESSAGES RECEIVED BY THE CONFERENCE

Message from Mr. Zhao Ziyang, Premier of the State Council of the People's Republic of China*

On the occasion of the convocation of the seventh session of the United Nations Conference on Trade and Development in Geneva, I wish to extend, on behalf of the Chinese Government and people, our warm congratulations to the Conference.

As a forum for discussing and resolving problems in trade and development within the United Nations system, UNCTAD has, for many years, played an important role in enhancing multilateral co-operation and promoting economic and trade development. We hope that at its seventh session the Conference, by adopting concrete actions and measures, will make a greater contribution to resolving the pressing problems of the developing countries, accelerating their economic development, revitalizing the world economy and expanding international trade.

I wish the Conference complete success.

Message from Mr. D. Sodnom, Chairman of the Council of Ministers of the Mongolian People's Republic**

On behalf of the Government of the Mongolian People's Republic, and in my personal capacity, I send greetings to the participants in the seventh session of the United Nations Conference on Trade and Development.

UNCTAD occupies an honoured place in the system of international economic organizations called upon to work for the restructuring of international economic relations on an equitable, democratic basis. Mongolia has from the outset actively supported the work of this representative international organization aimed at expanding all aspects of international trade on a basis of mutual advantage, equality and non-discrimination, seeking ways of arriving at an equitable solution to questions of international monetary and financial relations, stabilizing international commodity markets and establishing fair prices for raw materials and other goods. In Mongolia's view, problems relating to the trade and economic aspects of disarmament are becoming of ever more pressing importance in UNCTAD's activities.

During the years since the sixth session of the Conference, the world's economic, trade and financial problems have become more acute. The growth of international trade has slowed down. No progress is discernible in the process of restructuring international economic relations on an equitable and democratic

basis. The developing countries have found themselves in a particularly difficult situation with their external indebtedness increasing sharply. The situation is aggravated by the steady fall in world prices for basic commodities, the growth in protectionism and various discriminatory measures taken in international trade by the leading Western States in violation of the generally accepted rules of international law, the relevant provisions of the Charter of the United Nations and the progressive recommendations made by UNCTAD and other international bodies for the establishment of normal relations among States.

At the same time, the arms race, whipped up by imperialist circles, particularly in nuclear weapons, is not only increasing the danger of nuclear catastrophe but leading to disastrous consequences for the world economic, diverting enormous material, financial and intellectual resources which are so badly needed to solve the pressing socio-economic problems faced by all countries. It undermines the economic security of States which, together with disarmament, is the decisive element in a comprehensive system of international security.

All these circumstances call for constructive efforts and new approaches, by the world community as a whole and by UNCTAD in particular, towards finding solutions to the urgent problems of international trade and economic relations.

In Mongolia's view, the essence of such an approach lies in pursuing a policy of disarmament for development and actively promoting the adoption of measures to establish an equitable international economic order, in which all States, large and small, developed and developing would be shielded equally from adverse external factors.

The Mongolian Government will continue to support all measures and practical steps to that end.

I wish UNCTAD every success in the work of its seventh session and hope that it will make a worthy contribution to the efforts of the world's nations to normalize international economic relations and develop equitable trade and economic co-operation among States.

Message from Mr. Erich Honecker, General Secretary of the Central Committee of the Socialist Unity Party of Germany and Chairman of the Council of State of the German Democratic Republic***

On behalf of the German Democratic Republic, I wish to convey cordial greetings to you and the par-

---

* Initially circulated as TD/L.275.

** Initially circulated as TD/L.277.

*** Initially circulated as TD/L.278.

ticipants in the seventh session of the United Nations Conference on Trade and Development.

World-wide trade and economic co-operation for the benefit of all those involved offer genuine possibilities for deepening relations among States and peoples and are a contribution to détente and the safeguarding of peace. The German Democratic Republic regards the Conference as a significant forum for businesslike dialogue and result-oriented negotiations which conduce towards defusing the international economic situation and ensuring stability, predictability and a climate of trust in international economic relations.

If international trade is to live up to its role in promoting the economic and social progress of all countries and in generating international understanding, any artificial obstacles in its way must be removed and equality, non-discrimination and mutual advantage must prevail universally and permanently.

Changes in international economic relations, a growing complexity of international economic processes and an increasing interdependence of States require practical steps towards the normalization of international trade and the advancement of mutually beneficial economic and scientific-technological co-operation among nations. In the face of the great challenge of our time, i.e., to banish war forever from man's life and to ensure peace in the future, such steps are particularly important. The more international trade and economic co-operation are thriving, the greater the benefit for peace and for all nations.

Today, genuine results in the way of disarmament are possible, indeed imperative, in order to relieve humanity of the nightmare of a nuclear catastrophe. The decisions adopted at the Berlin session of the Political Consultative Committee of the States Parties to the Warsaw Treaty will be a stimulus to the solution of that issue which is of global importance. The conclusion of an agreement on the elimination of American and Soviet medium-range missiles in Europe can open the door to world-wide disarmament. This would also create favourable conditions for prospering international trade and propitious co-operation among States striving to resolve pressing international economic problems.

May I express hope that the seventh session of the Conference will give a major impetus to the development of international trade and thus help to build greater confidence and make peace more stable.

With this in mind, I wish the session every success and positive results.

Message from Mr. Fidel Castro Ruz, President of the Council of State and the Council of Ministers of the Republic of Cuba*

The seventh session of the United Nations Conference on Trade and Development, over which you preside—not only because of the prestige Zimbabwe has won for its struggle for national independence and peace and against *apartheid*, but also in recognition of your personal merits—is being held at a dramatic time: on the one hand, certain prospects for initiating denucleariza-

---

* Initially circulated as TD/L.279.

tion in Europe are beginning to be glimpsed and, on the other hand, the world economy, subject to permanent instability, is keeping the countries striving for development in the tragic situation of seeing their poverty and backwardness and the devastation of hunger increase, while all possibilities for a favourable change towards the future are closed to them.

I have maintained for some time that peace and development are inseparable. Peace, to which we all aspire, will be threatened and vulnerable as long as most of mankind is subjected to poverty and lives in economic backwardness. Once again, at the United Nations Conference on Trade and Development, this is the challenge that brings us all together.

Unfortunately, access to development has never faced so many adverse factors nor been so blocked by the unfair and outdated international economic order that now prevails. At the sixth session, in Belgrade, the United States Administration, combining its already failed policy of military supremacy with its attempt at economic supremacy aimed at imposing its interests on the entire world, once again rejected global negotiations and discredited UNCTAD as a negotiating forum.

Today, as the Conference meets in Geneva, the third world countries are feeling the strangling burden of a world economy that swings from crisis to economic restriction. Commodities, which are still their main source of income, have suffered a further price drop in the last few years, causing an economic catastrophe for them. Between 1980 and 1986, the real price index estimated by the World Bank for such goods dropped by 30 per cent and reached its lowest level since the 1930s crisis. This, together with regular increases in the prices of the industrial products, equipment and plant that these countries must import from the developed countries, has augmented the already unbearable debt burden, drastically reduced the underdeveloped countries' imports and turned them into net capital exporters, depriving them of a sizeable chunk of their financial resources. To cite the example of our region alone, in five years, Latin America and the Caribbean have transferred almost $120 billion to the international capitalist financial centres.

In the last few years, the mightiest capitalist Power of all time has lived parasitically off the savings of the rest of the world, which has been forced to finance that Power's fiscal and trade deficits while it promotes a headlong arms race.

International protectionism, which, as we all know, contributed decisively to the great depression of the 1930s, has become a trend among the developed capitalist countries. The multilateral system initiated in the post-war period, based on the growing liberalization of world trade, has been replaced by barriers that nullify the GATT projections and threaten to unleash a chaotic struggle in world trade, with even greater disadvantages for our countries.

In this intolerable situation, the external debt weighs oppressively on the third world.

I have said and say again that this debt is unpayable. Every day that passes confirms this. It rose to the figure of a trillion dollars in 1986, while its annual service this year came to more than $118 billion. Any alternative for paying it that can be dreamed up would be beyond economic possibility, as mathematics—so exact and implacable—shows us. Nevertheless, the developed capitalist countries, whose banking system fostered the third world's indebtedness in the days of surplus monetary liquidity, have turned a deaf ear to the cries of their impoverished debtors. The Venice statements, as we all know, are inadequate.

I have been accused of calling for a debtors' moratorium aimed at provoking an international financial catastrophe. However, those who have followed my statements seriously know that, far from acting to promote disasters, I have defended the formula that, by linking peace to development, will avoid this upheaval—an upheaval that will inevitably threaten us if urgent measures are not taken. I propose that a small part of the resources now allocated to building up arms and preparing us for a devastating war should be devoted instead to the orderly cancellation of this debt.

Today, the more we pay the more we owe, as I said at the Group of 77 meeting. Through financial manipulations, we are stripped of our scarce resources, and the transnational banks close off credits when we most need them, or grant them on terms like those of medieval usurers. I need not detail to you the consequences of the policies followed by the International Monetary Fund. The idea now is to convert our debts into equity. After mortgaging our future, they want to continue stealing our enterprises, land, industries and mines, without having to make new investments. The collection of the debt thus becomes a distraint on our dwindling resources.

Our scientific backwardness reinforces economic backwardness. A large number of commodities are being replaced by chemical products. Technological progress leads to inhuman decisions when it is not followed up by international rules to regulate the introduction of substitute products and thus allow the affected countries that can do so to re-export their products or transform the structure of their exports.

It is certainly not pessimism that leads us to enumerate all these elements to make up the drama of the third world. More than once I have called for struggle to remedy this intolerable burden.

If understanding prevails, UNCTAD is in a position to replace confrontation with agreement; it cannot be put off. UNCTAD is the most universal forum of our world economy. In it, all countries come together: those that demand development, the socialist countries and the countries euphemistically called "market-economy", which have the main responsibility—given the structure of the world economy—for finding appropriate solutions. We know that many of them have expressed their willingness to work out the necessary formulas. We should wish the possibilities now appearing of progress towards peace to be complemented by the appearance of paths leading to development.

Cuba will co-operate with any effort along these lines undertaken in this decisive forum. But for that it is indispensable that we should all understand the magnitude of the drama; that we should understand its real causes and not try to conjure them away through sterile, hackneyed theories. The hundreds of millions of children who die every year as a result of poverty will not allow their tragedy to be drowned in words.

It is time for action, united action. If the nuclear death that threatens us all has to be and can be stopped by the efforts of all, the poverty that overwhelms most of the inhabitants of this earth also requires the united efforts of all.

Message from Mr. Nicolae Ceausescu, President of the Socialist Republic of Romania*

I am very pleased to have this opportunity of conveying to the participants in the seventh session of the United Nations Conference on Trade and Development a friendly greeting and my best wishes for the success of this important international gathering.

Romania attaches great importance to the seventh session of the Conference, which will be called upon to consider extremely important matters of economic development and international trade, to work for the development and adoption of specific practical means of overcoming world economic problems and to promote the development efforts of all States. The session of the Conference is taking place at a time when the world economy is facing complex and difficult problems which affect all nations of the world, and particularly the developing countries. As a result of the world economic crisis, the unequal relationship of oppressor and oppressed fostered by the old imperialist, colonialist and neo-colonialist policies and the inequitable world financial system, the situation of the developing countries has become even more difficult of late. Their external debt has continued to grow, the gap between rich and poor countries has got wider, and all of this has had a devastating impact on the peoples of the world and international affairs in general. At the same time, negotiations between developing and developed countries—the so-called "North-South" dialogue—have remained at a standstill, yielding no concrete results to date. There is an ever more apparent tendency on the part of some developed countries to cling to their former privileges, to perpetuate the old international economic relations and to reject the forum offered by the United Nations for the analysis and solution of critical world economic problems.

The world economic situation has been made much worse by the fact that in recent years the arms race, particularly the nuclear-arms race, has been stepped up. This not only increases the threat of a catastrophic world war all the time, but also aggravates and amplifies the problems of world economic crisis and instability and places heavier and heavier burdens on peoples. The close interdependence between disarmament and development highlights ever more clearly the fact that an essential pre-condition for a satisfactory solution to the world's serious economic problems is to end the arms race once and for all and take practical steps to achieve disarmament and reduce military expenditure. Everything must be done to eliminate and destroy all nuclear weapons and all weapons of mass destruction and to build a world free from weapons and war, a world of peace and co-operation.

_____

* Initially circulated as TD/L.280.

In Romania's view, it is now more than ever necessary for all States to join in seeking, in the interests of peace and the progress of all peoples, a positive solution to the daunting problems facing the world today, including international economic problems. In this context, it is particularly important to intensify efforts to end the underdevelopment in which more than two thirds of the world's population subsists and to establish a new international economic order based on full equality and equity and capable of promoting faster progress in all countries, particularly the developing ones, giving peoples broad access to the latest achievements of science and technology and of modern civilization and ensuring the smooth progress and stability of the world economy.

Abolishing underdevelopment means first of all that the developing countries themselves should make every effort to make optimum use of their own resources on the basis of economic and social development programmes which, starting from each country's own priorities and real capabilities, will ensure the steady growth of their economic strength and a rising standard of living for their peoples. But the efforts of the developing countries, like the efforts of all States to achieve progress must be backed up by broad-based and unhindered international co-operation, firmly grounded in the principles of full equality, respect for national independence and sovereignty, non-interference in internal affairs, mutual advantage and the right of every people to dispose freely of their national wealth and to develop it in conformity with their own interests. In this sense, giving more support to the developing countries is not only a moral obligation for the developed countries, but also a compelling and objective necessity if world economic and political relations are to return to normal and progress and peace are to be ensured throughout the world.

In our opinion, this Conference could do much to encourage efforts to end underdevelopment and to establish a new international economic order by developing and promoting practical measures and programmes designed to place international economic and financial relations on a more equitable basis and to support the economic development programmes and efforts to mobilize the national wealth of the developing countries and all other peoples.

It is of prime importance to take resolute action to find a global political and economic solution to the problem of the developing countries' extremely high external debt and do everything possible to solve it on the basis of criteria and principles appropriate to the development levels of the countries concerned, their ability to repay and the efforts they have to make to achieve economic and social progress. Romania has submitted in the United Nations and other forums specific proposals for achieving these ends, notably by completely writing off the debts of the poorest countries, reducing, by appropriate amounts, the debts of all the other countries, and rescheduling, over a period of 15 to 20 years, the remainder of the debts at a modest rate of interest or no interest at all. A ceiling of not more than 10 per cent of export earnings should be established for annual payments by the developing countries on their external debts. It is also essential to achieve a general reduction in interest rates, including those applied by the World Bank and the International Monetary Fund, while at the same time ensuring a steady flow of new credits to the developing countries on advantageous terms and at reasonable interest rates, for their economic and social development.

It is necessary at the same time that at its seventh session the Conference should take action to solve the problem of prices, particularly for commodities, to guarantee their stability, which will make for greater order and fairness in the financial and monetary sphere. In general, the present inequitable financial and monetary system needs to be replaced by a new system based on principles of equity and equality and capable of giving real encouragement and support to the efforts of all States, particularly underdeveloped ones, to achieve development and progress.

Firmer action should also be taken to stop protectionism and liberalize economic exchanges among States, to eliminate all types of pressure and political and other strings from the economic sphere and to abolish all artificial limitations and obstacles to international trade, in order to promote economic relations grounded in full equality, respect for national independence and sovereignty, non-interference in internal affairs and mutual advantage.

In order to solve all these serious and complex problems, we believe it is necessary that the current session of the Conference should lead to the convening of a special conference by the United Nations, to be attended, on completely equal terms, by both the developing and the developed countries, to the initiation of effective negotiations and to the achievement of positive results in this area corresponding to the interests and aspirations for progress of all countries and the need for harmonious and steady development of the world economy. In Romania's view, it would be particularly useful for UNCTAD to establish a special working committee which, on the basis of the discussion at the current session and the proposals that are made, could formulate specific measures for solving these problems.

In conclusion, I wish to express the hope and the conviction that the measures and decisions to be adopted at this Conference will make a positive contribution to the solution of the great international economic problems and to global efforts to achieve the independent economic and social development of all peoples, to strengthen international co-operation and to promote détente, understanding and peace in the world.

In that conviction, I extend my best wishes for success to the seventh session of the United Nations Conference on Trade and Development.

Message from Mr. Nicolai Ryzhkov, Chairman of the Council of Ministers of the Union of Soviet Socialist Republics*

I cordially greet participants in the seventh session of the United Nations Conference on Trade and Development.

---

* Initially circulated as TD/L.281.

Over the years the Conference has shown itself to be an authoritative international forum for the consideration of vitally important problems in world economic relations. The Soviet Union greatly values the work of UNCTAD in promoting world development and trade, the restructuring of international economic relations on an equitable and democratic basis and the establishment of a new international economic order.

In our opinion, the work done in UNCTAD is becoming especially relevant at the present time, when the international economic climate in the world is deteriorating. As in the past, trade relations are still unequal, economic ties are widely used as a means of exerting political pressure, protectionism is on the rise and trade and currency conflicts are getting worse. The most acute problem, particularly for the developing countries, is foreign indebtedness, which has become a world-wide problem and has obvious political implications.

The time has come to tackle the vital economic problems confronting mankind. It is no longer possible to mark time, carrying on endless discussions and dodging constructive and realistic decisions.

The new mode of political thinking we call upon the world to adopt, which is based in particular on the growing interdependence of States and the priority of universal human values, should ensure a broad and long-term approach to international economic relations. At the Plenum of the Central Committee of the Communist Party of the Soviet Union held at the end of June, it was stressed that reorganization of the Soviet economy would help to develop wide-ranging international co-operation and thus improve international economic relations.

We are convinced that practical steps to reduce armaments and achieve disarmament, releasing vast additional resources for development purposes, would be an important factor in the socio-economic development of all States. UNCTAD is in a position to make its contribution to the formulation of principles for using the resources released by a reduction in military budgets for the benefit of the world community, including the developing countries.

UNCTAD remains the most universal international economic forum, both in its membership and in the range of issues it considers, and as such it could also play an active role in considering questions relating to the formulation of a plan for international economic security, which would help us to evolve joint approaches to the solution of world economic problems.

I wish the participants in the Conference success in their work, in the interests of the economic and social progress of all nations.

Message from Mr. Wojciech Jaruzelski, Chairman of the Council of State of the Polish People's Republic*

On behalf of the supreme authorities of the Polish People's Republic I have the honour to convey to the seventh session of the United Nations Conference on

---

* Initially circulated as TD/L.282.

Trade and Development our wishes for a fruitful debate.

The present session is evidence of the political will of the international community to find solutions to the burning issues currently confronting the world economy. Poland warmly supports all endeavours in this respect since mutually advantageous economic relations with developing countries constitutes one of the important elements of our foreign policy.

UNCTAD is one of the eminent universal bodies of the United Nations system active in the domain of trade and development. International efforts within its framework have contributed to the real progress achieved by the developing world in many fields.

The tasks ahead, however, are still enormous. The world economy is plagued by the chronic ailments from which the poorest countries suffer most severely. The heavy imbalance in trade, protectionism, monetary instability and the burden of indebtedness dangerously overshadow the future of the world economy. Mounting indebtedness represents a particularly acute problem. It should be conceived in global terms with the concurrent undertaking of indispensable steps in a spirit of common commitment and mutual co-operation by all the countries concerned.

Participating actively in the work of the United Nations from its very outset, Poland has always stressed the need to promote the comprehensive development of the developing countries and to diminish the gap between them and the more developed countries. We unwaveringly support the justified demands of developing countries for the establishment of the new international economic order aimed at the elimination of their underdevelopment. This was strongly emphasized in the Berlin Declaration on "Overcoming Underdevelopment and the Establishment of the New International Economic Order" of 29 May 1987.

Solutions should be found which take into account the interests of all parties to international exchange and are based on just and democratic principles, in particular those of mutual advantage and sovereignty.

International efforts in the area of trade and development should be reinforced by the world-wide acknowledgement of the urgent need to improve the political atmosphere for international trade and bring about increased rationality in international division of labour.

The arms race endangers the very existence of mankind, and absorbs huge material and intellectual resources. Checking the arms race and initiating the disarmament process would enable resources to be reallocated so as to achieve development objectives and thereby help to overcome many existing barriers to the expansion of international trade and co-operation. Therefore, all initiatives aimed at easing tension and building confidence in international political as well as economic relations require firm support. Our country has been for many years an active participant in that endeavour and will continue to do so.

In conclusion, I wish to reaffirm Poland's full support for the accomplishment of the lofty goals of the Conference.

Message from Mr. Pham Hung, Chairman of the Council of Ministers of the Socialist Republic of Viet Nam*

On the occasion of the convening of the seventh session of the United Nations Conference on Trade and Development, I would like to address to you, and through you to the Conference, the warmest greetings.

In the face of the present wide and profound changes in the world economy, especially the critical challenges faced by the developing countries, at its seventh session the Conference has a mission of great importance, namely, contributing to the finding of effective solutions to many burning economic problems in the field of money and finance, debt, primary commodity prices, trade, co-operation and development—primarily those affecting the developing countries.

In the past years, UNCTAD has made important contributions to the struggle for the establishment of a new international economic order and against policies resorting to economic and political pressure in international economic relations especially with the developing countries, and it has stimulated the expansion of economic relations among countries having different economic and social systems and among the developing countries.

At the same time, UNCTAD has also made its efforts in the common struggle of humanity against the arms race, for peace and international security with a view to creating a favourable international environment for the development of economies and of the economic relations among countries.

I am confident that at its seventh session the Conference will be able to carry out its important task, responding to the foremost aspiration of the international community for peace, co-operation and development.

In that spirit, I wish the Conference every success.

Message from His Holiness Pope John Paul II**

Prompted by a need to return to its source so as to revive the inspiration on which it was founded and to find new energy, the seventh session of the United Nations Conference on Trade and Development is being held in Geneva. I recall with pleasure that the Holy See was actively involved in the creation of this body in 1964 and has since extended to it its full support.

Exactly 20 years ago, my predecessor, Paul VI, wrote his Encyclical, *Populorum progressio*, speaking on behalf of starving peoples whose tragic plight was a challenge to the wealthy nations (para. 3), and devoting several pages to equity in trade relations (paras. 56 to 65). In my own first Encyclical (4 March 1979), I described our age as a gigantic tableau of the biblical parable of the feasting rich man and the poor Lazarus (*Redemptor hominis*)

Today, the picture is one of even greater contrasts than before, despite the planned and concerted efforts of the international community. Consequently, in a world broken and numbed by disillusionment, I should like to bring to those attending this session a message of hope—of hope now strengthened by our keener awareness of the equal dignity and collective responsibility of all men. It is not enough for countries to recognize their interdependence as a result of economic or political necessity. Only an ethical sense of genuinely shared responsibility will enable them to open the way for the attainment of international justice and to honour fully commitments which have been made jointly and are structurally linked.

In this spirit, you will be able resolutely to set about the important items on your present agenda, namely, the resources needed for development which are seriously impaired by the burden of international debt servicing; commodities, whose real prices have not been so low for half a century; international trade, where violations of international rules are ruining the chances of the weakest. Moreover, as you know, the courageous development efforts of "the least developed countries" themselves (most of them in Africa), to which you have been according special attention for some time, cannot succeed without the total and continuous support of all.

The external debt problem—an open sore in the side of international relations—has recently been studied, at my request, by the "Justitia et Pax" papal commission. I trust that its ethical reflections will quickly encourage "the various partners to reach agreement on the equitable sharing of adjustment efforts and the necessary sacrifices, bearing in mind the priority of the needs of the most deprived peoples. The wealthiest countries have a responsibility to accept a broader apportionment" (I,4).

Your task is the very exacting one of reviewing, in co-operation with other competent agencies, as I ventured to state in *Redemptor hominis*, the financial, monetary, productive and trade structures and mechanisms which govern the world economy and which have shown themselves incapable of remedying the injustices inherited from the past or responding to the urgent challenges [. . .] of the present (para. 16). Your task is very arduous, requiring you to be constantly on the alert to cope with the instability of exchange rates, the manipulation of markets, the hardening of protectionism and numerous other threats which feed on mistrust and self-interest.

Yet your task is also an uplifting one, since it transcends economics and addresses itself to man as a whole, with his cultural and spiritual dimensions. In that sense, developed and developing countries are not ranged on opposite sides. Every country is involved in man's overall development, and fortunately our age is less inclined to identify development with mere economic growth or the simple reproduction of industrialized country models. What is more, development cannot be spontaneous or instantaneous, decreed or granted. It calls for the vast and free participation of peoples themselves, patiently educated to become the masters of their own destiny.

With all my heart, I pray for divine blessing on your deliberations. This new appointment with the peoples of the world must not be missed. Expectations are too

---

* Initially circulated as TD/L.283.

** Initially circulated as TD/L.285.

great and too urgent for your Conference not to enter into new commitments or for those commitments not to be honoured by the political will of your countries. The time is ripe for you to open new avenues for the realization of the expectations of peoples.

Message from Mr. Alan García Pérez, President of the Republic of Peru*

The holding of the seventh session of the United Nations Conference on Trade and Development coincides with the worsening of the acute crisis which is being experienced by the whole developing world and which requires the adoption of urgent measures without delay. In this connection, I consider it imperative that recognition be given to the interrelationship of debt problems, protectionism, transfer of resources to the industrialized world and deterioration of the terms of trade, and to their effects in the outrageous regression of the living standards of the greater part of the third world to the levels of 30 years ago. Such recognition will make possible speedy action and will strengthen the negotiating role of UNCTAD as a body whose basic and primary purpose is the promotion of development.

External indebtedness is continuing to grow, more than ever undermining the social and political stability of the peoples of the third world and generating an irrational transfer of resources from our countries to the industrialized economies, which is unjustifiable and negative and which, if continued, will bring about the collapse of the entire world financial structure.

It is now unquestionably obvious to all that the debt problem must be accorded political treatment by all the actors involved: the creditor and debtor countries, international private banking and the international organizations.

A just solution can only be arrived at if the task is undertaken co-responsibly by all the parties concerned, and it is that objective which the work of the seventh session of the Conference must pursue.

I must also point out that commodities, on whose exports the economies of our countries largely depend, are continuing to suffer from falling export prices and volumes, owing to market controls, technological changes and deterioration of the terms of trade, without any glimpse of a coherent and effective alternative solution for their almost structural decline.

Our recognized need for development and growth in order that our contribution to international trade may generate benefits for all is being seriously limited by a system of subsidies and restrictive and protectionist measures which impede the access of our products to the markets of the industrialized countries, thereby perverting the principles of efficiency and comparative advantage.

For all the above reasons, I believe that unless, at the seventh session of the Conference and in other forums, effective commitments are not shortly arrived at which correctly, clearly and objectively deal with this critical situation of the international economy as a whole and especially of the developing countries, the day will soon come when this complexly interdependent world plunges into a state of chaos that will equally affect the countries of the developing South and the developed North. That is why I wish to re-emphasize that the occasion of the seventh session of the Conference constitutes the opportune moment to abandon the technocratic and compartmentalist scheme of things and to initiate responsibly and jointly a series of intersectoral measures to reverse the grave crisis in which we find ourselves and to promote the development of the countries of the third world, while respecting their own economic structures and systems.

I express my most fervent hope that this Conference will be sufficiently mature to meet the challenges and problems we are facing. You may be sure that the delegation of Peru will do all in its power to co-operate in the achievement of that objective, which we are certain you share.

Message from Mr. Guillermo Bedregal Gutiérrez, Minister of Foreign Affairs and Worship of Bolivia**

On behalf of the Government of Bolivia, I am pleased to convey my sincere hope that the seventh session of the United Nations Conference on Trade and Development will achieve the desired success in favour of the developing countries in the framework of fair and equitable negotiations between North and South. The Government of Bolivia, faithful to the principles of the new international economic order and the Charter of Economic Rights and Duties of States, has always defended the interests of developing countries. The spirit underlying the position of the Group of 77, framed at Havana, also reflects the thinking of Latin America on the socio-economic problems affecting the developing countries and now under consideration in the agenda of the seventh session of the Conference. Bolivia, a developing and, for the time being, land-locked country, has on various occasions expressed its concern regarding the low prices of commodities on the international market, protectionism, the rigid tariff barriers encountered by products exported from developing countries, as well as discrimination in preferential treatment against the products exported by land-locked developing countries. We are convinced that the seventh session of the Conference will bring the great majority of third world countries hopes for a solution of the grave economic problems hindering the normal growth of each country. We are sure that, with your worthy participation, arrangements between poor and rich countries will make feasible new formulas of common understanding.

Message from Mrs. Corazón C. Aquino, President of the Republic of the Philippines***

On behalf of the Philippine Government and the Filipino people, please accept my warmest congratulations on your election as President of the seventh session of the United Nations Conference on Trade and

---

* Initially circulated as TD/L.287.

** Initially circulated as TD/L.302.
*** Initially circulated as TD/L.305.

Development. It is my hope that under your able and wise leadership, the Conference will move forward towards the establishment of a new international economic order.

The developing world looks to the Conference as an opportunity where, together with its partners from the developed countries, policies can be adopted and measures taken to alleviate the current difficulties in the international economic situation. The crisis that has gripped the world economy is evidenced by the scarcity of developmental and financial resources available to the developing countries, mounting debt service, the deterioration of the terms of trade, and low commodity prices. This has been compounded by slow growth and widespread protectionism on the part of most developed countries. The seriousness of these problems is manifested in the acute social and political strains that are pervasive in most developing countries.

It is my hope that a consensus among developed as well as developing countries can be reached towards hastening the integration of developing countries into the world economy so that they may share equitably in the fruits of development. Progressive policies and forward-looking measures towards this end will, in the long run, be mutually beneficial to both developed and developing countries. This is the raison d'être for the creation of UNCTAD 23 years ago—the promotion of the well-being of all peoples through purposeful international co-operation as mandated by the Charter of the United Nations.

I wish you and the members of the Bureau a successful conference.

Annex V

A. THE HAVANA DECLARATION*

Final document of the Sixth Ministerial Meeting of the Group of 77, held at Havana, Cuba, from 20 to 25 April 1987

We, the Ministers of the Group of 77,

Having assembled in Havana, Cuba, from 20 to 25 April 1987, for our Sixth Ministerial Meeting,

Being convinced of the importance of reviewing and stating our collective appraisal of the world economic situation and of the perspectives for the development of our peoples' welfare,

Bearing in mind the Declaration of our three regional groups at their recent Ministerial Meetings in Dhaka, Addis Ababa and San José,

Adopt the following Declaration as a basis for concerted action in our economic relations with the developed countries and in our mutual economic co-operation and call upon the international community as a whole to work together for economic and social progress:

1. The 1980s have been the lost decade of development. The world economy is beset by contradictions and faces a crisis. The persistent stagnation of economic growth has severely retarded economic and social progress and, in several countries, has thrown that process into reverse. The inadequacies and inequities of the international economic system have led to adverse results, stifling trade, development and employment, instead of promoting them. Undue risk, uncertainty and unpredictability in the international economic environment have become major obstacles to national efforts to achieve long-term economic and social objectives.

2. While no country has been immune from these phenomena, the developing countries have been hardest hit. In particular the least developed countries and sub-Saharan African countries have suffered most. The economic situation in these countries still remains critical and their peoples are under the threat of hunger and starvation. It has become increasingly difficult for any developing country to pursue policies of self-reliant and equitable development, aimed at elimination of poverty, enhancement of human capacities, progressive modernization of the productive apparatus and enlargement of opportunities for participation in economic activity and in the benefits derived from it. Particular difficulties are experienced by the Palestinian people, whose living conditions have been deteriorating as a result of the Israeli occupation and who urgently need to be liberated from their occupation to enable them to develop their national economy; and by the people of southern Africa, and Namibia, particularly those of the front-line States whose painstakingly developed infrastructure and legitimate development programmes are undermined by the South African régime's destabilization policy.

3. This situation is beset with economic, social and political tensions, within and among countries. It poses a serious threat to democracy, social stability and international peace and security. Its reversal should command the political commitment and co-operation of all nations, which must work together to build an international economic system based on the principles of equity and justice, that would contribute to the establishment of the new international economic order.

4. This effort must be founded on the strict observance of the inalienable right of every State to social and economic development, to choose its economic and social system and to promote the welfare of its people in accordance with national plans and policies. It is unacceptable that this right should be constrained by the application by other States of economic measures intended to exert political and economic coercion, for purposes incompatible with the Charter of the United Nations and in violation of multilateral and bilateral undertakings and international law.

5. The members of the Group of 77 assume their responsibilities to strive for their own development. They are also determined to continue to strengthen their mutual economic co-operation. They are convinced that the effective solidarity of the Group strengthens its members, both in their national development efforts and in their external economic relations.

6. The members of the Group of 77 expect the developed countries to assume their responsibilities in the present world economic crisis, and to redesign their policies in order to contribute to an external environment more predictable and more supportive of growth and development. Those countries should realize that, by supporting the development process of developing countries, they can contribute effectively to revitalizing the world economy and thus to resolving their own economic problems, including persistently high unemployment.

I

7. The crisis in the world economy has many dramatic manifestations. For the developing countries, these include:

(a) The collapse of commodity prices and deteriorating terms of trade, which have deprived them

---

* Text issued at the Conference as TD/325.

of export earnings needed to sustain their development and to service their debt;

(*b*) The intolerable debt burden which has compelled many of them to adopt, with high social and political costs, adjustment programmes constraining their development potential. The debt cannot be serviced and repaid under present conditions and without sustained economic development;

(*c*) The stagnation of official development assistance and the sharp contraction in financial flows, particularly from commercial banks;

(*d*) All the previous factors have led to a net transfer of resources from developing to developed countries;

(*e*) The proliferation of protectionist and distortive measures and policies in developed market-economy countries, which are impeding developing country exports and obstructing structural adjustments which would permit the expansion of those exports;

(*f*) The erosion of respect for the disciplines of the multilateral trading system, which exposes the developing countries to arbitrary obstacles to their trade and leaves them without redress;

(*g*) The aggravation of the structural problems of the least developed countries, especially the land-locked and island developing countries, whose unique problems and inherent disadvantages have a particularly negative impact on their development.

8.   The manifestations of the crisis in the external environment for development also include volatile and misaligned exchange rates of major currencies; high interest rates in real terms; massive trade imbalances among the major economic powers and consequent tensions in the international trading system.

9.   The developed countries themselves are suffering from uneven and slow growth, and high levels of unemployment, resulting in intensification of protectionist measures and contraction of export markets for developing countries.

II

10.   The economic crisis is structural in nature. It has been aggravated by the long-term macro-economic policies of developed countries.

11.   Developed countries have maintained policies that negatively affect the international economic environment, weaken demand for developing countries' exports, put a downward pressure on commodity prices and aggravate the debt problem. The control of inflation, which is cited as a positive result of their policy stance, has, in fact, been brought about largely through the collapse of commodity and oil prices.

12.   Multilateralism has been on the wane. The stalemate in economic negotiations between developing and developed countries has hardened. The weakening of multilateral co-operation for development has led to a growing asymmetry in burden sharing and adjustment efforts between developing and developed countries. Many developed countries have shown a marked preference for bilateralism in their external economic relations, resorting increasingly to such policies for political purposes.

13.   Developing countries have not received substantial external resources commensurate with their development needs. This situation is illustrated in the inadequate implementation of the United Nations Programme of Action for African Economic Recovery and Development 1986-1990 and more generally in the plight of the least developed countries, whose efforts at domestic resource mobilization will not achieve their development objectives without substantial additional external resources and increased export earnings.

14.   Such a crisis coexists with important changes in the international economy. New and powerful actors are emerging, producing a multi-polar economic world. There is increasing interaction among countries with different economic systems. The economic interdependence of all countries has been intensified by the increasing share of external trade in national economic activity and by the internationalization of production and capital. Transnational conglomerates have become powerful actors enjoying unprecedented economies of scale and scope. A new wave of technologies is radically altering patterns of demand, production and trade. The concentrated control of these technologies is creating new strains in international economic relations. As a result of these changes the world economy is becoming more complex.

15.   In the present circumstances the potential for growth in the developing countries cannot be realized. If, however, external constraints are removed and the required systemic changes made, they can contribute to the sustained expansion of world trade and growth in the foreseeable future.

III

16.   The post-war international economic system has ceased to serve adequately its stated objectives of promoting world-wide economic and social progress.

17.   There has not been a meaningful and comprehensive policy initiative to enhance global economic co-operation on the basis of interdependence, equity and shared responsibilities. Instead, a new tendency has emerged in some quarters of the developed countries to play down the influence of the external economic environment on the development process and to insist on the primacy of domestic policy reform based on the efficacy of spontaneous market forces alone. This approach, not even applied by its major proponents, is inadequate to address development problems, carries the seeds of social and political instability and ignores the complexity of the contemporary world economy. This approach enables the transnational corporations to move freely goods, raw materials, services, data and capital across national frontiers, at their discretion.

18.   The international community should combine its forces and engage in dialogue to work out the characteristics and mechanisms of a comprehensive international economic system, based on the principles of equity, justice, harmony and universality and on the sovereign rights of States. Development, growth, employment and social progress should be its central objectives. The system should give full recognition to

the interdependence between money, finance, trade and development.

19. The expansion and diversification of trade, including trade among developing countries and among countries having different economic and social systems, is one of the most important instrumentalities for achieving these objectives. Trade expansion should be based on the principles of multilateralism and non-discrimination and be pursued within a framework of co-operative interaction among States. The ability of developing countries to expand trade presupposes expanded market access for their exports and increased availability of financial resources. Liberalization could only be pursued to advance their development objectives.

20. Such a framework for promoting development, growth and trade must have a sound and equitable counterpart in the monetary and financial spheres. This should facilitate a durable, global and equitable solution to the debt crisis. It should secure a substantial increase in flows of financial resources for development on an assured, continuous and predictable basis. Above all, it should lead to a substantially transformed international economic environment, responsive to and supportive of the process of development.

21. Development would be a fragile goal without peace. Peace without development would be unattainable. An international economic system, having as its central objectives development, growth, employment and social progress will promote peace and security. Such a system should facilitate the channelling of resources released by disarmament into productive use and consumption to better the human condition.

IV

22. UNCTAD is an institution born of the collective will of the international community. Its universal character, its historic development orientation and its unique, cross-sectoral and inter-disciplinary approach make UNCTAD an important link in the chain of international economic relationships. The crucial need for development calls for the enhancement of UNCTAD's effectiveness and its responsiveness to current and future problems, as well for maintaining the integrity of its mandate and its functions and of the means to fulfil them. The seventh session of the United Nations Conference on Trade and Development provides the member States with a signal opportunity to strengthen multilateral co-operation for develpment and to strengthen the institution of UNCTAD itself. The results of UNCTAD VII will have an important in-

fluence on the attitude of the developing countries towards other international negotiations and activities.

V

23. Developing countries cannot afford to rely only on external impulses to overcome the serious economic and social crises confronting them. The implementation of the Arusha Programme for Collective Self-Reliance and Framework for Negotiations[a] and the Caracas Plan of Action[b] has, therefore, acquired greater urgency. It is imperative further to expand and deepen economic co-operation among developing countries (ECDC) as an integral part of the efforts to promote a restructuring of international economic relations. The Global System of Trade Preferences among Developing Countries (GSTP) is the most important ECDC activity on which concrete and substantial progress is under way. Effective steps should be taken to complete the first round of negotiations under the GSTP at the Ministerial Meeting in Belgrade, as visualized in the Brasilia Declaration.[c]

24. We, the Ministers of the Group of 77, have presented our appraisal of the current international economic situation and outlined our approach towards the harmonious and equitable reconstruction of international economic relations aimed at ensuring development and employment for all. We have done this in the hope that our partners in UNCTAD would share with us their perceptions and approach. We believe that it is possible to further our co-operative search for a stable system of international economic relations, without necessarily compromising on our respective world views.

25. We believe that all the States members of UNCTAD share common interests and objectives. We also believe that we have a common stake in solving the present crisis. We expect our partners, particularly those who have relatively greater economic strength, to muster sufficient political will and seize the opportunity provided by UNCTAD VII. This occasion should be harnessed not only to launch a dialogue in a wider context for longer-range objectives but also to agree upon concrete measures in specific areas of the agenda of the Conference which need urgent solutions.

---

[a] Adopted at the Fourth Ministerial Meeting of the Group of 77, held at Arusha, United Republic of Tanzania, from 6 to 16 February 1979; see *Proceedings . . . Fifth Session*, vol. I, annex VI.

[b] See "Report of the High-Level Conference on Economic Co-operation among Developing Countries", Caracas, 13-19 May 1981 (A/36/333 and Corr.1).

[c] Adopted at the Meeting of the Negotiating Committee of the GSTP, held at Brasilia on 22 and 23 May 1986 (see GSTP/MM/BRASILIA/3/Part 3).

B. ASSESSMENT AND PROPOSALS BY THE GROUP OF 77 RELATING TO THE SEVENTH SESSION OF THE CONFERENCE*

PART I

ASSESSMENT

This assessment presents the views, expressions and analysis of the Group of 77 Ministers on the international economic environment which form the basis and rationale for the proposals, policies and measures adopted by the Ministers.

As the common position of the Group of 77 on the international economic situation, this assessment has been made to facilitate the understanding of the other groups and for a constructive dialogue and consultations prior to the commencement of negotiations at the seventh session of the United Nations Conference on Trade and Development.

1. INTRODUCTION

1. On the eve of the sixth session of the Conference the Group of 77, in placing before the international community the Buenos Aires Platform, summarized the then-prevailing economic situation and outlook in the following words:

> The world economy . . . is engulfed in the most pervasive and dangerous crisis since the 1930s. This crisis has already imposed incalculable costs on all groups of countries. It has taken a heavy toll of the international trade, monetary and financial systems. Recent indications point to some alleviation of economic stagnation in certain developed countries, but a sustained long-term recovery is nowhere in sight. The essential elements of the crisis remain unabated and the situation is displaying all the symptoms of a global depression. Unless resolved, the crisis will inflict even greater damage on the world economy, with far-reaching implications for peace and stability.[d]

2. On the eve of the seventh session of the Conference, none of the essential elements which have characterized the deepening malaise in the global economy has been resolved.

3. The developing world is facing a crisis of unprecedented gravity. In many developing countries the development process has been severely retarded. There is a widespread debt crisis. Primary commodity prices have fallen to unprecedented levels. Real interest rates are extraordinarily high, exchange rates volatile. The flow of financial resources, including ODA, has been much reduced and in fact several countries suffer substantial net outflows. Investment in infrastructure, machinery, and human resources has been drastically cut. Societies and political systems are under acute strain. The least developed countries, because of their structural vulnerability, are the most serious affected.

4. The policies of the major market-economy countries continue to compound this grim situation, itself a product of the interaction of those policies with the historical legacy of uneven world development manifested in asymmetrical capabilities as between developed and developing countries. Instead of providing remedies, industrialized countries with the capacity to do so are abdicating their responsibilities behind dogmatic assertions of faith in market forces and unrealistic assessments of the developing countries' ability to cope with the adverse external economic environment.

5. While the oil price decline of the last two years led to sizeable savings on the part of the industrialized countries, there has not been even an attempt to recycle the funds so saved for the purpose of development, and to offset illiquidity in many developing economies. Nor has there has been a corresponding reduction in prices of the industrialized countries' manufactures. Taken together with the fall in prices of other commodities in real terms, this combination of factors has enabled the industrialized economies to keep inflation rates low without stimulating growth in developing countries, a situation made inevitable owing to the enormously deflationary effect of unrequited reverse flows of real resources.

6. The development of their societies is the primary responsibility of developing countries and it is their objective to restructure themselves to reduce their vulnerability and derive advantage from producing for the world market. The deterioration of their external environment which underlines the present crisis is beyond the control of the developing countries. Neither their own efforts nor market forces can provide a solution in the absence of a fundamental change in the attitudes and policies of the industrialized countries.

7. Developing countries have a major stake in the proper functioning of the global economic system, since development itself is decisively conditioned by external trading and finance. The Group of 77 believes that the arduously negotiated agenda for the seventh session of the Conference provides a timely and valuable opportunity to the international community to devise a coherent multilateral strategy for revitalizing development, growth and international trade in a more supportive international environment.

8. It would be most unfortunate for the future prospects of a global economy if commitment to taking specific actions in several interrelated areas is delayed any longer. It would be even more unfortunate if the very painful and politically risky national policies and programmes already under way in the developing countries fail to produce positive results for these countries, as well as for the global economy, simply because those who have the power and the influence continue to hesitate to take measures in critical areas in need of immediate corrective action.

9. The seventh session of the Conference will be an opportune occasion for the international community to examine the interdependence of the world economy and

---

* Text issued at the Conference as TD/330 and Corr.1 and 2.

[d] See *Proceedings . . . Sixth Session*, vol. I, annex VI, section II, paragraph 2.

the consequences of the current economic situation for the trade and development of the developing countries.

10. The Group of 77, guided by its firm belief in multilateralism, expresses a fervent hope that its submissions on the various items of the agreed agenda for the seventh session of the Conference will persuade all participants to agree to take specific action in the areas covered by the agenda which constitute the essential elements for revitalizing development, growth and international trade. The decisions emerging from the seventh session of the Conference will have an important influence on the attitude of the developing countries in regard to other international economic negotiations and activities.

2. OVERALL TRENDS

11. The past few years have witnessed widespread breakdowns of the development process and an international debt crisis of unprecedented breadth, duration and gravity. Most developing countries have suffered a sharp reduction in their pace of economic growth, and a number have undergone contraction. Per capita incomes have fallen back to levels surpassed a decade ago, both capital accumulation and living standards have been cut, and investment in human resources and standards of education, health and nutrition have also been adversely affected. Thus, both actual growth performance and future development prospects have been severely damaged.

12. This constitutes a crisis in development that is unprecedented in breadth and depth. Its underlying cause has been the deterioration of the external trading and financial environment.

Real interest rates have become and remained extraordinarily steep.

Commodity prices in real terms have collapsed to their lowest levels since the 1930s Great Depression.

At the same time, developing countries have suffered a loss of export markets mainly owing to the intensification of protectionism and the slowing of growth in their principal markets.

Furthermore, as growth in developing countries has dropped, so has the dynamism of their mutual trade.

ODA in real terms has stagnated.

Exchange rates of the major world currencies have been volatile and misaligned and abnormal developments have occurred in current-account imbalances.

There has been a sharp contraction of international liquidity in relation to the volume of trade and the needs of developing countries.

13. Many developing countries, after incurring increased debt service charges as a result of higher interest rates and a shrinkage of capacity to service debt due to the deterioration of their terms of trade and export earnings, have also suffered an abrupt collapse of lending by international capital markets, commercial banks in particular. Indeed, several countries have suffered net outflows amounting to a significant portion of GDP. Yet, developing countries, generally, have continued to fulfil their commitments to service their debts.

14. Although ODA flows from developed countries have barely reached half of the internationally agreed targets in recent years, military expenditure has amounted to more than 5 per cent of world output and 20 times the total net flows of ODA. This is one of the principal underlying reasons for the failure of the international economic system to provide adequate resources for development. The quality of ODA flows has deteriorated, both through the increased tendency to utilize them for commercial purposes and through a more severe conditionality. Furthermore, policies and procedures of developed donor countries have become more stringent for recipient countries. The levels of direct foreign investment and of officially supported export credits have also dropped, in part due to the cutbacks in investment levels in developing countries following the tightening of the balance-of-payments constraints.

15. The combination of these adverse developments has caused the net flow of financial resources to developing countries to contract drastically and even to become strongly negative. In 1985 alone, developing countries made net outward transfers totalling $31 billion. This abnormal situation has forced a number of developing countries to resort to import compression, amounting to several percentage points of their national income, in order either to reduce their balance-of-payments deficit or to seek persistent trade surpluses—a burden which is additional to the income losses incurred through terms-of-trade deterioration and loss of export market growth. Thus, for the first time after the colonial era, developing countries as a whole are again becoming net suppliers of resources to industrialized countries. This is a grave set-back for the cause of development and threatens to further weaken the trade and payments system.

16. The massive reduction in absorption of goods and services required to make up for the worsened trading environment and financial haemorrhage has not only disrupted the economies of developing countries, but also has accentuated social tensions, and, in a number of countries, led to a deterioration of living standards and aggravated food shortages; and as different segments of society have sought to protect their real incomes from being eroded, it has greatly fuelled inflationary pressures.

17. At the international level, the extraction of trade surpluses from developing countries has intensified trade tensions and provided further impetus to the growth of protectionist pressure, by depressing output and employment in developed countries.

18. Despite the need to open markets further to accommodate the adjustments being made by developing countries, new and more sophisticated trade restricting measures have been applied in addition to the level of protectionism that hampers exports from developing countries.

19. The adjustment effort required of developing countries has been especially onerous because of the failure of developed countries to reverse the shocks that their restrictive macro-economic and trade policies have inflicted in developing countries. Consequently, real interest rates have remained extraordinarily high, and the demand for developing countries' exports low; commodity prices and the terms of trade of developing

countries have remained acutely depressed; and protectionism has continued to escalate, despite commitments regarding standstill and roll-back. The only significant achievement of the policy stance of the developed countries has been the conquest of inflation—and this has for the most part been gained at the expense of developing countries, through the downswing in oil and non-oil commodity prices.

20. Despite the public promotion by industrialized countries of market mechanisms as the solution to all problems, interventionism is increasingly resorted to by them to protect the lenders' interests, and "concerted lending" has been found expedient to avert default, to spread risks and to "discipline" the borrower. Bank rescues have often resulted in an extension of public ownership, despite their emphasis on privatization, and creditors increasingly press developing countries to nationalize the foreign debts of the private sector. At the same time, market principles continue to be flagrantly violated by industrialized countries in international trade through a wide array of increasingly restrictive barriers, particularly in the case of manufactures, quotas and through subsidies and support-price schemes in the case of commodities.

21. The interrelationship of money, finance, trade and development is still neglected in the attitudes and policies of the major developed countries. Thus, the absence of a co-ordinated and integrated set of policies directed at growth, together with deficiencies in the international monetary system which lacks a truly multilateral and coherent framework, have left the global economy deflated, and consequently unable to ensure the revitalization of international trade and development and mutually satisfactory resolution of the debt crisis. At the same time, the uneven approach being followed to the debt and development crisis, which parallels and reinforces other asymmetries and inequities in the international economic order, militates against a revival of the development process and renders the debt of developing countries a drag both on their development and on the growth of the world economy as a whole. It is clear that debt cannot be repaid under present conditions and without sustained economic development.

22. Developing countries thus cannot share the complacency regarding world economic trends which prevails in certain quarters in developed countries and stems from an inflexible attachment to restrictive and unco-ordinated policies, regardless of their global consequences. These consequences are extremely dangerous for all; indeed they even pose a threat to the international financial system and the functioning and credibility of the international trading system. Thus, the general economic environment induced by the policies of major industrialized countries constitutes an obstacle to the development efforts of developing countries.

23. At the same time, international control of the monetary situation is maintained by a few important industrialized countries, which attempt to influence it to favour their own national interest. International liquidity managed by the IMF is at its lowest level in years, and strains and stresses that have affected the financial system are becoming increasingly unmanageable. The case for an independent international reserve currency becomes stronger by the year, in view of the distortions and the stresses which continue to be experienced in the international monetary and trading systems, owing to the impossibility of reconciling national interests of one or a group of countries with those of the requirements of a sound, integrated international monetary, finance and trading system, serving the interests of all countries, developed as well as developing.

24. On the trade front, it is important to ensure that the Uruguay Round of negotiations contribute to the emergence of a truly international trade régime conducive to growth and development with a clear recognition of the needs of developing countries. However, as these negotiations get under way, prospects of implementation of the commitments on standstill and roll-back remain clouded. And if the re-negotiated MFA is a portent at all, it is one of pressing the developing countries to retreat into their own backyard, instead of providing them with a reason to hope for the establishment of a just and efficient international division of labour in accordance with each country's potential, as well as development. The aims of the Uruguay Round, even with the maximum effort at mutual multilateral accommodation, will be achieved only very partially, in the absence of commitments to deal with the essential elements of the global economy which demand resolute action.

25. The most serious development in the trade policy area in recent years has been the tendency on the part of some developed countries to seek linkages between trade in goods and other matters such as developing countries' policies in regard to foreign direct investment, protection of intellectual property, services and fair labour standards. Trade which is a means of self-reliant development is in danger of becoming an instrument in the hands of certain developed countries for imposing unacceptable linkages on developing countries dependent on trade.

26. The evolution of trade relations with the socialist countries of Eastern Europe, involving a relatively small number of developing countries, offers promising prospects for widening and deepening the process. The recent policy initiatives regarding export of a complete package of capital and technology, oriented towards joint ventures with developing countries, can make a steady contribution to capital formation within the economies of the developing countries, if increased resources are made available to assist in the build-up of necessary infrastructure as well as research and development efforts in the developing countries concerned.

27. Commodity-dependent developing economies have been severely emasculated in recent years owing to accumulating diminution of purchasing power resulting from prolonged decline in prices. For at least two decades, taking a long-term view of prospects for development of the countries dependent on commodity trade, concern has been expressed about how to achieve commodity-based development, price stabilization, market access and human resources development aimed at improving agricultural husbandry, processing and diversification, without which domestic measures and policies have a very limited impact.

28. It was to address these essential elements of a commodity-dominated economy that UNCTAD suc-

ceeded in evolving a comprehensive Integrated Programme for Commodities, including the Common Fund. The IPC/Common Fund scheme is intended, in a fundamental manner, to achieve price stabilization that is consistent with development. Until this central issue is dealt with decisively, the industrialized countries must provide adequate compensatory finance resources. If international trade is to have a sound and durable basis on which it can be sustained with benefit for all participants, then it must have healthy trading partners with a permanent stake in it. The international community must make every possible effort to give the IPC and the Common Fund a fair chance for the package to make a distinct and significant contribution to this process.

29. A cause of continuing concern to developing countries is the lack of concerted multilateral action in adopting and carrying out decisions of great importance to the international community. Small groups like the Group of Five agree among themselves on financial and monetary questions that affect the global economy as well as the economies of individual countries. There is a clear need to make full use of various multilateral institutions and forums established to handle economic issues, and the points of view of the developing world must no longer continue to be ignored.

3. Resources for development, including financial, and related monetary questions

30. More than four years after the emergence of the crisis the approach of developed creditor countries to the debt problem continues to be inequitable, one-sided and partial. Furthermore, neither the operational policies nor the time frame which the IMF and the World Bank adopt and recommend to the developing countries in the monetary, financial and trade spheres are coherent, thus causing adverse effects on their economies. While ostensibly "case-by-case", such approaches have in reality been based on certain uniform principles which fail to address the fundamental problems:

They have been designed exclusively to protect the short-term interests of creditors, and have been oblivious to differences in developing countries' capacity to pay.

They have wrongly assumed that the debt crisis stems from mismanagement by debtor countries, and have therefore ignored the need for symmetrical adjustment in developed and developing countries.

They have been based on simplistic preconceptions regarding appropriate policies, which fail to take due account of differences in the stage of development reached and in social and political conditions.

Instead of providing debtor countries with sufficient resources to allow them to strengthen and restructure their productive capacities, they have required the economies of debtors to be tightly squeezed to generate an outward transfer of resources. This has led furthermore to a negative social impact affecting the stability needed for sustained economic growth.

31. As a result of these flaws, responsibilities for dealing with debt problems have not been equitably distributed between the various parties involved: the ad-

justment costs, and the economic and social costs of debt service have been borne exclusively by the developing debtor countries. Maturity, grace and consolidation periods have remained short. The supply of new finance has sufficed only to keep debtor countries current on interest payments, allowing little or no margin for income growth even in per capita terms. This has been accompanied by the imposition of rigid and inappropriate conditions.

32. As the room for contractionary adjustment has become exhausted and the limits of political and social tolerance reached or even exceeded, recognition in principle has at last been given to the fact that, without resuming development, debtors will not be able to meet their obligations in the long run regardless of their aspiration to do so; and moreover, that without external resources, development and growth cannot be revived. However, there is a sheer contradiction between this recognition in principle of the need to place growth and development at the centre of the debt strategy and the continued calls upon developing countries to make further restrictive adjustments. The Group of 77 cannot but perceive an ironic note in these calls when developing countries are forced to transfer more resources to developed countries than they receive from them.

33. The inadequacy and insufficiency of recent initiatives such as the Baker plan are now fully evident. Their underlying approach is not consistent with the International Development Strategy. Such approaches merely seek to continue the shift towards laissez-faire policies in developing countries, by making available only a modest level of "involuntary lending" by banks and, now that the IMF has become a net taker of funds from the developing world, giving an enhanced role to the World Bank. They therefore fail to provide a meaningful strategy which would be commensurate with the scale and nature of the crisis and capable of restoring creditworthiness and the momentum of growth and development. They continue to misplace the onus of adjustment action on debtor countries instead of linking action on the debt front with action to revitalize the world economy as a whole. The latter would require coordinated action involving the participation of developing countries, not just the Group of Five to redress the present asymmetry in the international monetary system, and in particular to reduce real interest rates, strengthen commodity prices, expand liquidity, improve access to markets, and assure exchange rate stability.

By overestimating the extent and speed of the benefits that could flow from the structural policy reforms advocated and from direct foreign investment, and underestimating the difficulties and drawbacks of each, they call for further heavy sacrifices from the populations of debtor countries. The sacrifices already made have themselves been excessive.

They fail to recognize the need to tailor debt-service costs to debt-servicing capacity.

They fail to assure an adequate supply of resources, either from the private banks, or through the World Bank, and in particular IDA, the Special Facility for sub-Saharan Africa, or through the IMF's Structural Adjustment Facility. These facilities are very small in the light of their stated objectives. The Special Facility for sub-Saharan Africa, for example, has already committed more than half of its resources in the first year of its activity and will be discontinued effective July 1987.

34.   For most developing countries the debt situation remains the most severe strain on growth. Perspectives are gloomy if the framework is not changed since, for a number of developing countries, debt obligations exceed the capacities of their economies. What is even more intolerable is the increasing conditionality attached to the remaining and highly insufficient financial flows from developed to developing countries, which often tends to undermine their independence and sovereignty in the choice of their development priorities and their social and political system.

35.   The world economic crisis has extracted a heavy toll from all developing countries, especially those which for historical reasons have to contend with a large mass of poverty and living standards which provide little margin above the poverty line. Their adjustment efforts have reached and sometimes exceeded the limits of social tolerance. ODA flows have been stagnant and insufficient. Substantial additional concessional finance through multilateral sources is needed both for adjustment and development.

36.   Additional financing is needed. Funds must be mobilized and new instruments need to be devised to stop and reverse the negative transfer of resources now taking place, which hampers accumulation of capital, thus stifling development. Efficiency has to be part of the development process, but no change, within reach, in efficiency in the use of resources through structural adjustment can offset the siphoning of resources as a result of their transfer abroad. Without resources there can be no expansion and without expansion it will be impossible to create the dynamic climate needed to stimulate investment, the only path to growth.

37.   However, the magnitude of the problem is such that an increase in external financial flows alone would not be sufficient for its solution. Parallel and co-ordinated action is needed to lower interest rates, ease the liquidity shortage experienced by developing countries, raise commodity prices, achieve exchange-rate stability, increase access to developed countries' markets for products of developing countries, etc. Co-ordination is needed to redress the present asymmetry in the functioning of the international monetary system. The aim of the system—to serve equitably the international community—cannot be achieved with the present extremely high concentration of decision-making power among a few most developed countries. Co-ordination is inconceivable without the active participation of the developing countries. The world can no longer sit back and watch a spectacle in which the fate of all is decided by the few.

38.   In promoting enhanced and equitable international co-operation in the field of money and finance including debt, UNCTAD has a unique role to play, being the essential organ for the consideration of financial and monetary questions related to trade and development. The seventh session of the Conference should, *inter alia*, aim at translating the elements contained in General Assembly resolution 41/202 on the external debt crisis and development into a broader set of more

concrete operational guidelines and action-oriented measures.

39.   If the necessary commitments are not undertaken in these areas, the developing countries will face an extremely serious situation which will force them to limit resource transfers to the industrialized countries in order to avoid greater social and political instability.

4. COMMODITIES

40.   Two thirds of developing countries' export earnings come from commodities. One of the alarming features of the economic recession of the first half of the 1980s has been the persistent decline in the prices of primary commodities and the terms of trade of developing countries. Despite a short-lived mild recovery in 1983-1984, the general trend for commodities has been sharply downwards. Thus, the annual average index in 1986 was about 30 per cent lower than at the beginning of the decade in current United States dollars and about 20 per cent in real terms. Commodity prices are now at their lowest level since the Great Depression of the 1930s. The prices for petroleum have substantially declined since 1982. All commodity categories—food, agricultural raw materials and minerals—have suffered these declines in prices.

41.   The volume of developing countries' commodity exports rose by only 11 per cent during the period 1980-1986 and thus their real earnings from these exports were 20 per cent lower in 1986 than in 1980. This decline has aggravated their budgetary, debt-servicing and balance-of-payments difficulties.

42.   This situation poses an especially serious problem for Africa and other subregions in view of the generally higher dependence of the countries of this region on primary commodity exports, particularly on food and beverages and minerals and metals; their declining market share for commodity exports; and their lower level of commodity processing and manufacturing.

43.   The major factors which have influenced commodity markets are both cyclical and structural. Cyclical factors include the deflationary macro-economic policies of developed countries, exchange rate fluctuations and high real interest rates. Structural factors also include macro-economic policies of developed countries such as subsidies and support price mechanisms, protectionist measures, as well as technological developments and substitution. All have contributed to the persistent downward fall of prices.

44.   In the short and longer term the outlook for commodity prices is not expected to improve significantly. Slow growth in the industrial countries, continued protectionist practices and subsidized exports by these countries, supply pressures and underutilized capacities are among the factors that constrain the recovery of most commodity prices.

45.   The developed countries have sharply curtailed their import needs through increased production of various commodities. Protectionist measures and other massive support policies for domestic producers as well as strategic objectives have encouraged production and

generated large surpluses of agricultural products and increased the stock of minerals and metals in the developed market-economy countries, placing the commodities of developing countries at a competitive disadvantage and adversely affecting commodity prices.

46. In this connection, it is interesting to note that, although developing countries have together earned about $75 billion annually from their agricultural commodity exports during the past few years, the United States, the European Economic Community and Japan have spent approximately $42 billion annually on their agricultural support programmes.

47. Protectionist measures introduced by the developed countries have shut off commodity markets, as for example, the EEC market for meat, the Japanese market for rice and the reduction of the sugar market in the United States through quota restrictions. Internal taxes on tropical products have also put these products at a disadvantage *vis-à-vis* the alternative products originating in the developed countries. Such taxes also have negative influences on the consumption of these products.

48. The economic recovery of the developed countries from the recession of the early 1980s was not strong enough or long enough to influence the commodity economy significantly. It therefore failed to carry with it a parallel increase in the level of aggregate demand for commodities and in the export earnings and import capacities of the developing countries.

49. It should also be stressed that exchange-rate fluctuations have disruptive influences on the prices of commodities and impose additional management and adjustment responsibilities on developing countries.

50. In this context, and in view of the decline of prices and the subsequent shortfall in export earnings, a number of developing countries resorted to increasing their commodity exports in the hope of maintaining their import capacity and facing their financial obligations.

51. Globally, rising stock levels, with interruptions in 1979 and 1983, and increasing production have outrun consumption ever since 1978. Although there were some variations between the various product groups, the cyclical downturn in consumption was much more marked and the subsequent recovery failed to close the gap.

52. Competition over a narrow range of products in a limited and depressed market, therefore, often led to market gluts and consequently to price slumps.

53. The situation is alarming. Therefore, any effort aimed at revitalizing growth and development of developing countries should lend particular focus to the critical short-term and long-term issues of commodities.

5. INTERNATIONAL TRADE

54. The developing countries' share of world trade continues to decline. Despite the stated objectives of the international community, their exports of manufactures have ceased to grow, and their share of world production of manufactures has increased only marginally. Although developing countries have been obliged to reduce imports, their economies continue to provide markets for exports from developed countries and a buffer against the unemployment problems of these countries.

55. It is difficult to envisage any progress in this respect in the current international trading environment. Protectionist pressures are on the rise and are being manifested in new legislation and trade restrictive actions in the developed countries. Such actions have been largely aimed at products where developing countries have achieved a comparative advantage, and there has been a proliferation of measures applied against developing countries on a discriminatory basis, in conflict with the rules and principles of the international trading system. A clear tendency exists towards an extension of market-sharing arrangements to cover more products and more developing countries; in fact, the international trading system threatens to become a web of market-sharing arrangements rendering irrelevant the rule of non-discrimination and comparative advantage. There has been little progress in particular in working out specific programmes of action to facilitate structural adjustment in industrial countries in those economic sectors in which they have applied protectionist measures during long periods or on repeated occasions on account of loss of comparative advantage.

56. Trade policy actions of developed countries are being characterized by a growing disregard for multilaterally agreed principles and concepts, arbitrariness and patent infringements of international commitments. An atmosphere of indiscipline prevails in the trading system. Bilateral solutions are increasingly being sought outside the framework of multilateral rules and principles and multilateral reciprocity is giving way to the bilateral balancing of trade. Major trading countries are unilaterally imposing their criteria as to what constitute "unfair" trade practices, and assuming the right to take retaliatory measures against the trade of developing countries, often in response to their domestic policies outside the trade field, such as in the areas of foreign direct investment, protection of intellectual property and services. Trade sanctions have been and continue to be applied against developing countries for political reasons, despite the condemnation of such actions by the General Assembly.

57. Developing countries have also become the innocent victims of trade disputes among the major economic powers, as witnessed by the current competition in the agricultural subsidies.

58. In such an environment, the multilaterally agreed principles of differential and more favourable treatment and non-reciprocity in favour of developing countries have been seriously eroded and even called in question by the developed countries. The most striking examples have been the unilateral application of "graduation" by the developed countries and their growing tendency to condition the continuation of GSP benefits upon reciprocal actions by developing countries, including with respect to services, investment and other issues outside the trade field.

59. International trade is increasingly characterized by oligopolistic structures, and inter-firm trade of transnational corporations has become a major portion

of such trade. The concentration of market power in these corporations has been enhanced by conglomerate mergers. Restrictive business practices instituted by such entities have constituted impenetrable barriers to the expansion of trade of developing countries. The lack of binding multilateral rules on restrictive business practices has facilitated the circumvention of international trade commitments.

60.   There has been a striking lack of progress in the implementation of the commitments accepted at the sixth session of the Conference. The application of the repeated commitments with respect to standstill and roll-back have not been reflected in actual performance, even in the light of the most recent Ministerial Declaration on the Uruguay Round. Little progress has been made towards a comprehensive understanding on safeguards, based on the MFN principle, essential to the proper functioning of the trading system. At the same time, the harassment of developing countries' trade by anti-dumping and countervailing actions has intensified.

61.   Furthermore, the recognized need for international co-operation to strengthen agricultural and agro-industrial production in developing countries—of particular importance to African countries—has not materialized. In fact, barriers to market access for such products have continued and even increased.

62.   Conference resolution 159 (VI) instructed the Trade and Development Board to review and study developments in the international trading system with a view to making recommendations on principles and policies related to international trade and proposals on strengthening and improving the system with the aim of giving it a more universal, dynamic and development-oriented character. This resolution derived from the fundamental mandate of UNCTAD as spelled out in General Assembly resolution 1995 (XIX), which also assigned to UNCTAD the function of initiating action where appropriate, in co-operation with the competent organs of the United Nations, for the negotiation and adoption of multilateral legal instruments in the field of trade.

63.   The inaction in the areas described above can be attributed to the prevalence in certain quarters of preconceived ideologies questioning the very basis of multilateralism and of the basic approach underlying UNCTAD philosophy. Attempts are being made to focus debate in UNCTAD on the autonomous development policies pursued by developing countries. At the same time, trade is becoming an instrument in the hands of certain developed countries for imposing unacceptable linkages on developing countries with respect to such development policies, and for expanding the economic space of the TNCs. The lack of progress in the trade area in UNCTAD and the systematic attempts to transpose the dialogue on trade and development to less universal and narrowly conceived forums merely go to confirm this.

64.   UNCTAD has—and must continue to play—a central role in the formulation, negotiation and implementation of measures in the sphere of international trade and its interrelation with debt, money and finance issues in a development context. The seventh session of the Conference offers the much-needed opportunity to reaffirm the validity of, and the need for, continuing with the basic approach informing UNCTAD. In this context, the major role of UNCTAD in the years to come should be that of continuing to provide a universal forum for bringing about the establishment of a truly international trading system with the major aim of facilitating self-reliant development of developing countries.

65.   The successful conclusion of the Uruguay Round of multilateral trade negotiations is a necessary condition for the evolution of a truly international trading system. However, such a system cannot be expected to emerge as a natural, much less inevitable, consequence of the multilateral trade negotiations. UNCTAD, with its mandate, character and history, is the only forum in which to forge a trading system which is truly non-discriminatory, universal and comprehensive. Moreover, its unique, cross-sectoral and inter-disciplinary approach is ideally suited to developing such a trading system as part of the harmonious and equitable reconstruction of international economic relations.

Trade relations among countries having different economic and social systems

66.   UNCTAD, as a universal organization, has succeeded in elaborating multilateral guidelines and criteria with a view to assisting the member countries in developing trade and economic relations among countries having different economic and social systems. This is within the framework of the mandate given to UNCTAD by General Assembly resolution 1995 (XIX) and subsequent resolutions and decisions adopted by UNCTAD. These resolutions aimed at, and in fact contributed considerably to, the achievement of greater harmony of policies and performance relating to issues of trade and economic co-operation between different groups of countries. East-South trade and economic relations have thus been accentuated and reinforced through the implementation of resolutions and decisions of UNCTAD regarding inter-system trade. In view of the interdependence of all trade flows, it is considered that the expansion of trade and economic relations between East and West would positively affect the expansion of international trade as a whole, including East-South trade.

67.   It has been observed that since the sixth session of the Conference in 1983, UNCTAD has enlarged the scope of its activities and intensified its efforts in the area of trade relations among countries having different economic and social systems. Considering the growing interdependence among countries, confidence-building and economic security in international economic relations have assumed importance in inter-system trade.

68.   As regards prospects for East-West-South trade in the remaining 1980s, the position remains uncertain in the context of the current international economic environment. There are constraints and problems to be overcome to restructure the composition of exports and imports and to reinforce the elements of stability and predictability in trade exchanges, in order to achieve sustained expansion and diversification of trade and

economic relations among different groups of countries. In respect of East-South trade, major problems that remain to be solved are the low level of diversification of the developing countries' exports to socialist countries and the fact that the bulk of this trade still involves only a limited number of developing countries. Experience, however, suggests that there are, in principle, good prospects for further growth of trade and economic relations between the two groups of countries.

69. The socialist countries of Eastern Europe, which are responsible for one third of the total world industrial output, are already playing a significant role in the world economy. The recent process of modernization of the foreign trade system and management, structural adjustments and reforms in their economies, as well as various changes in their economic and foreign trade policies in accordance with the requirements of their national economies and the evolution of the international environment—all these trends offer potential for expanding and diversifying their trade and economic relations with all groups of countries. These developments could bring forth innovations in their economic relations and enable them to play a more effective role, contributing to the better functioning of the world economy and in particular the development processes of developing countries. There is, however, an urgent need for a new approach and concerted efforts on the part of all groups of countries to adopt constructive policy measures and initiatives to eliminate and overcome all impediments and obstacles in order to ensure the smooth expansion of inter-system trade flows.

70. There is a growing need for new approaches and a meeting of minds on confidence-building, since the evidence available indicates that the progress made in implementing various Conference resolutions and Board decisions is far from satisfactory. An analysis of the developments and trends in inter-system trade also shows that these developments still correspond neither to the economic potential of the trading partners nor to the existing possibilities or challenges of the 1980s and 1990s.

6. PROBLEMS OF THE LEAST DEVELOPED COUNTRIES, BEARING IN MIND THE SUBSTANTIAL NEW PROGRAMME OF ACTION FOR THE 1980s FOR THE LEAST DEVELOPED COUNTRIES

71. The continuing economic crisis in the LDCs, which are the poorest and economically weakest among the developing countries and are faced with the most formidable structural problems, has been a cause of grave concern to the international community. The structural deficiencies of these countries are manifested in extremely low levels of per capita income, a high proportion of population in the subsistence sectors, a high rate of population growth, low agricultural productivity, a low level of exploitation of natural resources, weak institutional and physical infrastructure, an acute scarcity of skilled personnel, an insignificant share of manufacturing value added in GDP, and the recurrence of natural disasters. These factors constitute the main causes of their extreme economic and social difficulties. The land-locked and island LDCs, which constitute over half of the group of LDCs, continue to face additional problems in their development because of their serious

geographical handicaps. The number of LDCs, instead of decreasing, increased to 40 countries in 1986 from a level of 31 in 1981 when the Substantial New Programme of Action was adopted. This situation indicates the worsening economic conditions of developing countries in general and of the LDCs in Africa, where the number has increased from 21 to 27 countries. It was in recognition of the difficult economic situation of the LDCs that the international community undertook a commitment in the Substantial New Programme of Action to provide substantially enlarged assistance to these countries to bring about structural transformation of their economies and to enable them to break away from their past and present situation and their bleak prospects, towards self-sustained development.

72. In spite of the increased attention given by the international community, and the international organizations, to finding a lasting solution to the problems of the LDCs, mainly through the adoption of the Substantial New Programme of Action in 1981, there has been a significant deterioration in the overall socio-economic situation of these countries since 1981. Despite the existence of the Substantial New Programme of Action, African LDCs experienced a persistent deterioration in their economic growth between 1981 and 1984, as a result of the deepening domestic crisis occasioned by a hostile international economic environment as well as natural calamities and disasters, notably the drought since 1982.

73. Other LDCs have also suffered considerably owing to cyclones and recurrent floods. These natural disasters have considerably reduced the potential for agricultural production, the main source of value added, and led to the reorientation of efforts for relief and rehabilitation activities rather than the pursuit of development programmes.

74. The already very low per capita GDP of the LDCs as a group declined during the first half of the 1980s and the majority of them registered negative per capita growth rates. The average annual rate of GDP growth during this period was 2 per cent, which amounted to an average annual decline of 0.5 per cent in per capital terms. This was against a positive average annual GDP growth rate of 4 per cent in the 1970s. Although there was a marginal improvement, to 2.7 per cent in the GDP growth rate during 1985, that rate remained far short not only of the Substantial New Programme of Action target of 7.2 per cent, but also of the growth rate of 4 per cent actually achieved in the 1970s.

75. The performance in the agricultural sector continues to be the main factor determining overall growth in the LDCs. The agricultural production per capita continued to decline during the first half of the 1980s at an average annual rate of 0.6 per cent. Per capita food production also registered an average annual decline of 0.9 per cent during the same period. The main bottlenecks include drought, which is widespread especially in Africa and is still being experienced in many parts of the continent. This seriously jeopardized food and livestock production and resulted in low productivity generally.

76. The record of progress in manufacturing activities, energy consumption, development of transport

and communication, etc., was also disappointing during the first half of the 1980s. The average growth rate of real GDP arising from manufacturing in most of the LDCs in 1984 was only 1.3 per cent. The consumption of energy remained at an extremely low level of 313 kg per capita in 1984, as compared to 669 kg in developing countries as a group. In the area of transport and communications, particularly in the 15 land-locked and 9 island LDCs, the situation remains critical.

77.   The external trade and payments position of most of the LDCs continued to suffer from depressed conditions in world commodity markets, worsening terms of trade, increased protectionism, and reduced ODA and other types of financial flows and workers' remittances. The exports of the LDCs were 10 per cent lower during the first three years of the present decade than the level attained in 1980. Although there was a slight recovery in 1984, the exports started declining again in 1985 and reached a level of 7.2 per cent below the 1980 figure. The prices of almost all primary commodities of export interest to the LDCs dropped by a large margin, and the average annual shortfall in export earnings from such commodities was about $770 million during the period 1978-1983. The decline in export earnings had an adverse impact on capacity to import, which also declined by 6 per cent between 1980 and 1985.

78.   The worsening of the economic situation in the LDCs during the first half of the 1980s was due, *inter alia*, to the following factors:

(*a*) Net ODA receipts by the LDCs stagnated at around $7 billion per annum during the period 1980-1984, as compared with an average increase of about 70 per cent per annum in ODA flows during the 1970s. The total level of ODA in 1984 was only 44 per cent above the average level attained in 1976-1980 in nominal terms, as against the commitment undertaken by the donor countries in the Substantial New Programme of Action to double such flows by 1985. Total ODA flows in 1984 were 0.08 per cent of the donors' GNP, as against the target of 0.15 per cent fixed in the Substantial New Programme of Action;

(*b*) Aid from multilateral agencies registered a decline in 1985, whereas in the Substantial New Programme of Action there was a specific commitment for a significant increase in multilateral assistance to the least developed countries;

(*c*) Non-concessional financial flows, which had increased by an average of more than 100 per cent every year during the 1970s, underwent a steady decline in the 1980s, falling to only $457 million in 1984. This was against total non-concessional flows of $1.1 billion in 1980. Total external assistance provided to LDCs declined from $8.2 billion in 1980 to only $7.5 billion in nominal terms in 1984;

(*d*) The commitments undertaken in the Substantial New Programme of Action to improve aid modalities in favour of the LDCs did not materialize. The average grant element of concessional assistance, which had increased from 86 per cent in 1981 to 89 per cent in 1983, declined to about 85 per cent in 1984. About 80 per cent of total aid from DAC countries to LDCs in 1984 was tied. Some initiatives have recently been taken by a number of donors to give more emphasis to programme

aid including sectoral assistance, general import financing and balance-of-payment support, as well as commodity aid, food aid, local-cost financing, and recurrent cost financing, but these measures are totally inadequate to meet the needs of the least developed countries;

(*e*) The external debt of the LDCs, which grew rapidly in the 1970s, worsened considerably during the first half of the 1980s as a result of the adverse impact of the world economic crisis on the debt-servicing capacity of these countries. Their total external debt, including short-term debts, is estimated to have been over $39 billion at the end of 1985, a 13 per cent increase as compared to the previous year. In addition, their use of IMF credit was estimated at $2.2 billion. Debt service payments in 1985 amounted to $2 billion, representing well over 20 per cent of the value of the combined exports of the LDCs. Debt service payments arising from non-concessional debts have continued to form the main part of LDCs' total debt service payments. Although some debt relief has been provided by 15 DAC member countries for their ODA debt to 33 LDCs under Trade and Development Board resolution 165 (S-IX), the debt service problem remains critical for many LDCs. The problem has been exacerbated by a sizeable proportion of non-commercial debt and by the significant increase in the multilateral debt which is not within the purview of resolution 165 (S-IX) and is subject to multilateral reschedulings. Since the adoption of the Substantial New Programme of Action in 1981, 13 LDCs have had recourse to the Paris Club to reschedule their official debt and 5 LDCs to the London Club to reschedule commercial debt. Moreover, a number of LDCs had to ask for another rescheduling in order to cope with their increased debt liabilities. However, these reschedulings have also proved to be inadequate as they provide only temporary relief and do not entail a diminution of debt stocks. Eventually they add to the debt burden.

(*f*) Since the adoption of the Substantial New Programme of Action in 1981, 19 LDCs have formulated an adjustment programme supported by a stand-by arrangement with IMF. These programmes, in the absence of increased inflow of external financial resources, have resulted in sharp cuts in imports, investments, budgets and social outlays, thus further slowing down economic growth;

(*g*) The continuance of tariff and non-tariff barriers in important markets still inhibits expansion of LDCs' exports. In spite of commitments undertaken in the Substantial New Programme of Action, the 1982 GATT Ministerial Declaration[e] and, most recently, the Punta del Este Declaration of 1986[f] many developed countries continue to impose various types of restrictions on exports from LDCs. Moreover, the land-locked and island LDCs suffer from high transportation costs which make their products uncompetitive in the world market;

(*h*) In view of the fact that almost 85 per cent of the LDCs' exports consist of primary commodities and are concentrated on only a few products, these exports have

---

[e] GATT, *Basic Documents and Selected Instruments, Twenty-ninth Supplement* (Sales No. GATT/1983-1), p. 9.

[f] *Ibid., Thirty-third Supplement* (Sales No. GATT/1987-1), p. 19.

been hard hit by the collapse of international commodity prices and the deteriorating terms of trade. The prices of almost all primary commodities of export interest to the LDCs have dropped precipitously. This has adversely affected the foreign-exchange earnings of the LDCs. The compensatory financing available to them under the existing financing schemes is inadequate and this has resulted in depletion of their monetary reserves and overall capacity to mobilize finance for development. The commitments undertaken in the Substantial New Programme of Action for special provisions in favour of the LDCs in terms of compensating their commodity-related export earnings shortfalls have not been fully realized;

(*i*) Assistance so far provided to land-locked and island countries among the LDCs and measures taken in implementing the relevant resolutions are still very inadequate in terms of alleviating the problems confronting them.

79. The LDCs, for their part, have implemented several measures to improve their economic conditions. These include, among others, adoption of effective policies to mobilize domestic resources, expand food and agricultural production and develop their external trade. Since the adoption of the Substantial New Programme of Action, almost all the LDCs have designated focal points for the implementation, follow-up and monitoring of the Substantial New Programme of Action. Twenty-eight LDCs have had a country review meeting as envisaged by the Substantial New Programme of Action. Five more LDCs are preparing for the convening of such meetings.

80. Low and often declining per capita income notwithstanding, several LDCs were able to achieve domestic savings rates exceeding 10 per cent and, in a few areas, exceeding 15 per cent during the period 1980-1984. In an effort to further improve mobilization of domestic resources, several LDCs have implemented measures to make their tax system simpler and more broadly based and to improve tax administration. Measures have also been initiated in several LDCs to improve the performance of public sector enterprises. The development and mobilization of human resources, through eradication of adult illiteracy, expansion of public education, including vocational training, and development of entrepreneurial capacities, is an important element in the development plans and programmes of several LDCs. Adult illiteracy rates decreased by more than 20 percentage points between 1970 and 1985 in seven LDCs. Almost all LDCs decreased their illiteracy rate between 1980 and 1985. The number of students undertaking vocational training in the LDCs increased in 24 per cent between 1980 and 1984. In the field of food and agricultural production, many LDCs have taken steps to increase production and productivity, *inter alia*, by increasing the use of the market mechanism, mobilizing the rural population and diversifying production. In order better to respond to the adverse and changing economic environment, many LDCs have adopted appropriate policy measures to enhance the effective implementation of their adjustment programmes. Many LDCs have taken measures for improvement of the institutional and physical infrastructure, in spite of limited resources. The assistance provided by other developing countries in the context of ECDC has reinforced the efforts of the LDCs themselves to alleviate some of their problems. In spite of all these positive measures the development prospects of the LDCs remain bleak owing to the extremely adverse external environment.

PART II

POLICIES AND MEASURES, INCLUDING THOSE RELATED
TO THE INTERDEPENDENCE OF ISSUES

SECTION I

Resources for development, including financial and related monetary questions

A. *Policies and measures aimed at the elaboration and implementation of a growth-oriented strategy for tackling the problems of debt and development, based on the principles of shared responsibility, political dialogue and co-ordination among all the parties concerned: Governments of developed creditor and developing debtor countries, banks of developed countries and international financial institutions*

The Conference

1. Recognizes that the lack of a durable solution to the debt problem of the developing countries is a major impediment to the recovery of a reasonable rate of growth on a sustained basis in those countries, and a source of instability in world financial markets and distorts trade flows, affecting negatively the ability of debtor countries to import and achieve their development objectives, as well as the capacity of creditor nations to export and secure sustained growth and employment.

2. Agrees on the urgent need to halt and reverse the net flow of financial resources from developing debtor countries to developed creditor countries.

3. Further agrees on the imperative need for a political dialogue aimed at implementing a new, comprehensive debt strategy based on growth, development and shared responsibility in order to reach a lasting solution to the continuing debt crisis, taking into account the close interrelationship of the monetary, financial and trade issues and bearing in mind General Assembly resolution 41/202. Such a strategy should be implemented through, *inter alia*, the following measures:

(*a*) Adapting debt-service payments of developing countries to their real debt-servicing capacity through measures such as limiting payments to a percentage of export earnings and establishing, as appropriate, a relationship between the amount of debt service and GDP, the evolution of commodity prices or other relevant indicators of the economic situation of each indebted developing country;

(*b*) Significantly increasing the availability of resources of the multilateral financial institutions through: (i) the expansion of capital; (ii) raising of the borrowing authority or of the lending ratio; (iii) setting up of trust funds;

(*c*) Consideration by developed donor countries of further cancellation of the ODA debt of poorer developing countries, in particular as regards the LDCs least developed countries and the countries of sub-Saharan Africa, bearing in mind Trade and Development Board resolution 165 (S-IX) and the commitments undertaken at the thirteenth special session of the General Assembly on the critical economic situation in Africa;

(*d*) Immediate implementation of the recommendations of the mid-term global review of the Substantial New Programme of Action for the 1980s for the Least Developed Countries;

(*e*) Consideration by Governments of developed creditor countries and international commercial banks of a significant lengthening of consolidation, maturity and grace periods as well as of the reduction of bank margins to a minimum in the context of debt reschedulings;

(*f*) Consideration should also be given to introducing distinctly concessional interest rates to be applied on the rescheduling of official and officially guaranteed loans extended before 1987 to developing countries. In this connection, special arrangements should be made in regard to the debt of the LDCs, countries in sub-Saharan Africa, and small hard-hit developing countries in Africa, Asia and Latin America and the Caribbean, to developed creditor countries;

(*g*) Extension of the procedure of negotiating debt rescheduling of developing countries' debt to developed creditor countries without prior agreement with IMF;

(*h*) Adoption by Governments of developed creditor countries of appropriate regulatory and other measures which would give international commercial banks flexibility to reschedule interest payments on debts contracted before 1987, to provide new loans to indebted nations, as well as to take measures of a debt-relief nature, such as partial writing-off of the principal and application of concessional rates of interest.

4. The Conference, in view of the critical nature of the present situation, welcomes and fully supports the initiative of creating, within the Interim and Development Committees, a Committee of Ministers from developing and developed countries to take up the examination of the debt problem, including specific solutions for low income countries, particularly those in sub-Saharan Africa, and recommend appropriate measures.

B. *Policies and measures aimed at substantially increasing the flows of financial resources from developed to developing countries, provided through multilateral institutions, export credit agencies,* *bilateral ODA, the banking system and foreign investors*

The Conference

5. Urges developed countries to redouble efforts to achieve as quickly as possible the internationally agreed targets on ODA to developing countries, in compliance with the recommendations of the Task Force on Concessional Flows, so as to place ODA on an increasingly assured, continuous and predictable basis in accordance with the development needs of developing countries.

6. Recognizes the need for adapting the conditionality criteria and the characteristics of the operations of the international financial institutions to the need of achieving adequate rates of growth and of adjusting under conditions where external imbalances are caused by exogenous factors; co-ordination between IMF, the World Bank and other multilateral financial institutions should not lead to cross-conditionality.

7. Agrees that urgent actions should be undertaken to strengthen the role of the World Bank as a development institution, through the doubling of its capital, the improvement of its lending ratios, the increase of its financial leverage, as well as other measures aimed at enhancing its catalytic role in order to ensure a sufficient volume of net transfer of resources to developing countries.

8. Recommends a significant increase of IDA resource in real terms, assuring their adequate replenishment, while improving the quality of its resources.

9. Urges the World Bank to mobilize additional resource commitments from developed donor countries for sub-Saharan Africa.

10. Recommends an increase in the size of the Structural Adjustment Facility of IMF while improving its essential features, particularly its growth orientation, low conditionality and the provision of supplementary resources.

11. Stresses the need to strengthen the Asian, African and Latin American development banks and funds through, *inter alia*, the increase of their capital and lending programmes, while maintaining their essential developmental and regional nature and their equitable decision-making process.

12. Calls upon industrialized countries to make a greater effort for increased participation in IFAD's third replenishment and urges other contributors to the Fund in a position to do so, to make additional efforts to contribute to the resources of the Fund with a view to ensuring the highest possible level of replenishment while preserving the institution and its unique structure.

13. Urges that the possibility be considered to establish appropriate mechanisms for the recycling of the large current-account surpluses of some developed countries for utilization by developing countries for their mutual benefit.

14. Urges developed countries to increase the financial support of their export credit agencies to developing countries under suitable terms and conditions. Measures should be taken to avoid coverage suspension, including such as may be politically motivated.

15. Calls upon Governments of developed countries to encourage resumption and increase of bank lending to developing countries.

16. Recommends that Governments of developed countries encourage foreign investments to developing countries in accordance with national legislations and development objectives of host countries.

17. Urges that ways and means be considered to enhance the participation of developing countries members of multilateral institutions engaged in development financing in the formulation and approval of the credit policies of these institutions so as to adapt them to the development objectives of the borrowing countries.

18. Urges developed countries and international financial institutions to increase the flow of resources in real terms to African countries in accordance with the decisions contained in the United Nations Programme for African Economic Recovery and Development 1986-1990, adopted at the thirteenth special session of the General Assembly on the critical economic situation in Africa.

19. IMF and the World Bank should, at their next meetings, acquire specific commitments with a view to improving the IMF Compensatory Financing Facility so as to respond to the deterioration in international commodity prices and establish an additional facility for relieving the debt-service burden caused by high real interest rates.

C. *Policies and measures aimed at promoting the reform of the international monetary system so as to make it truly stable, multilateral, equitable and responsive to the development needs of developing countries*

The Conference

20. Calls upon all States members of UNCTAD to support the early convening of an international conference on money and finance with universal participation, with the objective of reforming the international monetary and financial system so as to make it truly stable, multilateral, equitable and responsive to the development needs of the developing countries. As a matter of urgency, and without prejudice to the comprehensive reform of the system through the convening of the conference, the following measures should be implemented for the improvement of the functioning of the existing system:

(a) IMF should exercise effective multilateral surveillance, particularly with respect to the principal industrialized countries, giving special attention to the evolution of exchange rates, trade and capital flows and fiscal equilibrium in conformity with the growth objectives provided for in article 1 of its Articles of Agreement;

(b) A supply of adequate international liquidity on an increasingly assured, continuous and predictable basis, consistent with the growth requirements of the world economy and meeting in particular the needs of the developing countries, should be ensured. In this context, IMF should agree on a new substantial special drawing right allocation totalling SDRs 25/30 billion

for the first year and on regular annual allocations throughout the fifth basic period to satisfy the established long-term global need for reserves, while ensuring the unconditional nature of special drawing rights and their link to the development needs of developing countries. Developed countries should consider forgoing their shares, for the benefit of developing countries in need of reserves;

(c) Repayment periods for drawings from IMF should be extended significantly and conditionality criteria brought into line with the development objectives of developing countries. Fund agreements should as a norm make provisions for additional support if GDP growth were to fall below a pre-agreed level;

(d) Expansion and improvement of the IMF Compensatory Financing Facility;

(e) Continuation and further improvement of the enlarged access policy, necessitated, *inter alia*, by the inadequacy of quotas and by the reduction in access limits;

(f) Undertaking necessary actions related to the ninth review of quotas, which should lead to a substantial increase of developing countries' quotas, keeping in view that the eighth review not only fell short of requirements, but led to retrogressive results for developing countries;

(g) Increasing the voting share and level of participation of developing countries in policy formulation and in the decision-making process of IMF.

21. The Conference, in view of the need for immediate action, welcomes and fully supports the call for the creation of a representative Committee of Ministers from developing and industrialized countries to examine the proposals for reform and improvement of the international monetary system. This Committee could perhaps take the form of a joint sub-committee of both the Interim and Development Committees to examine the proposals for reform and improvement of the international monetary system.

SECTION II

Commodities

I

1. Since the beginning of the 1980s, world commodity markets have been suffering a crisis of unprecedented dimensions. Prices have collapsed to their lowest level since the Great Depression of the 1930s. The macro-economic policies, pursued by developed market-economy countries, with scant regard for their ultimate impact on the fragile economies of developing countries, have constituted a major factor in the prevailing sharp deterioration in commodity prices. In particular, protectionist policies blocking market access, subsidies and price support schemes, inflation first and then deflation, high real interest rates and volatile exchange rates, as well as manipulation of markets by commodity speculators, have been responsible for the dramatic loss of export earnings experienced by developing countries during this period. This situation has in turn greatly constrained the economic and social

development of developing countries. It has also led to a deterioration in the terms of trade of these countries, seriously affecting further their capacity to meet their external financial obligations, creating a climate of instability and uncertainty in international economic relations and hindering a reactivation of the world economy.

2. The present critical situation fully confirms the continued validity of the objectives and international measures agreed to in Conference resolution 93 (IV) on the Integrated Programme for Commodities (IPC). It calls for prompt and full implementation of the IPC, particularly in view of the close link between the fall in commodity export earnings and the accumulation of debt. There is also greater need than ever for improved market access coupled with stable and remunerative prices for products of export interest to developing countries in order to stimulate growth and development. We therefore reaffirm our strong commitment to the IPC and call for the following measures to be effectively implemented as set out below.

II

A. *International commodity agreements/ arrangements*

3. International commodity agreements/arrangements (ICAs) should be strengthened and include economic clauses, and new ones should be negotiated taking into account the provisions of Conference resolution 93 (IV), including the objective of ensuring remunerative and just prices for producers. The international community should provide the necessary financial and political backing for such arrangements to be viable and effective. All producers and consumers of the commodities concerned should support such arrangements.

4. The Secretary-General of UNCTAD is requested to make the necessary arrangements for the convening of preparatory meetings on individual commodities not covered by ICAs and which are included in the indicative list of resolution 93 (IV). This should be followed, when appropriate, by negotiating conferences, with a view to reaching comprehensive international agreements with economic provisions, or arrangements containing appropriate measures, including those of a developmental character, needed to solve the problems faced by these commodities in the international market. A programme of negotiations should be carried out and completed by 1990 as far as possible.

5. The UNCTAD secretariat should continue to provide the necessary assistance to establish the means for mutual consultations enabling the strengthening of co-operation and co-ordination among producing countries required for negotiations on commodities.

6. Complementary to specific price stabilization efforts, co-operation between producers and consumers within ICAs should also be encouraged to facilitate greater transparency, research and development, and market promotion, including new end-uses, as well as remedial measures for special problems in the commodity field.

B. *The Common Fund for Commodities*

7. The Conference should appeal to developing countries and developed market-economy countries which have not yet done so, and to socialist countries of Eastern Europe, to ratify the Agreement Establishing the Common Fund for Commodities. It should appeal also to the United States of America to reconsider its decision not to ratify the Agreement. A meeting of interested countries should be called in 1988 to review the status of the Agreement and to recommend measures to accelerate its full implementation.

C. *Processing, marketing and distribution*

8. The UNCTAD secretariat's work, including the elaboration of frameworks, should continue on processing, marketing and distribution, including transportation, of commodities. In particular, attention should be given to North-South as well as South-South actions that would ensure a greater participation of developing countries in these areas. Technical and financial support should be provided by developed countries, and by multilateral and financial institutions, to developing countries for training and research on these subjects. International co-operation in these fields should be strengthened by identifying the needs of developing countries and the forms of international assistance by which they can be addressed.

D. *Diversification*

9. Developed countries and multilateral funding organizations are called upon to make resources available, including through special facilities for financing horizontal and vertical diversification of commodity production and exports on favourable and concessional terms and conditions for developing countries. Such medium-term and long-term financing should be complemented with technical assistance for feasibility studies and infrastructural developments as an indispensable component. The UNCTAD secretariat is requested to follow the activities in this field more closely in co-operation with relevant international organizations.

E. *Compensatory financing*

10. The ongoing programme of work aimed at establishing an additional facility to compensate developing countries for their shortfalls in commodity export earnings should be concluded. Strengthening and improving the existing compensatory financing facilities should also be undertaken. Special arrangements should be made to ensure simplified access for the LDCs to the IMF Compensatory Financing Facility.

F. *Market access*

11. The developed countries should demonstrate their political will to eliminate totally the obstacles to trade in agricultural, tropical and natural resources-based products of developing countries. The UNCTAD secretariat should provide technical assistance to developing countries in the negotiations in the Uruguay Round. This assistance should be oriented towards improving access conditions in developed countries'

markets for developing countries' exports and in particular identifying ways and means of applying differential and more favourable treatment for such exports.

12. Developed countries are called on to cease providing subsidies and other unfair forms of assistance to their domestic commodity producers and to their commodity exports and to eliminate tariff escalation on commodities in their processed and semi-processed forms and quantitative restrictions on commodities of export interest to developing countries.

G. *Synthetics and substitutes*

13. Developed countries should support the efforts of the developing countries to improve the competitiveness of natural products. To this end, support should be extended to research and development activities in developing countries and to facilitating transfer of technologies. Measures for promoting demand for natural products of developing countries, new end-uses and exchange of market information should also be implemented. Assistance should also be given to improving transportation and other infrastructural facilities for such exports.

14. In cases where increased substitution of natural products derives from protectionist policies and from support prices in developed countries at levels not consistent with prevailing international market prices, such administered domestic prices should be brought into line with international levels. To this end protectionist barriers should be dismantled in order to allow exports of natural products from developing countries to compete more freely with substitutes.

H. *Disposal of non-commercial stocks*

15. In regard to the sale of non-commercial stocks, an international code of conduct should be concluded expeditiously so as to halt the prevailing adverse effects on commodity markets, bearing in mind the principles agreed to in decision 4 (V) of the Committee on Commodities[g] and other international instruments relating to this matter. To this end the Secretary-General of UNCTAD should be requested to take necessary measures to give effect to this objective.

I. *The role of UNCTAD*

16. The negotiating and leading co-ordinating role of UNCTAD as well as the provision of technical assistance in the area of commodities should be strengthened. UNCTAD should actively carry out its responsibilities of promoting a general and integrated approach to commodities in co-operation with other relevant institutions and of taking specific actions in the commodity field. Such actions should include review of commodity policies world wide and, in particular, their impact on developing countries, as well as monitoring of progress in the area.

---

[g] See *Official Records of the Trade and Development Board, Tenth Session, Supplement No. 3* (TD/B/317), annex I.

Section III

International trade

PROPOSALS OF THE STATES MEMBERS OF
THE GROUP OF 77
IN THE AREA OF INTERNATIONAL TRADE

In order to translate the approach outlined in the Assessment[h] into a programme of action, the following specific policy measures and decisions should be adopted:

A. *International trading system*

1. UNCTAD should initiate work on a blueprint for a universal, non-discriminatory, comprehensive, stable and predictable trading system which will respect fundamental principles underlying the international legal order. The system should aim at facilitating the increase of developing country participation in world exports, and at achieving an equitable distribution of the gains from trade. The improved and strengthened trading system shall thus be oriented towards development and growth and incorporate differential and more favourable treatment for developing countries as an integral part of, not as an exception to, its rules and principles. It should take into account the special problems of the least developed countries. It should be fully responsive to development objectives in the area of commodities and contain a mechanism for redressing restrictive business practices, particularly those of TNCs. Such a system should be seen as part of a new paradigm of harmonious and equitable international economic relations. To this end, it should be founded on the new international consensus to be generated on the objectives of development and employment.

2. Action relating to monetary and financial matters, transfer of technology, services and other relevant areas should be made compatible and consonant with the established objectives of the system. The adoption of support measures would be required in the international monetary and financial sphere to allow for improved conditions which, as a whole, will facilitate dealing with the developing countries' debt, based on an integrated strategy oriented towards development and growth.

B. *Protectionism and structural adjustment*

3. Developed countries shall respect multilateral trade rules and principles, including their commitments to provide differential and more favourable treatment to developing countries, and strictly comply with the standstill and roll-back commitment. All protectionist measures applied by developed countries should be notified to the Surveillance Body set up under the Uruguay Round. Information on all such measures should be communicated to the Secretary-General of UNCTAD for the periodic review of protectionism and structural adjustment. UNCTAD should provide advice on identifying such measures and concerting the appropriate action to ensure their removal.

---

[h] See part I above of the present annex V, B.

4. Developed countries shall not impose economic and trade sanctions against developing countries for political reasons, and shall remove such sanctions currently being applied.

5. Developed countries shall establish a transparent and independent mechanism at the national level to examine the need for protectionist action sought by firms/sectors, and the implications of such action for the domestic economy as a whole. This mechanism shall also monitor the observance of the standstill and roll-back commitments. Periodic reports shall be sent by this mechanism to UNCTAD for its consideration in the Trade and Development Board.

6. Developed countries shall establish a transparent and independent mechanism at the national level to (*a*) draw up programmes for facilitating structural adjustment in sectors of particular export interest to developing countries; (*b*) monitor the implementation of such programmes; and (*c*) report progress periodically to UNCTAD for consideration in the Trade and Development Board.

C. *Market access*

7. Developed countries shall:

(*a*) Improve the access to their markets for products of export interest to the developing countries, including manufactures and semi-manufactures;

(*b*) Liberalize agricultural trade by eliminating restrictions and distortions, particularly those regarding non-tariff and tariff barriers and subsidized exports, by bringing all measures affecting import access and export competition under strengthened and more operationally effective GATT rules and disciplines;

(*c*) Ensure total liberalization of trade in tropical products and those derived from natural resources;

(*d*) Liberalize the trade régime in textiles and clothing by removing discriminatory restraints on exports from developing countries and take steps to integrate the régime into the General Agreement on the basis of strengthening the rules and disciplines of the General Agreement;

(*e*) Eliminate escalation of tariff and non-tariff barriers affecting the products of export interest to developing countries at higher stages of processing.

The Trade and Development Board should keep under review, on a regular basis, the implementation of these measures.

8. Developed countries shall continue to improve the GSP, *inter alia*, through the expansion of product coverage; and without any impairment of the multilaterally agreed principles upon which the system is based, in particular those relating to its generalized, non-discriminatory and non-reciprocal character. The Secretary-General of UNCTAD is requested to prepare a special report on the observance of such principles by preference-giving countries, to be considered by the Trade and Development Board at the second part of its thirty-fourth session, in the first half of 1988.

9. Developed countries are invited to provide financial and technical support to the UNCTAD Technical Assistance Programme in the field of GSP; UNDP is in-vited to consider favourably requests for increased financial resources for this Programme.

10. Special problems of the LDCs shall be kept in view while undertaking these tasks, particularly for the liberalization of tariff and non-tariff barriers and other restraints on the exports of the LDCs, keeping in view the Agreement relating to the Framework for the Conduct of International Trade (Enabling clause).

11. The particular problems facing the land-locked and island developing countries on account of their geographical situation and other inherent disadvantages shall be kept in view while undertaking these tasks.

12. Observance of multilaterally agreed commitments with respect to trade in goods shall not be linked to concessions in such areas as investment, intellectual property and services. No linkages shall be established between the negotiations on trade in goods and negotiations in areas such as trade in services, intellectual property and investment.

13. Restrictive business practices, particularly of TNCs, shall be brought squarely within the operation of the trading system through:

(*a*) An obligation in regard to transparency and consultation procedures;

(*b*) The establishment of a special committee on restrictive business practices within the framework of UNCTAD to monitor the application of the Set of Multilaterally Agreed Equitable Principles and Rules for the Control of Restrictive Business Practices;[i] and

(*c*) Continuing work in UNCTAD towards the establishment of a legally binding framework.

D. *The role of UNCTAD in connection with the Uruguay Round of multilateral trade negotiations*

14. The Trade and Development Board should follow closely developments in the Uruguay Round and appraise such developments as to their implications for the trade and development interests of the developing countries. In this regard, the Board should study particular aspects of the negotiations with a view to formulating specific recommendations which could be transmitted to the appropriate bodies. In carrying out this exercise, the Board should give priority to the implementation of the roll-back of protectionist measures against the trade of developing countries and to reaching a comprehensive understanding on safeguards based upon the MFN principle.

15. The Secretary-General of UNCTAD is requested to provide advice and technical assistance to developing countries as regards the MTNs to enable them to participate more effectively in the negotiations. UNDP is requested to consider favourably requests from UNCTAD and individual countries to make increased financial resources available for this exercise.

16. In order to carry out effectively the above tasks, adequate arrangements should be made for the Secretary-General of UNCTAD to follow the work in Uruguay Round bodies.

---

[i] United Nations publication, Sales No. E.81.II.D.5.

E. *Services*

17. The Secretary-General of UNCTAD is requested to analyse, from the point of view of developing countries and in the context of promoting and ensuring their autonomous development and economic growth, the implications of the issues being raised in the context of trade in services by developed countries. The objective is to ascertain the need for, and examine the implications of, a multilateral framework for trade in services, and not "liberalization" of, or removing "the barriers" to, trade in services. This analysis should bear in mind that, for developing countries, the issues of transfer of technology and the restrictive business practices of TNCs, among others, are of paramount importance in the area of services.

18. The UNCTAD secretariat should be asked to analyse the wider implications of any international régime governing trade in services. These implications should include political, cultural and security aspects.

19. The Secretary-General of UNCTAD is requested to work out appropriate problematics for trade in services, keeping in mind that the revolutionary changes in telecommunications and telematics provide a new and easy medium for transactions in services around the globe. More often than not, new technologies are making transactions in services across national borders more difficult to monitor and control. The problematics for trade in services must take this into account; an approach based on the General Agreement on Tariffs and Trade may not be relevant or adequate.

20. UNCTAD should be provided with adequate resources to carry out effectively its mandate to assist developing countries in studying the contribution of services to their development process, and, when requested, to provide assistance to the developing countries in undertaking national studies, as defined in Trade and Development Board decision 309 (XXX). The Secretary-General of UNCTAD should present at the next session of the Trade and Development Board a programme on technical assistance to developing countries to improve the statistical basis on trade in services. UNDP is invited to respond positively to requests from UNCTAD and its member States for financial support for the above purposes. The developed countries are also invited to make available financial and technical resources for such studies.

21. The Secretary-General of UNCTAD should explore the possibility of establishing a programme of co-operation on services within UNCTAD as a mechanism for channelling financial and technical assistance to developing countries with the aim of strengthening the service sector in those countries.

F. *Trade relations among countries having different economic and social systems*

22. Taking note of the informal text annexed to Conference decision 145 (VI) and the ideas contained in TD/B/1104, the Group of 77 proposes:

(*a*) To request the socialist countries of Eastern Europe to take measures: to contribute fully and effectively to the efforts of the developing countries to diversify and intensify their trade, and to provide a growing share of their imports, including semi-manufactures and manufactures, from developing countries; to make further improvements in their GSP schemes; to improve the terms and conditions of credits to the developing countries; to enlarge their economic assistance; to increase the share of convertible currencies in resources made available for financing developing countries' projects; to develop a flexible and efficient payments mechanism in trade operations; to pay special attention to the specific needs and requirements of the LDCs;

(*b*) To request the Secretary-General of UNCTAD to carry out the necessary consultations with the relevant Governments on the possibility of initiating a process of negotiations leading to a further strengthening of trade and economic co-operation between the developing countries and the socialist countries of Eastern Europe;

(*c*) In the areas of technical assistance and consultative activities, to intensify the existing UNCTAD operational programme for the promotion of East-South trade;

(*d*) To request the Trade and Development Board to keep the implementation of these activities under periodic review.

Section IV

Problems of the least developed countries, bearing in mind the substantial new programme of action for the 1980s for the least developed countries

SPECIFIC POLICY MEASURES SUGGESTED FOR ADOPTION

At the end of the mid-term global review of the implementation of the Substantial New Programme of Action, conducted by the Intergovernmental Group on the Least Developed Countries in September/October 1985, a number of recommendations were made for the improvement of the condition of the LDCs and for full implementation of the Substantial New Programme of Action. It would be necessary to implement fully and expeditiously all these recommendations and conclusions, along with other measures included in the Substantial New Programme of Action itself. The following, *inter alia*, deserve reiteration and expeditious action by the countries concerned within the context of the Substantial New Programme of Action:

A

The LDCs reaffirm their primary responsibility for their overall development.

B. *Financial and technical assistance*

1. The international community should support the efforts of LDCs to increase their per capita food production and, in view of the energy problems, provide financial and technical assistance for research, exploration and development of energy resources; and should assist in maximizing capacity utilization of their productive economic units.

2. Donors should endeavour to provide emergency assistance and financing of costs involved in the

management and relief operations in African and other LDCs affected by food and other emergencies.

3. The Substantial New Programme of Action should be fully and effectively implemented, and a substantially enlarged volume of financial assistance in real terms should be given to LDCs on terms which correspond to their immediate and long-term development needs.

4. Within the context of the Substantial New Programme of Action, donor countries which have not yet done so should attain 0.15 per cent of their GNP as ODA to the LDCs before the end of the decade or should attain, on a priority basis, a doubling of their ODA (a target which was originally to be achieved by 1985).

5. The multilateral assistance to the LDCs through such channels as IDA, IFAD, regional development banks and their funds, UNDP, the Special Measures Fund for the Least Developed Countries, UNCDF, UNV, etc., should be significantly increased to meet the increased needs of the LDCs, and donors should channel a substantial part of their aid through these institutions and agencies.

6. The Eighth Replenishment of IDA should be significantly higher than the previous levels, keeping in view the critical importance of IDA for the LDCs.

7. Relevant international institutions should continue their concerted efforts to consider new mechanisms and arrangements, which include proposals for, *inter alia*, international tax schemes for development, further gold sales by IMF, the linking of the creation of special drawing rights to development assistance, and the use of interest-subsidy techniques. IMF should undertake a fundamental review of the principles on which its conditionality rests in such a way as to reflect the peculiar social, economic and political priorities of the LDCs, and allocate substantial portions of special drawing rights, Trust Fund facilities and compensatory financing facilities to these countries.

8. Concerned donors should provide timely assistance on appropriate terms to mitigate the adverse effects of adjustment programmes and should support the efforts of the LDCs in implementing the required policy changes.

C. *Compensatory financing*

9. In the event that a complementary facility for fully compensating the export earnings shortfalls of the developing countries is established, it should ensure special provision for the LDCs. Special measures should be taken to strengthen the commodity markets and enhance export receipts of the LDCs from such commodities. The existing Compensatory Financing Facility of IMF should be improved, with provision for special treatment for the LDCs ensuring full coverage of their export earnings shortfalls, subsidization of their interest payments on outstanding drawings and a longer repayment and grace period than hitherto.

10. All developed countries which have not yet done so should expeditiously adopt special measures in order to compensate fully the export earnings shortfalls of the LDCs.

D. *Aid modalities*

11. With regard to aid modalities, immediate steps should be taken to provide ODA to the LDCs fully in the form of grants and to provide loans without discrimination on highly concessional terms, at least as concessional as those provided by IDA.

12. Urgent steps should be taken by donor countries to provide ODA, loans and grants to LDCs on an untied basis. They should also take steps to improve the quality and effectiveness of aid, and eliminate the time-lag between aid commitment and disbursement. In this regard, a mechanism that would ensure automaticity and predictability of disbursement should be created.

13. Advance payments should be made by the donors concerned against their commitment in order to minimize delays in disbursement and improve the effectiveness of assistance.

14. Donor countries should take steps for increased local-cost as well as recurrent-cost financing.

15. Concerned donors should provide increased balance-of-payments support as well as commodity aid, programme aid, including sector assistance and general import financing, and their terms should be flexible enough to facilitate their effective use. Such balance-of-payments support in general must not be used to exercise political pressure on the LDCs and should not be dependent on acceptance by these countries of measures and programmes which involve social costs and hinder their basic aims, objectives and priorities or compromise their political independence and national sovereignty.

E. *Debt problems of the least developed countries*

16. Developed countries should fully implement Trade and Development Board resolution 165 (S-IX) expeditiously and convert all outstanding bilateral ODA loans of all the LDCs into grants, without discrimination.

17. Creditors should provide substantial and multi-year scheduling of private debts, including the waiving of service payments and/or outright cancellation of the debt.

F. *Access to markets*

18. Steps should be taken by developed countries to further improve GSP or MFN treatment for products of the LDCs, with the objective of providing duty-free access to such products, and to eliminate non-tariff measures affecting exports of LDCs. Special schemes should be prepared by each of them to realize these objectives. Flexible rules of origin should also be applied in favour of LDCs to facilitate expansion of their export trade.

19. Increased technical assistance should be given to the LDCs for promotion of trade and expansion of production facilities for export. In particular, developed countries and international organizations should also assist the LDCs to create industries for on-the-spot processing of raw materials and food products, and the development of integrated projects for the expansion of

exports and to provide adequate resources to overcome all supply bottle-necks.

20.   The developed countries should assist the LDCs in entering into long-term arrangements for exports, as called for in the Substantial New Programme of Action.

G.   *Land-locked and island developing countries*

21.   In accordance with the United Nations Convention on the Law of the Sea of 1982 and Conference resolutions 137 (VI), 138 (VI) and Trade and Development Board resolution 319 (XXXI) and other relevant resolutions of the United Nations as adopted on the specific needs and problems of land-locked and island countries among the LDCs and the extremely acute nature of the problems:

(*a*) Transit countries should intensify co-operation with the land-locked countries among the LDCs to alleviate the transit problems;

(*b*) Concerned donors, while providing technical and financial assistance to land-locked and island countries among LDCs, should particularly focus on capital input in infrastructural development;

(*c*) International bodies, in particular UNDP and the regional commissions, should continue to support those LDCs with measures required to alleviate their specific transit-transport and communications problems.

H.   *Country review mechanisms*

22.   The country review meetings which are the mechanisms for the periodic review and implementation of the Substantial New Programme of Action should be further strengthened and improved to make them more effective. UNDP and the World Bank, as the lead agencies, should expand their technical assistance to the LDCs to enable them to prepare efficiently for these meetings. Donor countries should be represented at an adequately high level. The meetings should result in firm commitments and secure increased mobilization of resources to the LDCs.

23.   Developed donor countries and international financial institutions participating in country review meetings for LDCs, such as the UNDP-sponsored Round Table Processes (RTPs), should not link their commitments of development resources to the condition that the LDCs should have effective operational IMF/World Bank adjustment programmes; these country review meetings should be seen essentially as addi-

tional measures for increasing financial resources to the accelerated development of LDCs.

I.   *Equitable benefits of assistance*

24.   In the application of all measures, it should be ensured that the assistance benefits all LDCs according to their individual requirements on a just and equitable basis.

SECTION V

Interdependence of issues

1.   The policy actions in the four interrelated areas of the provisional agenda of the seventh session of the United Nations Conference on Trade and Development, as proposed here, are mutually supportive. Many of the most pressing needs of developing countries—including a new and comprehensive strategy to reach a lasting solution to the problem of debt—can be hoped to be successfully met only through the implementation of a coherent set of agreed measures spanning the above areas.

2.   Developed countries should adopt more expansionary macro-economic policies including an easing of monetary policies and of fiscal stances where appropriate, with a view to substantially lowering interest rates, stabilizing and correcting misalignment in exchange rates, reducing protectionist pressures, expanding trade and financial flows, and reversing the declining trend in commodity prices.

3.   The areas covered in UNCTAD call for commensurate action in other important current and forthcoming multilateral economic activities, in particular the Uruguay Round and in the framework of the IMF and the World Bank.

4.   In order to enhance UNCTAD's capacity to exercise its central role and to ensure effective action in the interrelated areas of money, finance, debt, commodities, development and trade, the Trade and Development Board should strengthen its reviewing and monitoring on a regular basis of decisions and measures in these areas.[j]

---

[j] At the closing meeting of the Technical Committee it was unanimously agreed that the Chairman of the Committee should read out the following statement:

"It is recognized by all that, in order to make the work of the Trade and Development Board on this subject fruitful, it will be necessary for the UNCTAD secretariat to make adequate and careful preparation."

Annex VI

DOCUMENTS SUBMITTED BY REGIONAL GROUPS AND CHINA ON AGENDA ITEM 8*

A. *Document submitted by the United Kingdom on behalf of the States members of Group B*

Communiqué of the Council of the Organisation for Economic Co-operation and Development**

1. The Council of OECD met on 12 and 13 May at ministerial level. The meeting was chaired by Dr. Martin Bangemann, Federal Minister of Economics of the Federal Republic of Germany. The Vice-Chairmen were Mr. Uffe Ellemann-Jensen, Minister for Foreign Affairs, and Mr. Palle Simonsen, Minister of Finance, of Denmark; and Mr. Roger Douglas, Minister of Finance of New Zealand. On the fortieth anniversary of his Harvard speech, the Council paid a tribute to the vision of international co-operation framed by General George C. Marshall.

I. Improving growth prospects

2. The economic strategy of the OECD countries has, over recent years, brought inflation down to its lowest level for a generation, at the same time maintaining positive growth rates. The long-term effort must be pursued, taking account of developments, in order to strengthen the prospects for stable and sustainable growth; to reduce substantially the levels of unemployment—unacceptably high almost everywhere; to correct the massive current-account imbalances of the major countries; to consolidate the improvement in exchange rate configurations while achieving greater stability; and to improve the economic performance of developing countries. The first and foremost contribution that the OECD countries can make to world prosperity is to foster vigorous economies in an open multilateral trading system.

3. In order to achieve these objectives, Ministers agree upon the following wide-ranging and mutually reinforcing actions. They are based on a common will to use to the full the possibilities of international co-operation and to exploit for the best the interactions between macro-economic and structural adjustment policies. Improved policies in both fields are interrelated elements in the strategy for stronger growth of output and employment. Both are essential. Macro-economic policies stabilize expectations, build confidence for the medium-term and strengthen growth prospects. Micro-economic policies create a more dynamic and responsive environment, in which growth and adjustment forces are stronger and macro-economic policies are more effective.

II. Macro-economic policies

4. Macro-economic policies must respond simultaneously to three needs: maintaining medium-term orientations which contribute to the stability of expectations and building confidence; unwinding the present exceptionally large external imbalances of the major countries; exploiting to the full the potential for non-inflationary growth and thus for stronger job creation. International complementarity and compatibility of policies are essential in order that adjustment takes place in the perspective of growth and of exchange rate stability. Each country must make its contribution to the collective effort. In particular, the effective implementation of the commitments in the "Louvre agreement", together with those in the recent communiqué of the Group of Seven countries, shall be achieved quickly. Member countries will reinforce their co-operation, continue to review the policy requirements of the situation and introduce further measures as necessary.

5. Monetary policies, supported by fiscal policies, should remain geared towards growth of monetary aggregates and maintenance of financial market conditions consistent with low inflation objectives and real growth potential; they should also contribute to the orderly behaviour of exchange rates. In view of the outlook for low inflation in many countries, a further decline of interest rates in these countries—in particular a market-led decline of long-term rates—would be helpful.

6. Since the possibilities for monetary policy, by itself, to improve prospects are limited, these need to be enhanced by further action on the fiscal front.

7. In the United States, the process of reducing the Federal budget deficit—which is coming down from 5.2 per cent of GNP in 1986 to less than 4 per cent in 1987—must and will continue in the years ahead. Holding firm to this course is essential for external and

* For the agenda of the Conference, see annex I above.

** Initially circulated as TD/334. This communiqué was issued in OECD press release PRESS/A(87)27 of 13 May 1987. Terminology, including country terminology, is that employed by the authors of the communiqué and not that of the United Nations.

domestic reasons. The confidence of economic agents, in the United States and elsewhere, depends heavily upon it; so do, consequently, the prospects for moderate interest rates and stable exchange rates, sound economic activity with an adequate flow of funds into productive investment, and resistance to protectionist temptations. These highly beneficial effects of reducing the Federal budget deficits should over time outweigh any short-term damping effect in the United States. Exchange rate changes have improved the cost competitiveness of United States products and are having a positive effect on net exports.

8.   For Japan the objective is to achieve stronger growth with domestic demand increasing more rapidly than output, accompanied by a rapid growth in imports, consistent with the substantial terms of trade gains which have taken place. The reaffirmation by the Japanese Government of its intention to further improve access to its domestic markets for foreign goods and services is also welcome. The Japanese authorities will take further substantial fiscal and other measures to strengthen the growth of domestic demand. This will not prejudice medium-term budgetary objectives of the central Government. In this regard, it is to be noted that the recently announced Japanese initiative to expand domestic demand is part of the far-reaching longer-term effort to reorient the Japanese economy.

9.   In Germany, also, the growth of domestic demand, and particularly of private investment, must exceed substantially the growth of potential output. In order to support growth and external adjustment, the German Government has already announced that some scheduled tax cuts will be accelerated to 1 January 1988 and a broader tax reform will be implemented in 1990. This will have a favourable influence on investment. In addition, further measures of structural adjustment, including reduction of subsidies, will be implemented. Taken together, these actions will contribute to an increase of the general budget deficit relative to GNP between now and 1990. Fiscal prudence over recent years permits this kind of action. Should there be a serious risk to the sustained expansion of domestic demand, especially private investment, the medium-term strategy for growth and higher employment would be adjusted as a consequence.

10.   Other countries with substantial current-account surpluses should also take appropriate action to encourage domestic demand growth relative to sustainable output.

11.   Some countries face tight constraints in so far as fiscal policy is concerned. For countries which have large budget deficits, priority must continue to be given to correcting them. There are a few countries in Europe, however, where budget deficits are not large but where current-account considerations constrain policy. Scope for fiscal action on the part of these countries would be increased and growth prospects improved if demand strengthened in their major trading partners. In this latter respect, and as an example, a co-operative economic strategy of the EEC countries could take advantage of their interdependence and be accompanied by other European countries.

III.   Structural adjustment policies

12.   Ministers welcome the *Report on Structural Adjustment and Economic Performance.*[a] Despite progress in recent years, OECD economies are still hampered by major distortions and rigidities. These compound current macro-economic problems and retard growth. Increasing competition in product markets, responsiveness in factor markets and effectiveness in the public sector will contribute significantly to growth potential in all countries. Priorities in reforming structural policies will vary in individual countries reflecting differing national situations but also international requirements. It is thus essential that concerted action be guided by common principles. To ensure the greatest gains from reform, action must be broad, bold, sustained and, to the extent possible, built on international economic co-operation. The effects of such action will emerge mainly in the medium term. Implementation now, by expanding opportunities and bolstering confidence about the future, will underpin present efforts to strengthen non-inflationary growth and to reduce unemployment. Successful structural adjustment can simultaneously increase fairness and offer improving opportunities for all. Increasing social dialogue is an integral part of this process.

13.   Industrial subsidies, to the extent they are a source of domestic and international distortions and an impediment to structural adjustment, should be reduced. The work on industrial subsidies initiated by OECD is, therefore, to be encouraged and pursued actively.

14.   The conclusions drawn by the Economic Policy Committee[b] on the report on structural adjustment were endorsed and will guide action in the forthcoming years. The Secretary-General is requested to report, at appropriate intervals, on the work of the organization on micro-economic and structural issues at subsequent meetings of the Council at ministerial level.

Trade policies

15.   International trade provides, through competition, the most powerful means of promoting economic efficiency and growth. Measures which impede or distort the functioning of international markets tend to impair structural adjustment, preserve outdated economic structures, damage consumer interests, weaken incentives for efficient investment and thus hinder economic growth. Therefore, it is of paramount importance to reverse recent trends towards restrictive trade measures, notably of a bilateral or a discriminatory nature, and to act with determination to strengthen and extend the open multilateral trading system. OECD will intensify its monitoring of the various aspects of trade policies.

16.   The Uruguay Round presents a unique opportunity to create an improved framework for trade in the 1990s and beyond. It is essential to ensure that renewed signs of protectionism and conflict management on a bilateral basis should not be allowed to undermine con-

[a] OECD, Paris, 1988.

[b] See OECD press release PRESS/A(87)25.

fidence in the Punta del Este Declaration or in the negotiating process it has initiated. Ministers affirmed the determination of their countries to resist these trends and to work for rapid, sustained and substantive progress in the negotiations towards a balanced global result which would be of benefit to all, developed and developing countries alike. OECD countries will prove this determination by submitting in the coming months comprehensive proposals covering the various fields of the negotiations, by carrying out the standstill and rollback commitments they have entered into and by opposing domestic protectionist pressures. In keeping with the Punta del Este Declaration, Ministers reaffirmed that the conduct and the implementation of the outcome of the negotiations shall be treated as parts of a single undertaking. However, agreements reached at an early stage may be implemented on a provisional or a definitive basis by agreement prior to the formal conclusion of the negotiations. Early agreements shall be taken into account in assessing the overall balance of the negotiations.

17. Ministers noted the welcome progress on trade in services in the organization. This is of particular importance in the light of the inclusion of services in the Uruguay Round. Further related work will be needed to refine the concepts for liberalization of trade in services as well as continuing efforts to strengthen the OECD Codes of Liberalisation of Invisible Operations and of Capital Movements. This will be pursued actively.

18. Ministers welcome the agreement recently reached by the Participants in the Arrangement on Guidelines for Officially Supported Export Credits in response to directives from the 1984 and 1985 meetings of the Council of the OECD at ministerial level. The agreement will strengthen substantially the Arrangement and reduce the risk of trade and aid distortions. Ministers also welcomed the recent agreement on the related DAC guiding principles. These are a tangible sign of co-operation in a difficult period.

Agriculture

19. The joint report of the Trade and Agriculture Committees[c] was approved. This important work clearly highlights the serious imbalances that prevail in the markets for the main agricultural products. Boosted by policies which have prevented an adequate transmission of market signals to farmers, supply substantially exceeds effective demand. The cost of agricultural policies is considerable, for government budgets, for consumers and for the economy as a whole. Moreover, excessive support policies entail an increasing distortion of competition on world markets; run counter to the principle of comparative advantage which is at the root of international trade; and severely damage the situation of many developing countries. This steady deterioration, compounded by technological change and other factors such as slow economic growth or wide exchange rate changes, creates serious difficulties in international trade, which risk going beyond the bounds of agricultural trade alone.

20. All countries bear some responsibilities in the present situation. The deterioration must be halted and

---

[c] *National Policies and Agricultural Trade* (OECD, Paris, 1987).

reversed. Some countries, or groups of countries, have begun to work in this direction. But, given the scope of the problems and their agency, a concerted reform of agricultural policies will be implemented in a balanced manner.

21. Reform will be based on the following principles:

(*a*) The long-term objective is to allow market signals to influence by way of a progressive and concerted reduction of agricultural support, as well as by all other appropriate means, the orientation of agricultural production; this will bring about a better allocation of resources which will benefit consumers and the economy in general.

(*b*) In pursuing the long-term objective of agricultural reform, consideration may be given to social and other concerns, such as food security, environment protection or overall employment, which are not purely economic. The progressive correction of policies to achieve the long-term objective will require time; it is all the more necessary that this correction be started without delay.

(*c*) The most pressing need is to avoid further deterioration of present market imbalances. It is necessary:

  (i) On the demand side, to improve prospects as much as possible inside as well as outside the OECD area;

  (ii) On the supply side, to implement measures which, by reducing guaranteed prices and other types of production incentives, by imposing quantitative production restrictions, or by other means, will prevent an increase in excess supply.

(*d*) When production restrictions are imposed or productive farming resources withdrawn by administrative decision, these steps should be taken in such a way as to minimize possible economic distortions and should be conceived and implemented in such a way as to permit better functioning of market mechanisms.

(*e*) Rather than being provided through price guarantees or other measures linked to production or to factors of production, farm income support should, as appropriate, be sought through direct income support. This approach would be particularly well-suited to meeting the needs of, amongst others, low-income farmers, those in particularly disadvantaged regions, or those affected by structural adjustment in agriculture.

(*f*) The adjustment of the agricultural sector will be facilitated if it is supported by comprehensive policies for the development of various activities in rural areas. Farmers and their families will thus be helped to find supplementary or alternative income.

(*g*) In implementing the above principles, Governments retain flexibility in the choice of the means necessary for the fulfilment of their commitments.

22. The Uruguay Round is of decisive importance. The Ministerial Declaration of Punta del Este and its objectives provide for the improvement of market access and the reduction of trade barriers in agriculture and will furnish a framework for most of the measures necessary to give effect to the principles for agricultural reform agreed upon by OECD Ministers, including a progressive reduction of assistance to and protection of

agriculture on a multi-country and multi-commodity basis. As agreed in paragraph 16 above, the Uruguay Round negotiations will be vigorously pursued and comprehensive negotiating proposals submitted over the coming months, in this as in other fields. In the Uruguay Round appropriate account should be taken of actions made unilaterally.

23. In order to permit a de-escalation of present tensions and thereby enhance prospects for the earliest possible progress in the Uruguay Round as a whole, OECD Governments will carry out expeditiously their standstill and roll-back commitments and, more generally, refrain from actions which would worsen the negotiating climate: they will, *inter alia*, avoid initiating actions which would result in stimulating production in surplus agricultural commodities and in isolating the domestic market further from international markets; additionally, they will act responsibly in disposing of surplus stocks and refrain from confrontational and destabilizing trade practices.

24. Agricultural reform is not solely in the interests of member countries. Developing countries which are agricultural exporters will benefit from a recovery on world markets. Developing countries which are importers of agricultural produce will be encouraged to base their economic development on more solid ground, by strengthening their own farm sector.

25. Agricultural reform poses vast and difficult problems for member countries. Strengthened international co-operation is needed to overcome these problems. OECD will continue to contribute to their solution by deepening further its work; by updating and improving the analytical tools it has begun to develop and which will prove particularly valuable in many respects; by monitoring the implementation of the various actions and principles listed above. The Secretary-General is asked to submit a progress report to the Council at ministerial level in 1988.

Financial markets

26. The process of liberalization in financial markets and financial institutions must continue. In order to secure the clear benefits deriving from this process and to ensure the viability and stability of these markets, efforts will be intensified in the appropriate forums with a view to increasing compatibility and convergence of policies regarding prudential supervision of these markets.

Tax reform

27. Most OECD countries have undertaken or are considering major tax reforms. Well-constructed tax reform can considerably enhance performance at both macro- and micro-economic levels. Tax reform should focus on simplicity, equity and reducing distortions affecting incentives to work, save and invest. The competent bodies of the organization will actively contribute to reflection on tax reforms in member countries and consider the best means of achieving them with due respect given to international aspects.

Technological change

28. The development and diffusion of technology is central to the growth of output, employment and living standards. The process of technological change provides opportunities that must be grasped. Much work has already been done within the organization on analysing and interpreting various elements of this process. It now seems necessary to define an integrated and comprehensive approach to the different technology-related questions, to deepen the analysis in order to understand better, and make better use of, technological advances. The Secretary-General's intention to develop and carry out such an approach was welcomed. A progress report will be made to Ministers at their meeting in 1988.

Employment and socio-economic reform

29. In view of the seriousness of unemployment problems in most countries, three areas of socio-economic reform are particularly important—all involve, in varying degrees, the private sector and the social partners as well as Governments. First, there is a pressing need in many countries to improve the quality of education and training systems, and to adapt them more to the needs of societies and economies undergoing rapid structural change. Secondly, more flexible labour markets are needed to facilitate access to the new jobs emerging as structural and technical change accelerates. Thirdly, employment and social protection policies need to evolve so that displaced and unemployed people are given not only income support but also—especially through training—opportunities and incentives to get back into work or other useful activities such as local employment initiatives. OECD work in these areas will be intensified, a key aim being to prepare a new framework for labour market policies as agreed at the meeting of the Manpower and Social Affairs Committee at ministerial level in November 1986.

Environment

30. There is general agreement that environmental concerns have to be given a high priority in government policies, in order to safeguard and improve the quality of life as well as to preserve the resource base needed for sustained global economic development. Member countries will develop, within OECD, approaches and methods for more systematically and effectively incorporating environmental considerations into the policy-making process. Work will be intensified on policies needed to prevent more effectively the release of hazardous substances to the environment, including from large-scale accidents. In this connection, international co-operation should be reinforced. The recently presented report of the World Commission on Environment and Development, *Our Common Future*,[d] will be studied closely in member Governments and in the organization.

Energy

31. The past year has seen considerable falls in the prices of oil, gas and coal. Although lower energy prices

---

[d] Oxford, Oxford University Press, 1987.

have broad economic benefits, they tend to increase consumption and reduce indigenous production of energy. The Chernobyl reactor accident has underlined the safety aspects of nuclear power. These developments could intensify the tightening of energy markets expected for the 1990s. The Governing Board of the International Energy Agency, meeting at ministerial level on 11 May 1987, agreed to strengthen existing policies in a number of areas in order to advance the objectives of energy policy while continuing to secure the general benefits of lower energy and oil prices. These areas include indigenous energy production, the efficient use of energy, diversification of sources of primary energy, particularly those used in the generation of electricity, the promotion of free and open trade in energy, measures to respond to an interruption in oil supplies, and due recognition of environmental concerns.

IV. Relations with developing countries

32. In a world characterized by an increasing level of interdependence, the economic problems and performance of developing countries have become increasingly diverse. Although a number of developing countries, particularly in Asia, have made significant progress, many others have suffered economic set-backs in recent years. Economic co-operation with developing countries must respond to varying capacities and needs in the critical areas of development, trade, debt and finance. Developed countries must strive to ensure a better environment for developing countries' growth and exports in the interest of these countries as well as of the international economy more generally. In this regard, the implementation of the policy directions and objectives set out in this Communiqué will represent a significant contribution by OECD countries to better global prospects.

33. Economic policies in developing countries themselves will remain a major factor in their own performance. Upon them depend heavily confidence, savings and investment, both domestic and foreign. The wide range of developing countries presently implementing economic policy reforms to establish a sound development process must be supported and encouraged by all possible means including improved market access and official development assistance. In this regard, it is important to maintain and as far as possible increase the flow of development assistance, as well as to improve its quality and effectiveness. Those developing countries whose economic strength is already significant should progressively play their full part in the rights and obligations of the multilateral

trading system. It is important that the potential offered by the private sector be fully exploited.

34. Large debt burdens remain a major impediment to growth in certain heavily indebted middle-income countries. There is no feasible alternative today to the co-operative strategy adopted for the solution of these problems. Only enhanced co-operative action, on a case-by-case basis, by all parties involved—debtor and creditor Governments, the international financial institutions and private banks—will permit reducing the strains in a growth-promoting environment. For some countries notable progress has been made in this process. However, in some cases difficulties in the adjustment and financing processes point to the need for improvements. The trend towards innovative and more flexible approaches on the financing side, both private and official, should play a key role in making debt burdens more manageable and restoring capital flows.

35. Even more constraining are debt problems among low-income countries. Proposals have recently been made by OECD countries for additional action to reduce the debt-servicing burden of the poorest countries, especially in sub-Saharan Africa, undertaking strong growth-oriented adjustment programmes. Early results from the current discussions among creditor Governments will be urgently sought.

36. For poorer developing countries, provision of adequate concessional finance is essential. OECD countries' record in this respect is already substantial but should be further enhanced. The volume and forms of aid must be commensurate with the growing requirements of policy reform programmes and broader development efforts. The new DAC guiding principles for using aid to support improved development policies and programmes and strengthening aid co-ordination with developing countries are welcomed.

37. Commodity-dependent developing countries face difficult problems in view of the outlook for many commodities. An acceleration in world growth would improve the prospects for these countries. New efforts should be made to diversify their economies and to address the structural and development dimensions of commodity dependence. Action to remove measures distorting trade in commodities will make an important contribution to export prospects for commodity-dependent developing countries.

38. The seventh session of the Conference provides an opportunity to discuss with developing countries the major problems and policy issues in the global economy with a view to promoting common perceptions and effective policies for trade and development.

B. *Approach of the countries members of Group D and Mongolia to the major items of the provisional agenda of the seventh session of the United Nations Conference on Trade and Development**

I. Introduction

The seventh session of the United Nations Conference on Trade and Development, which is to be held in Geneva from 9 to 31 July 1987, will constitute the year's most important international meeting devoted to trade and economic problems.

It will be taking place in a context reflecting the complexity of and contradictions inherent in the development of the world economy and of multilateral trade and economic co-operation.

The realities of today's world make it vitally necessary for Governments and peoples to change their way of thinking, particularly in view of the high stakes involved, namely, the preservation of civilization and the survival of mankind. A new understanding of the ultimate responsibility of all for the future of development is emerging in the world at the present time. This implies that the international community must, as a matter of urgency, develop new approaches to the solution of vitally important foreign policy and world economic problems, specifically by turning its back on outdated political and economic thinking and by reviewing unjustified assessments of outstanding problems and methods of their solution.

The exposure of national economies to the external environment, in this modern interrelated and interdependent world of ours, is increasing considerably owing to the growing complexity of international economic relations. The new thinking called for in this sphere should result in the complete replacement of confrontation in the international arena by a joint search for solutions to the most difficult problems presented by today's world economy, ensuring its stability and predictable development. This new, realistic and constructive thinking within UNCTAD should lead to broad, genuinely equitable and mutually advantageous co-operation between all groups of countries and to joint efforts to solve complex problems in that field.

The need for an approach of this kind is explained not only by the complexity of the problems involved but also by the fact that they can be solved only through concerted action by the international community as a whole, for which there is no mutually acceptable and reasonable alternative. All countries in today's world are linked by a community of vital interests, notwithstanding differences in their political systems, ideologies and views. In view of the increasing interdependence of States, it is not only difficult but quite out of the question for them to solve their problems alone or in isolated groups. Their solution calls for concerted efforts by all countries of the world, regardless of their social system and level of economic development.

Specifically, progress in this direction could be made by the achievement of international economic security, the concept of which is at present being studied within the United Nations in accordance with General Assembly resolutions 40/173 and 41/184. The assurance of stable, predictable and equitable economic relations could serve as a basis for this concept. The concept of international economic security, far from replacing the idea of establishing a new international economic order is, on the contrary, capable of contributing to its realization in accordance with the wishes of the developing countries, expressed specifically in the Economic Declaration adopted by the Eighth Conference of Heads of State or Government of Non-Aligned Countries, held in September 1986 at Harare.[e] At the present stage, the concept of international economic security, presented as a general idea concerning the need for international economic security, not only provides impetus in the right direction but constitutes a starting-point for the efforts that are implied. However, it requires further elaboration and definition in detail, and it can obviously be developed only through broad, constructive and unbiased discussion.

This is precisely the purpose of the proposals made by the socialist countries on matters relating to the relationship between disarmament and development. The realization of the "disarmament for development" principle, which should replace the "armament instead of development" principle, would be of considerable economic advantage to all countries, including the developing countries.

If effective arms limitation and reduction measures were implemented, part of the resources released as a result of disarmament could be used for economic and social development, particularly that of the developing countries. Not only the development process but also international economic co-operation would be considerably stimulated by the implementation of agreed disarmament plans accompanied by measures to strengthen confidence and expand co-operation between States. These issues have a direct bearing on the work of

---

* Initially circulated as TD/333 and Corr.1.

[e] See A/41/697, annex.

UNCTAD, in which they could be examined from a practical point of view.

The policy adopted by many socialist countries aimed at effecting changes in their national economies with a view to their accelerated development similarly opens up further possibilities for the expansion of international economic co-operation. The restructuring process also covers the foreign economic sphere. These objectives cannot be achieved unilaterally. Their atteinment also implies commensurate efforts on the part of countries which are interested in developing economic co-operation with the socialist countries and in creating a climate of confidence and equality in economic relations, particularly between East and West, removing obstacles on this path, doing away with the shackles of the past and eliminating artificial barriers to mutually advantageous economic exchanges. The achievement of a favourable climate in this sphere also calls for new thinking, a broad and impartial dialogue, and a patient search for mutually acceptable solutions. This approach corresponds to the realities of today's world and offers the most promising alternative solution for the complex problems faced by the Conference at its seventh session, which will have to devise new approaches in order to increase the effectiveness of international co-operation in the interest of the economic and social progress of all peoples.

*

* *

In the light of the above, the delegations of the Group D countries will contribute actively to the resumption of a constructive multilateral dialogue within UNCTAD on the most urgent international economic problems with a view to the establishment of secure and predictable economic conditions in the interest of all countries. This would not only be in line with UNCTAD's mandate but would also have the effect of strengthening it as a universal international organization, searching for mutually acceptable solutions to world-wide economic problems in the interrelated areas of international trade, monetary and financial matters, commodities and economic development. UNCTAD should reaffirm its own undisputed place in the modern world among international economic organizations. And in this respect the interests of all countries should be taken into account.

II. Assessment of the present state of international economic relations

International economic relations developed in a complex and contradictory manner during the period following the sixth session of the Conference. On the one hand, the international division of labour continued, the economic interdependence of States increased following a decline during the 1980-1982 crisis, and foreign trade once again started to expand.

On the other hand, many of the economic and trade policy problems that were discussed at the sixth session of the Conference became even more acute, and new obstacles emerged to hamper equitable international economic exchanges. The general world market situation deteriorated and instability increased and the irregular pattern of economic development became more pronounced throughout the world economy.

The expansion of international trade also slowed down as a result not only of a slackening of economic growth but also of increasing deficits in the trade and payments balances of many countries, the high level of external indebteness, falling commodity prices, exchange rate instability, traditional as well a new forms of protectionism, and a general deterioration in the situation as regards trade policy.

Multilateral economic co-operation was considerably weakened. Many progressive solutions to the problem of improving international economic relations adopted by various bodies, including UNCTAD, were not implemented and attempts were made to review and even cancel programmes and recommendations that had already been adopted. Discrimination against the socialist countries and a number of developing countries was maintained and in some cases even intensified, sometimes for political reasons.

The economies of the socialist countries in general expanded steadily. However the general deterioration of the international economic situation had a negative impact on their development as well. These countries were, at one and the same time, obliged to find solutions to a number of complex problems connected with the restructuring of their economies, switching over from extensive to intensive methods of development and seeking ways of participating more actively in the international division of labour.

The structural adjustments being made to the economic machinery of a number of socialist countries through the improvement of economic management methods are designed to speed up their economic development and will help to expand their external economic relations not only with other socialist countries but with other countries of the world as well.

In most of the developed capitalist countries production growth rates were low and unstable, structural imbalances became more pronounced, high unemployment levels persisted and assumed a chronic character, State budget deficits increased, financial systems were disrupted and the exchange rates of the major currencies experienced sharp fluctuations.

The policies pursued by the Governments of the developed capitalist countries failed—to the extent required—to bring about the structural changes conducive to economic expansion. Furthermore, these policies had the effect of transferring some of the problems created by the adaptation and structural adjustment of their economies to other countries, particularly the developing countries.

The internal and external economic situation of most of the developing countries deteriorated considerably owing to the continued growth of their external indebtedness, increasing protectionism, declining commodity prices, the outflow of their resources in various ways to the developed capitalist countries, the activities of TNCs and a number of other unfavourable developments. The economic growth of this group of countries as a whole virtually ground to a halt and it was impossible to attain the objectives laid down in the International Development Strategy for the Third United Nations Development Decade.[f]

In most of these countries problems connected with employment and the task of supplying the population with foodstuffs became more acute, and government social programmes, investments and appropriations for research and development were curtailed. Differences between the developing countries became more pronounced.

III. Monetary and financial questions

Present international monetary and financial relations are characterized by considerable instability and the existence of serious crisis factors which suggest the possibility of further disruptions not only in the financial and economic spheres and in world trade, but in all other areas of international economic and political relations as well.

The external indebtedness of the developing countries, which now exceeds $1,000 billion, continues to be a source of increasing concern. The seriousness of the situation is obvious from the fact that this amount accounts for about 50 per cent of the GNP of the developing countries and that debt-servicing payments exceed one quarter of their export earnings.

One of the main development problems of the mid-1980s is the outflow of resources from the developing countries. Whereas in the 1970s this outflow was accompanied by the relatively rapid growth of certain parts of the third world, the outflow of resources from many developing countries has assumed such proportions in the 1980s that they are experiencing a sharp drop in income, stagnation and the undermining of the development process. For the first time in the postcolonial era a net transfer of financial resources from the developing to the developed capitalist countries occurred; it is estimated that in 1985 the amount in question was $31 billion. The actual outflow, in the opinion of the socialist countries, is much greater.

The situation has become one in which the developing countries no longer receive financial resources but have become a source of financing for the developed capitalist countries. The most important contributing factors in this respect include higher interest rates on loans, the remittance of profits from foreign direct investments, the covert remittance of profits by subsidiaries of TNCs through transfer prices, the flight of capital, etc.

At the same time the flow of financial resources to the developing countries has declined. For example, since the sixth session of the Conference the amount of ODA made available by the developed capitalist countries has not reached the 1982 level. The conditions on which export credits were granted have in general had the result of an increase in the cost of imports of the developing countries from the developed capitalist countries.

The socialist countries of Group D are of the view that present international monetary and financial prob-

lems must be solved as rapidly as possible so that the development process can be resumed, international trade expanded and equal economic security assured for all States.

External indebtedness

The socialist countries consider that, with respect to the problem of external indebtedness, the developed capitalist countries bear considerable responsibility for the present international monetary and financial crisis and the deterioration of the economic situation of the developing countries. The relations of the socialist countries with the developing countries are based on principles of equality and mutual advantage, and have never been the cause of the payments difficulties experienced by their developing country partners.

They call for the solution of the external indebtedness problem in the light of the interests of all countries and in the context of the restructuring of international economic relationships on a just, equitable and democratic basis.

Such solutions could include:

The reduction of inflated interest rates on loans;

The stabilization of exchange rates;

Concerted efforts by the international community to seek effective means of arriving at a just solution of the indebtedness problem and ensuring general economic security;

Reduction of the outflow of resources from the developing countries; and

Agreement to refrain from using the monetary and financial difficulties of individual countries as a means of exerting political pressure and interfering in the internal affairs of sovereign States.

The General Assembly, at its forty-first session, adopted resolution 41/202 which specifically makes provision for action within the United Nations aimed at resolving external debt problems. In this respect UNCTAD could, within its area of competence, also contribute to their solution. Specifically, it could help to create general conditions conducive to the improvement of international monetary and financial relations on the basis of equality and mutual advantage and subject to the understanding that States refrain from the use of monetary and financial factors as a means of exerting political pressure and threatening the economic security of other States.

Outflow of resources from the developing countries

The socialist countries of Group D abide by their consistent position on the question of the outflow of resources from the developing countries, a question which they have always regarded as an important reason for the monetary and financial difficulties of those countries. They consider that this problem should be interpreted in a broad manner and that the elements used in calculating its magnitude should include deterioration of the terms of trade, monopolistic price formation practices, the flight of capital, the impact of exchange rate fluctuations of the major currencies of the developed capitalist countries, etc.

---

[f] General Assembly resolution 35/56 of 5 December 1980, annex.

The socialist countries are of the view that in accordance with Economic and Social Council resolution 1986/56, which calls upon organizations of the United Nations system "to take appropriate and effective measures in the fields of money, trade and finance . . . in order to halt and reverse the net transfer of resources from developing to developed countries", UNCTAD should adopt specific recommendations in this area and begin to work actively on the problem of the net outflow of resources.

Official development assistance

The socialist countries of Group D provide the developing States with all kinds of economic, scientific and technical assistance.

They support the position adopted by the Group of 77 concerning the inadmissibility of exerting political pressure on the developing countries in deciding whether or not they should be granted ODA.

The socialist countries wish to point out that the possibilities of an increase in the availability of obtaining the additional resources that are so necessary to satisfy economic and social requirements, including those of the developing countries, are offered by disarmament and the reduction of military expenditures. The implementation of the programme for the general reduction of armaments presented by the socialist countries will enable all the developed countries of the world to allocate additional resources to development.

Group D considers that UNCTAD should contribute to the elaboration of principles of using—for the benefit of the international community, and above all that of the developing countries—a part of the resources that will be released as a result of the reduction of military budgets.

Mobilization of domestic resources

The position of the socialist countries on this question is based on the possible balanced development of the State, co-operative and private sectors. However, Group D emphasizes the priority of the first sector in the main branches of the economy and the need for effective State regulation of the public and private sectors.

High interest rates, which are the result of the macro-economic policy of certain developed capitalist countries, considerably undermine the financing of development from domestic sources since a significant proportion of resources must be used to service the external debt. A reduction of interest rates and the solution of the external debt problem will considerably enhance the savings and investment potential of the developing countries.

Military expenditures on armaments constitute a serious obstacle to development for many developing countries. The aggregate military expenditures of the developing countries as a proportion of world military expenditures are greater than their share of the world GNP.

The implementation of a programme of general and complete disarmament as rapidly as possible will have the effect of making available for development purposes domestic resources at present being used unproductively in addition to supplementary external resources (ODA).

The reform of the international monetary system

Group D:

Supports the idea of more rapid action to reform the international monetary and financial system in the interest of all countries;

Supports the idea of strengthening the role of international currency units, including the need for a supplementary issue of special drawing rights and the withdrawal from the system of international settlements of surplus United States dollars by means of "substitution accounts";

Supports the proposal to mitigate extensive and prolonged fluctuations in currency exchange rates;

Considers that UNCTAD should, in accordance with its mandate, make greater use of its possibilities of influencing the development and improvement of the international monetary system.

IV. Trade in commodities

Overall assessment

A striking feature of the current situation in international commodity markets has been their growing instability.

More frequent and abrupt rises and falls in commodity prices have distorted long-term market trends, creating an uneven distribution of productive resources, and this in turn has been causing even greater instability on commodity markets.

The sectoral and macro-economic policies of the developed capitalist countries have together contributed to the present aggravation of these trends. Increased protectionism, particularly in the agricultural sectors, and the growing direct and indirect subsidization of the production and exports of commodities have substantially deformed an already imperfect market mechanism, weakened the relationship between supply and demand, and added to the disarray on many commodity markets. This, combined with high interest rates, the instability of exchange rates and an enormous rise in the indebtedness of the developing countries and debt-servicing costs, is clouding prospects of achieving economic security for the developing countries, which depend on the production and exports of commodities.

The Group D countries believe that the above-mentioned adverse trends should be counteracted by co-ordinated efforts on the part of the international community aimed at the greatest possible intensification of co-operation between the producers and consumers of commodities.

Since the sixth session of the Conference, work has continued on implementing the Integrated Programme for commodities. The elaboration of an International Tropical Timber Agreement was completed. A new International Cocoa Agreement, 1986, came into force and may be regarded as the first in a new generation of international commodity agreements. Negotiations on the International Natural Rubber Agreement were successfully completed. A new International Olive Oil Agreement was concluded. Terms of reference were agreed upon for the International Nickel Study Group. As a result, a larger number of commodities are now covered by international commodity agreements or other arrangements. UNCTAD became somewhat more active in co-ordinating the work of the intergovernmental commodities bodies.

In co-operation with international commodity organizations, UNCTAD carried out extensive analytical work to study the operation, effectiveness and role of ICAs in attaining the objectives of the IPC. This work resulted in the adoption by the Committee on Commodities in December 1985 of recommendations to improve the machinery of ICAs[g] which took into account the main deficiencies of previous ICAs and outlined ways of overcoming them. Within the framework of UNCTAD, efforts were undertaken during the inter-sessional period to intensify work on problems in the area of processing, marketing and distribution, including transportation, of commodities.

The Group D countries reaffirm the need to strengthen by every possible means the role of UNCTAD in dealing with world commodity trade problems, in accordance with its mandate as defined in General Assembly resolution 1995 (XIX) and other basic resolutions (for example, Conference resolution 93 (IV)), and also emphasize the role of UNCTAD in co-ordinating the activities of other bodies in the field of commodities. Work on commodity problems should be accorded priority in UNCTAD's future activities.

Integrated Programme for Commodities

The Group D countries share the view that the IPC is of continuing relevance. Work on the conclusion of ICAs, as well as in the area of processing, marketing and distribution, including transportation, of commodities and on the problems of protectionism, trade liberalization and increased access to markets should be pursued.

International commodity agreements

The countries of Group D consider that, notwithstanding the difficulties in negotiating new ICAs or renegotiating existing ones with a stabilization mechanism, such agreements are still the most acceptable instrument for international co-operation in the field of commodity trade, since they take into account the interests of both exporters and importers of commodities, bring about the conditions required to eliminate fluctuations in prices, limit the opportunities for TNCs to manipulate the commodity markets in their own interests and, to some extent, restrain speculation in the commodity markets. The basic approach of the Group D countries to the elaboration of ICAs is consistent with the above-mentioned recommendations made by the Committee on Commodities at its eleventh session.

Group D supports the proposal by the Group of 77 for the continuation within UNCTAD of preparatory work on commodities not covered by ICAs.

Processing, marketing and distribution, including transportation, of commodities

The socialist countries of Group D consider that, since the control of the TNCs over the processing and marketing of commodities has increased considerably in recent years, effective national and international controls on the activities of TNCs in the area of processing, marketing and distribution, including transportation, of commodities are essential.

The question of increasing the role of the developing countries in the system of marketing the commodities they produce is also closely bound up with the problems of liberalizing trade in processed commodities, the need to improve access to the markets of the developed capitalist countries and efforts to combat protectionism in agricultural commodities.

The socialist countries of Group D consider that some attention also deserves to be given to evaluating and promoting horizontal and vertical diversification in the commodity sectors of the developing countries. Insufficient importance has so far been attached in UNCTAD to this question, yet a number of developing countries have been successfully applying such policies and their experience merits attention.

Group D intends to contribute to the achievement of positive results at the seventh session of the Conference in the area of the normalization of world commodity trade.

V. International trade, including structural adjustment, trade in services and trade relations among countries having different economic and social systems

Trade policy

The seventh session of the Conference will take place against an extremely complicated background as regards trade policy, one which is characterized by continuing erosion of the system of international trade and increasingly widespread use of protectionist measures in world trade, and which thus threatens the economic security of States.

The main aspects of these negative processes in the area of international trade are:

Even more frequent and harmful departures from the basic principles of international trade policy (MFN treatment and non-discrimination);

The frequent imposition of restrictions in trade, based on political motives;

The widespread violation of international treaty obligations in the field of trade practised by the leading Western States, which are also the largest trading partners.

A particularly complicated situation as regards trade policy has occurred in those sectors of world trade which, practically, are not covered by General Agreement rules (for example, agriculture) or in which depar-

---

[g] See *Official Records of the Trade and Development Board, Thirty-second Session, Supplement No. 4* (TD/B/1085), annex I, decision 23 (XI).

tures from multilateral General Agreement rules have been legalized (textiles and clothing).

Various new non-tariff trade restrictions are being imposed on a wide scale to circumvent General Agreement rules (for example, so-called "voluntary export restraints"). Wider use is being made of restrictions by trading firms (restrictive business practices), this being associated above all with the activities of TNCs. These various restrictions affect the trading interests of the socialist and developing countries in particular. They are a serious threat to international trade as a whole.

In the present situation, the socialist countries consider that:

(1) It is in the long-term strategic interest of all countries to create conditions in international trade and economic relations that will ensure their economic security. To this end, the principle of the sovereign equality of States must be fully realized in international economic relations, an objective which can only be achieved, however, through application of non-discrimination and MFN treatment in international trade.

The existing principles and rules of the system of international trade are consistent with these requirements. International trade relations, therefore, have worsened not because these principles and rules are now irrelevant or obsolete, but because many countries are pursuing trade policies which ignore these international principles.

(2) The socialist countries are firmly convinced that the existing principles and rules of international trade, such as the principles of MFN treatment and non-discrimination, are in the interest of all countries, and for this reason they will oppose the legitimization of departures from these principles.

(3) Our commitment to MFN treatment and non-discrimination does not mean that the socialist countries dispute the right of the developing countries to differential and more favourable treatment. The trade preferences granted to the developing countries do not constitute a violation of the basic principles of the system, but rather are exceptions recognized internationally.

The socialist countries continue to support the need for preferential and differential treatment in trade for the developing countries.

(4) The socialist countries recognize the importance of reaffirming commitments to "standstill" and "roll-back" and their observance on a universal basis.

(5) The socialist countries are in favour of all interested countries having the opportunity to participate in the Uruguay Round, since the new round of negotiations on the problems of world trade effects the interests of all those taking part in it. The socialist countries consider it important that, as in the case of the Tokyo Round, UNCTAD should review and evaluate the results of the Uruguay Round.

(6) The socialist countries also note the interrelationship between protectionism and structural adjustment, i.e., the fact that the wave of protectionism is mainly due to the inadequacy of the structural changes taking place in the developed capitalist countries. They call for continued discussion in UNCTAD of the question of protectionism and structural adjustment.

Structural adjustment

In considering the questions of structural adjustment in the world economy, the socialist countries take the view that the effective implementation of structural adjustment in individual countries and their greater participation in the international division of labour is an objective necessity for the further development of the world economy. This process should take into account the economic interests of all groups of countries and contribute to the establishment of democratic and equitable international economic relations. When discussing structural changes within the framework of the United Nations, consideration must at the same time be given to all the various social, economic and political aspects of this process. Appropriate structural adjustment in the world economy can be carried out successfully only in conditions of mutual confidence among States and of good will on their part. As for the developing countries, structural changes should help in gradually overcoming their economic and technological backwardness and in meeting the domestic needs of their economies in general, and should also contribute to appropriate social transformations.

The socialist countries support:

(*a*) The establishment of a system of international economic security and confidence among States, which is essential in creating a favourable climate for the development of economic co-operation among States;

(*b*) The exercise of the requisite political will to help in solving the economic problems of the developing countries;

(*c*) The adoption of specific measures aimed at limiting the arms race and gradually achieving disarmament, reducing the arms spending of all countries and using the resources thus released for social and economic development, including that of the developing countries.

International trade in services

For objective reasons services are becoming an increasingly important factor in the economic development of all countries.

Trade in services differs substantially from trade in commodities and involves not only economic but also social issues, and at times even the sovereignty of States.

Growing importance is justifiably being attached to the problems of trade in services in international economic organizations, including UNCTAD.

In this regard, the socialist countries consider it important that the UNCTAD secretariat should undertake the preparation of basic comprehensive studies, taking particular account of the important role of service in the process of economic development of all countries and in improving the overall international competitiveness of their economies. They will be of assistance in the formulation of relevant proposals in this area.

In connection with the Uruguay Round of multilateral trade negotiations which have now commenced, dealing, *inter alia*, with matters relating to trade in services, the socialist countries believe that UNCTAD should serve as a forum for the discussion of the progress and results of these negotiations, with a view to protecting the interests of all parties concerned in the international trade in services.

Trade relations among countries having different economic and social systems

The approach of the socialist countries to trade relations among countries having different economic and social systems is based on the following principal considerations.

(1) They reaffirm the universal nature of UNCTAD's mandate in accordance with General Assembly resolution 1995 (XIX).

(2) They express their readiness to develop a constructive dialogue and co-operation with every group of countries, in view of the interdependence of all trade flows, for the purpose of removing existing obstacles and establishing favourable conditions for reciprocal trade while fully observing the principle of the sovereign equality of all countries.

(3) They call for a business-like and constructive discussion of the problems, prospects and ways of developing the trade of the socialist countries with the developed capitalist and developing countries, making active use of the analytical report of the Secretary-General of UNCTAD, particularly chapter IV. They support the harmonization and adoption of an extensive document on further promotion of trade and economic co-operation among countries having different economic and social systems, based on the proposals of the UNCTAD secretariat in TD/B/1104 and the acceptable elements of the draft resolution annexed to Conference decision 145 (VI).

(4) They call for the expansion of UNCTAD activities to provide technical assistance in trade between the developing and socialist countries, first and foremost with resources from UNDP.

VI. The least developed countries

The socialist countries share the view that progress achieved thus far in this area is very modest indeed. The economic and social situation of the LDCs is continuing to deteriorate. Implementation of the Substantial New Programme of Action for the 1980s for the Least Developed Countries is proceeding slowly. The situation facing the LDCs is to a considerable extent the result of existing inequitable international economic relations.

It has also become obvious that the cyclical economic revival in some leading industrialized capitalist countries in the mid-1980s has not had a positive impact on the developing countries.

The socialist countries believe that, in discussing this question, the Conference should focus attention on the following two aspects:

An analysis of the reasons for the failure to implement fully the decisions which have already been adopted on this problem;

The identification of internal and external factors likely to stimulate the socio-economic development of the LDCs.

Bearing in the mind the recommendations of the mid-term review of implementation of the Substantial New Programme of Action, the socialist countries intend, in the latter half of the 1980s, to pursue trade and economic policies likely to bring about greater co-operation with the LDCs as a result of an extension of its geographical framework; further diversification of a mutually advantageous division of labour with interested LDCs; supplying these countries with the machinery, equipment and other producers' goods they require; increasing exports of their domestic output to the socialist countries, including the development of exports on a long-term basis; assisting the LDCs in strengthening their State planning systems in the economic field; and providing assistance where possible to interested LDCs for the development of industry and of some other sectors.

The socialist countries are sympathetic to the proposal regarding the need to enhance the role of UNCTAD within the United Nations system in addressing the problems of the LDCs. On the other hand, our countries believe that the United Nations regional commissions should make a more substantial contribution to the implementation of the Substantial New Programme of Action, and also participate in monitoring progress in the implementation of that programme.

The socialist countries consider that the UNCTAD secretariat should, on a regular basis, prepare up-to-date information regarding the situation of the LDCs, and analyse the results achieved in implementing the Substantial New Programme of Action. This analysis and information should be made available to all countries participating in UNCTAD.

C. *Position paper of the People's Republic of China on issues to be considered at the seventh session of the Conference**

The seventh session of the United Nations Conference on Trade and Development is being convened against the background of a critical international economic situation, characterized by weak growth of the world economy, a volatile monetary and financial situation and a slow development of international trade. The developed countries are experiencing slow economic growth, and the economic and trade conflicts among

---

* Initially circulated as TD/331.

them have intensified. As for developing countries, their economies are stagnating, while the external economic environment continues to deteriorate. Rising protectionism and the drastic falling of commodity prices have substantially reduced the export earnings of the developing countries. This situation, coupled with the shortage of resources for development and increasing indebtedness, has seriously hindered their economic development. As a result, the gap between the North and the South is widening.

The international community is confronted with the two interrelated challenges of peace and development. Peace is a prerequisite for economic development, while economic development in turn contributes to peace and stability. At a time when there is an increasing interdependence in international economic relations, the economic development of individual countries depends both on their own efforts and policies and on a favourable external environment and international co-operation. Developing countries are shaping their social and economic systems and development strategies in accordance with their own development needs and specific social and economic conditions. Many of them are carrying out arduous adjustment processes for a rapid development in the light of their respective conditions. However, these difficulties have been exacerbated by the deteriorating international economic environment. The developed countries, particularly the major developed countries, should thus give full consideration to the interests of developing countries when formulating their domestic economic policies and co-ordinating their macro-economic policies, so as to avoid an adverse impact on the developing countries and help improve the external conditions for the economic development of those countries. The developed countries should give priority to improving the market access and the transfer of funds and technology to the developing countries. Stable and enduring economic prosperity of the developed countries can be achieved only through the economic development and the elimination of poverty in the developing countries.

As a forum in the United Nations system for both developing and developed countries to discuss trade and development issues and hold substantive negotiations, UNCTAD should take the opportunity offered by the seventh session of the Conference to actively promote North-South dialogue and improve the economic relation between the North and the South. The session should contribute to the strengthening of multilateral co-operation, finding solutions for the urgent problems facing the developing countries, promote the development of international trade and the international economy and facilitate the establishment of a new international economic order. China notes with appreciation the correct propositions and reasonable proposals put forward by the Group of 77 at its Sixth Ministerial Meeting and hopes that they will be given due attention by the Conference.

China wishes to clarify its principled position as follows *vis-à-vis* several substantive items on the agenda for the session, so as to facilitate discussion with other delegations.

I. Resources for development

At present, the developing countries are suffering from a serious shortage of resources for development and an increasing debt burden. The difficulties confronting them cannot be resolved without (*a*) expanding the sources of their development resources; and (*b*) reducing their external debts.

The developed countries should increase their financial flows to developing countries, especially their ODA. Some developed countries have reached or surpassed the ODA target established by the United Nations, but there are still many which have not done so. Developed countries, especially the major economic powers, including those countries with huge trade surpluses, should make serious efforts to attain the above target as soon as possible. At the same time, the developed countries should expand their export credit to the developing countries. They should encourage their own enterprises while respecting the laws of host countries to increase their direct investment in the developing countries. They should also urge their commercial banks to increase commercial lending to developing countries on more favourable terms.

Creditor countries, commercial banks, international financial institutions, and the debtor countries themselves should share the responsibility in solving in debt problem. This should be done through the economic growth of debtor countries, i.e. by increasing their capacity to repay their debt, rather than at the sacrifice of their development process. In addition, the solution of the debt problem should be associated with an improvement in the terms of trade of the developing countries and with an easier access by developing countries to the markets of the developed countries. The reasonable proposals by some debtor countries to limit their debt repayments to a certain ratio of their own economic growth rate and export earnings should be given serious consideration. Developed creditor countries should make a serious effort to implement Trade and Development Board resolutions 165 (S-IX) and 222 (XXI) by lowering interest rates and liberalizing repayment terms for the benefit of the developing countries.

Moreover, solving the problems of resources for development and debts confronting the developing countries requires a more favourable international financial environment and a more rational and more stable international monetary system. International financial institutions should contribute to mobilizing resources for development for the developing countries by increasing concessional loans for them. IMF should, as soon as possible, make a new allocation of special drawing rights. The international community should make further efforts to reform the international monetary system, strengthen the regulation of rational flow of international capital and improve the terms on which the developing countries can find access to the international financial markets.

II. Commodities

During the 1980s, the situation regarding commodities has steadily deteriorated. Commodity prices have fallen to their lowest level since the Great Depression of the 1930s, inflicting extremely adverse impact on the healthy development of the world economy, especially on the economic development of the developing countries. For this reason, the international community should take effective measures to stabilize commodity prices and to improve the worsening terms of trade afflicting the developing countries, so as to promote their socio-economic development.

At the seventh session, the Conference should promote the full implementation of the Integrated Programme for Commodities and the early entry into force of the Agreement Establishing the Common Fund for Commodities.[h] In an effort to break the deadlock over commodities, it should urge those major powers that have not yet done so to ratify the Agreement as soon as possible.

In the spirit of the IPC and according to the specific characteristics of the different commodities, the international community should continue its efforts to conclude ICAs containing price stabilizing and other measures. In order to enhance research development in the field of commodities and to increase market transparency, it should give serious consideration to additional measures which would help stabilize prices and increase the export earnings of the developing countries.

The international community and the developed countries should emphasize, and provide financial support for, the diversification of the commodities produced and exported by the developing countries. One important way of achieving such diversification and increasing export earnings is to ensure greater participation by the developing countries in the processing, marketing and distribution, including transport, of commodities. The developed countries should end their tariff escalation and other protectionist measures against the processed and semi-processed products of the developing countries. They should also provide active support and assistance to the developing countries in finance, technology and human resources development, so as to create favourable conditions for the diversification of their production and exports.

In order to stabilize the export earnings of the developing countries, it is vitally important to establish within UNCTAD compensatory financing facilities for the shortfalls in export earnings. At the same time, the international community should make a serious effort to improve the existing compensatory facilities so that their potentials can be fully realized.

Since its establishment, UNCTAD has done an enormous amount of fruitful work on commodities. It should continue to play its unique role in that field with a view to helping the developing countries to change the unfavourable situation confronting them on the international commodity market.

III. International trade

Since the sixth session of the Conference, protectionism in the developed countries has seriously under-

---

mined the fundamental principles of the international trading system. It has hampered the development of world trade and by reducing their share in it, endangered the economic development of the developing countries.

The developed countries should therefore adopt concrete and effective measures to implement the commitments on the standstill and roll-back of protectionism they have made in UNCTAD and other international forums. They should, in particular, reduce and eliminate the protectionist measures against products which are of export interest to the developing countries, such as textiles, clothing, footwear and agricultural products, and give them more favourable differential treatment. They should open up their markets to the developing countries and review their trade legislation and regulations relating to anti-dumping and countervailing, and exempt the exports of the developing countries from unreasonable obtacles. At the same time, the developed countries should take effective measures to control restrictive business practices that are unfavourable to the trade of the developing countries.

To help the economic development of the developing countries, the developed countries should fulfil the commitments they entered into at previous sessions of the Conference to take effective measures in the structural adjustment of industries which have lost their competitive advantage. In this connection, the Trade and Development Board should further strengthen its annual review of protectionism and structural adjustment.

The developed countries should respect the principles of the GSP, namely those of generality, non-discrimination and non-reciprocity. They should improve their GSP schemes by expanding the coverage of preferential products and simplifying the application procedure, so that the developing countries can benefit from them.

UNCTAD should play an active role in the new round of multilateral trade negotiations. It should provide the necessary advice and technical assistance to the developing countries, so that their needs can fully be taken into account in the new round of negotiations and tangible results can be achieved in combating protectionism, strengthening and improving the international trading system and promoting the development of world trade.

Expanding international trade, including that between countries with different economic and social systems, is one of the most important means of promoting the development of the world economy and international trade. When considering this item, however, at the seventh session the Conference should take full account of the needs of the developing countries.

IV. The least developed countries

The LDCs have long been facing very serious economic difficulties. The better part of the 1980s has been a witness to stagnated production, declining per capita income and aggravated poverty in these countries, which have aroused the serious concern of the international community.

---

[h] United Nations publication, Sales No. E.81.II.D.8 and corrigendum.

The special difficulties of the LDCs have met with China's deep sympathy. To the extent of its capacity, China supports them in their efforts to overcome their backwardness and has provided assistance for their endeavour.

Support and assistance from the international community is of vital importance to the economic development of the LDCs. The developed countries should assume responsibility for assisting the economic recovery of the LDCs. They should take effective measures to implement adequately the Substantial New Programme of Action and the resolutions concerning the LDCs adopted by the General Assembly and by UNCTAD and to attain as soon as possible the targets for development assistance established by the United Nations.

In considering the question of the LDCs, the Conference should highlight the causes for the failure to implement adequately the Substantial New Programme of Action, with a view to an early attainment of the target set therein. It should formulate proposals for an overall review of that programme in 1990. When considering such items as resources for development, commodities and international trade, the Conference should take full account of the special difficulties of the LDCs and keep in mind their special demands.

Since its establishment, UNCTAD has been constructively carrying out the mandate given to it by the General Assembly in its resolution 1995 (XIX). It has played an important role in promoting North-South dialogue and South-South co-operation. In the present situation, this role should be strengthened further rather than weakened. In view of the important role of UNCTAD in the field of development, the international community should make a concerted effort to improve its effectiveness and its responsiveness to both immediate and long-term issues.

Annex VII

REPORT OF THE CREDENTIALS COMMITTEE[a]

1. At its 205th and 210th plenary meetings, on 13 and 27 July 1987, respectively, the United Nations Conference on Trade and Development, in accordance with rule 14 of its rules of procedure, appointed a Credentials Committee consisting of the following member States: Barbados, Burma, China, Ghana, Netherlands, Rwanda, Union of Soviet Socialist Republics, United States of America and Venezuela.

2. The Credentials Committee met on 24 July 1987.

3. Mr. Adolfo Raúl Taylhardat (Venezuela) was unanimously elected Chairman of the Committee.

4. The UNCTAD secretariat informed the Committee on the status of credentials of representatives as at 23 July 1987. Credentials issued by the head of State of Government or by the Minister for Foreign Affairs, as provided for in rule 13 of the rules of procedure of the Conference, had been submitted by 103 member States. The appointment of the representatives of 13 member States had been communicated to the Secretary-General of UNCTAD by means of a cable from the Minister for Foreign Affairs or from the Ministry of Foreign Affairs. The appointment of the representatives of 20 member States had been communicated to the Secretary-General of UNCTAD by means of a letter from the permanent representative or a note verbale from the permanent mission in Geneva. The appointment of the representative of 5 member States had also been communicated to the Secretary-General of UNCTAD. The Committee also had before it document TD/342.

5. The representative of the *Union of Soviet Socialist Republics* objected to the acceptance of the credentials for the representatives of so-called "Democratic Kampuchea", stating that, in the view of the Soviet delegation, those credentials were null and void.

6. The representative of *China* objected to the statement by the representative of the USSR and stated that, in the view of the Chinese delegation, the credentials of Democratic Kampuchea were valid, referring to the fact that the Government of Democratic Kampuchea had been recognized by the General Assembly of the United Nations as the sole legitimate Government of that country.

7. With regard to the participation of Afghanistan in the seventh session of the Conference, the representative of China reiterated the position of his country as reflected in the report of the Credentials Committee of the General Assembly at its forty-first session.[b]

8. With regard to the participation of Chile in the seventh session of the Conference, the representative of the *Union of Soviet Socialist Republics* reiterated the position of his country as reflected in the report of the Credentials Committee of the General Assembly at its forty-first session.

9. The representative of the *United States of America* stated that the credentials of the representatives of Democratic Kampuchea and Chile were in order, fulfilled the requirements of rule 13 of the rules of procedure, had been accepted by UNCTAD in the past and should be accepted at the current session. The Credentials Committee's work should be of a technical nature, and not based on the views of Governments about the policies of member States. Out of respect for the technical nature of the credentials exercise, the United States was not objecting to the acceptance of the credentials of the representatives of Afghanistan, but pointed out that the position of his delegation about the unrepresentative nature of that Government, installed as a result of aggression by the Soviet Union, was reflected in the report of the Credentials Committee of the General Assembly at its forty-first session, and remained unchanged.

10. The representative of the *Union of Soviet Socialist Republics* stated that the statement made by the United States representative concerning Afghanistan was a conscious and evil attempt to distort the historical and political reality in that country. That statement could not change the fact that the Democratic Republic of Afghanistan was a sovereign, non-aligned State which was a full and equal Member of the United Nations. The comment by the United States representative was an attempt to interfere in the internal affairs of Afghanistan and was contrary to the Charter of the United Nations and to the interests of normalization of the situation in South-West Asia, a process that was being assisted by the personal efforts of the Secretary-General.

11. The representative of the *Netherlands* reiterated the position of his country as reflected in the report of the Credentials Committee of the General Assembly at its forty-first session, namely that the Committee had a technical task to perform—it was not its function to make political judgements regarding the Governments that issued the credentials. Accordingly, his delegation would accept the credentials of the representatives of all the States participating in the Conference.

12. The representative of *Ghana* stated that the position of his country on the credentials of Afghanistan, Chile and Democratic Kampuchea remained the same as that stated in the Credentials Committee of the General Assembly at its forty-first session.

---

[a] For the discussion of this report in plenary meeting, see part three above, section F.2.

[b] A/41/727 and Add.1.

13. The representative of *Rwanda* stated that the position of his country on the credentials of Afghanistan, Chile and Democratic Kampuchea remained the same as that stated in the Credentials Committee of the General Assembly at its forty-first session.

14. The representative of *Barbados* stated that he was prepared to accept the credentials of representatives submitted in accordance with the relevant rules and procedures for the submission of such credentials.

15. The *Chairman* proposed that, taking into account the statements made by members of the Committee, which would be reflected in its report, the Committee should decide to accept the credentials of the representatives of the member States referred to in paragraph 4. In connection with the credentials which had not yet been submitted in due form, the Chairman proposed that the Committee accept the assurances given by the representatives concerned, on the understanding that their credentials, in conformity with rule 13 of the rules of procedure of the Conference, would be submitted promptly to the Secretary-General of UNCTAD. There was no objection to this proposal.

16. The *Chairman* then proposed the following draft resolution for adoption by the Committee:

"*The Credentials Committee,*

"*Having examined* the credentials of the representatives of the seventh session of the United Nations Conference on Trade and Development,

"*Accepts* under the terms of rule 14 of the rules of procedure of the Conference, the credentials of the representatives to the seventh session of the Conference and recommends to the Conference that it approve the report of the Credentials Committee."

17. The Committee adopted the above draft resolution without a vote.

18. The *Chairman* then proposed that the Committee should recommend to the Conference the adoption of the draft resolution in paragraph 19. The proposal was adopted by the Committee without a vote.

19. In the light of the foregoing, the present report is submitted to the Conference.

RECOMMENDATION OF THE CREDENTIALS COMMITTEE

The Credentials Committee recommends to the Conference the adoption of the following draft resolution:[c]

"*Credentials of representatives to the seventh session of the Conference*

"*The United Nations Conference on Trade and Development*

"*Approves* the report of the Credentials Committee."

---

[c] For the text adopted, see resolution 168 (VII).

Annex VIII

CHECK-LIST OF DOCUMENTS

Note: Unless otherwise indicated in the column "Observations and references", the
documents are mimeographed. The abbreviated title "*Proceedings*" refers to *Proceedings
of the United Nations Conference on Trade and Development, Seventh Session.*

A. DOCUMENTS IN THE GENERAL SERIES

Document No.	Title	Agenda item	Observations and references
TD/327	Note by the Secretary-General of UNCTAD transmitting the provisional agenda, with annotations, for the seventh session of the Conference	6	For the agenda as adopted, see annex I above
TD/328 and Add.1-5	Revitalizing development, growth and international trade—assessment and policy options: report by the UNCTAD secretariat (Foreword and Executive Summary, and chapters I to V)	8	See TD/328/Rev.1 and Add.1
TD/328/Rev.1	*Idem* (Foreword and chapters I to V)	8	United Nations publication, Sales No. E.87.II.D.7; see also *Proceedings*, vol. III
TD/328/Rev.1/Add.1	*Idem* (Executive Summary)	8	See also *Proceedings*, vol. III
TD/329/Rev.1	Reviving multilateral co-operation for growth and development: report by the Secretary-General of UNCTAD	8	*Ibid.*
TD/330 and Corr.1 and 2	Note by the Secretary-General of UNCTAD transmitting the document entitled "Assessment and proposals by the Group of 77 relating to the seventh session of the Conference"	8	See annex V above
TD/331	Note by the Secretary-General of UNCTAD transmitting the position paper of the People's Republic of China on issues to be considered at the seventh session of the Conference	8	See annex VI above
TD/332	Note by the UNCTAD secretariat concerning the reports submitted by the Trade and Development Board since the sixth session of the Conference	9	
TD/333 and Corr.1	Note by the Secretary-General of UNCTAD transmitting the document entitled "Approach of the socialist countries members of Group D and Mongolia to the substantive items of the provisional agenda for the seventh session of the Conference"	8	*Idem*
TD/334	Note by the Secretary-General of UNCTAD transmitting the Communiqué of 13 May 1987 of the Council of the Organisation for Economic Co-operation and Development	8	*Idem*
TD/335	Note by the Secretary-General of UNCTAD transmitting the Havana Declaration, adopted on 25 April 1987 at the Sixth Ministerial Meeting of the Group of 77	8	See annex V above
TD/336	Pre-Conference Meeting of Senior Officials: report by the Chairman of the Meeting		
TD/337	Note by the UNCTAD secretariat transmitting the document entitled "Basic provisions for a fundamental reform of economic management", submitted by the delegation of the Union of Soviet Socialist Republics		
TD/338	Agenda of the Conference, as adopted at its 201st plenary meeting, on 9 July 1987	6	See annex I above
TD/339	Note by the UNCTAD secretariat transmitting the Pyongyang Declaration and Plan of Action on South-South Co-operation, adopted on 13 June 1987 by the Extraordinary Ministerial Conference of Non-Aligned Countries on South-South Co-operation	7, 8	
TD/339/Add.1	Note by the UNCTAD secretariat transmitting documents of the Extraordinary Ministerial Conference of Non-Aligned Countries on South-South Co-operation	7, 8	

Document No.	Title	Agenda item	Observations and references
TD/340	Note by the UNCTAD secretariat transmitting the text of a resolution adopted by the 77th Conference of the Inter-parliamentary Union	8	
TD/341	Note by the UNCTAD secretariat transmitting the document entitled "Economic and technical assistance of the USSR to developing countries"	8	
TD/342	Letter dated 9 July 1987 to the Secretary-General of UNCTAD from the delegations of the following States participating in the seventh session of the Conference: Algeria, Bahrain, Democratic Yemen, Djibouti, Iraq, Jordan, Kuwait, Lebanon, Libyan Arab Jamahiriya, Mauritania, Morocco, Oman, Qatar, Saudi Arabia, Somalia, Sudan, Syrian Arab Republic, Tunisia, United Arab Emirates and Yemen; and from the Palestine Liberation Organization	5	
TD/343	Declaration by the Socialist People's Republic of Albania	8	
TD/344	Note by the UNCTAD secretariat transmitting the document entitled "Foundation for sustained growth in a changing world", submitted by the delegation of the United States of America	8	
TD/345	Note by the UNCTAD secretariat transmitting the document entitled "Economic assistance provided by the Czechoslovak Socialist Republic to developing countries and national liberation movements in 1986"	8	
TD/346	Report of the Credentials Committee	5 (b)	See annex VII above
TD/347	Note by the UNCTAD secretariat transmitting the document entitled "Resources for development: net outflow of capital from developing countries", submitted by the delegation of the Ukrainian Soviet Socialist Republic	8	
TD/348	Letter dated 29 July 1987 from the Permanent Representative of Israel to the Secretary-General of UNCTAD	5	
TD/349	Communication dated 28 July 1987 from the head of the delegation of the Yemen Arab Republic to the seventh session of the Conference, co-ordinator of the Arab Group, addressed to the Secretary-General of UNCTAD	5	
TD/350 and Corr.1	Final Act of UNCTAD VII		See part one above, section A.1
TD/351	Report of the United Nations Conference on Trade and Development on its seventh session		For the printed version, see TD/352 (vol. I)
TD/352 (vol. I)	*Proceedings of the United Nations Conference on Trade and Development, Seventh Session, vol. I, Report and Annexes*		United Nations publication, Sales No. E.88.II.D.11
TD/352 (vol. II)	*Ibid., vol. II, Statements and Summary Records*		United Nations publication, Sales No. E.88.II.D.12
TD/352 (vol. III)	*Ibid., vol. III, Basic Documents*		United Nations publication, Sales No. E.88.II.D.13

B. DOCUMENTS IN THE LIMITED SERIES

Document No.	Title	Agenda item	Observations and references
TD/L.273	Designation of intergovernmental bodies for the purposes of rule 80 of the rules of procedure—application by the International Tropical Timber Organization: note by the UNCTAD secretariat	9	
TD/L.274	*Idem*—application by the International Textiles and Clothing Bureau: note by the UNCTAD secretariat	9	
TD/L.275	Message from Mr. Zhao Ziyang, Premier of the State Council of the People's Republic of China		See annex IV above
TD/L.276	Statement by Mr. Kenneth K. S. Dadzie, Secretary-General of UNCTAD, at the 201st plenary meeting, on 9 July 1987		See *Proceedings*, volume II
TD/L.277	Message from Mr. D. Sodnom, Chairman of the Council of Ministers of the Mongolian People's Republic		See annex IV above
TD/L.278	Message from Mr. Erich Honecker, General Secretary of the Central Committee of the Socialist Unity Party of Germany and Chairman of the Council of State of the German Democratic Republic		*Idem*
TD/L.279	Message from Mr. Fidel Castro Ruz, President of the Council of State and the Council of Ministers of the Republic of Cuba		*Idem*
TD/L.280	Message from Mr. Nicolae Ceausescu, President of the Socialist Republic of Romania		*Idem*

Document No.	Title	Agenda item	Observations and references
TD/L.281	Message from Mr. Nicolai Ryzhkov, Chairman of the Council of Ministers of the Union of Soviet Socialist Republics		*Idem*
TD/L.282	Message from Mr. Wojciech Jaruzelski, Chairman of the Council of State of the Polish People's Republic		*Idem*
TD/L.283	Message from Mr. Pham Hung, Chairman of the Council of Ministers of the Socialist Republic of Viet Nam		*Idem*
TD/L.284	Statement by Mr. Bernard T. G. Chidzero, Minister of Finance, Economic Planning and Development of the Republic of Zimbabwe, President of the seventh session of the United Nations Conference on Trade and Development, at the 201st plenary meeting, on 9 July 1987		See *Proceedings*, vol. II
TD/L.285	Message from His Holiness Pope John Paul II		See annex IV above
TD/L.286	Address by Mr. Lazar Mojsov, President of the Presidency of the Socialist Federal Republic of Yugoslavia (host country to the sixth session of the Conference), at the inaugural ceremony on 9 July 1987		See annex III above
TD/L.287	Message from Mr. Alan García Pérez, President of the Republic of Peru		See annex IV above
TD/L.288	Note concerning two documents submitted by the Organisation for Economic Co-operation and Development		
TD/L.289	Address by Mr. Mohamed Hosny Mubarak, President of the Arab Republic of Egypt, at the 202nd plenary meeting, on 10 July 1987		See *Proceedings*, volume II
TD/L.290	Statement by Mr. Javier Pérez de Cuéllar, Secretary-General of the United Nations, at the inaugural ceremony on 9 July 1987		See annex III above
TD/L.291	Address by Mr. François Mitterrand, President of the French Republic, at the 202nd plenary meeting, on 10 July 1987		See *Proceedings*, volume II
TD/L.292	Welcoming address by Mr. Pierre Aubert, Federal Councillor, President of the Swiss Confederation, at the inaugural ceremony on 9 July 1987		See annex III above
TD/L.293	Address by Mrs. Gro Harlem Brundtland, Prime Minister of Norway and Chairman of the World Commission on Environment and Development, at the 203rd plenary meeting, on 10 July 1987		See *Proceedings*, volume II
TD/L.294	Address by Colonel Denis Sassou Nguesso, President of the People's Republic of the Congo, current Chairman of the Assembly of Heads of State and Government of the Organization of African Unity, at the 203rd plenary meeting, on 10 July 1987		*Ibid.*
TD/L.295	Economic situation in the occupied Palestinian territories: draft resolution submitted by Cuba on behalf of the States members of the Group of 77	9	Adopted; see resolution 169 (VII)
TD/L.296	Statement by Mr. Uffe Ellemann-Jensen, Minister for Foreign Affairs of Denmark and President of the Council of the European Communities, on behalf of the European Community and its member States, at the 202nd plenary meeting, on 10 July 1987		See *Proceedings*, volume II
TD/L.297	Statement by Mr. Ricardo Cabrisas Ruiz, Minister of Foreign Trade, as representative of the head of State of the Republic of Cuba, at the 202nd plenary meeting, on 10 July 1987, to present the results of the Sixth Ministerial Meeting of the Group of 77, preparatory to the seventh session of the Conference		*Ibid.*
TD/L.298	Address by Mr. Gamani Corea, former Secretary-General of UNCTAD, at the 209th plenary meeting, on 15 July 1987		*Ibid.*
TD/L.299	Address by Mr. Robert G. Mugabe, Prime Minister of the Republic of Zimbabwe and Chairman of the Non-Aligned Movement, at the 207th plenary meeting, on 14 July 1987		*Ibid.*
TD/L.300	Draft report of the Conference on its seventh session	10	For the final report, see TD/351
TD/L.301	Structural adjustment and economic performance—synthesis report: document submitted by the Organisation for Economic Co-operation and Development	8	
TD/L.302	Message from Mr. Guillermo Bedregal Gutiérrez, Minister of Foreign Affairs and Worship of Bolivia		See annex IV above
TD/L.303	Report of Committee III: amendments and additions to TD(VII)/C.III/L.2	8 (c)	

Document No.	Title	Agenda item	Observations and references
TD/L.304 and Corr.1	Statement by Mr. Tian Jiyun, Vice-Premier of the State Council of the People's Republic of China, at the 204th plenary meeting, on 13 July 1987		See *Proceedings*, volume II
TD/L.305	Message from Mrs. Corazón C. Aquino, President of the Republic of the Philippines		See annex IV above
TD/L.306	Report of Committee II: amendments and additions to TD(VII)/C.II/L.2	8 (*b*)	
TD/L.307	Report of Committee IV: amendments and additions to TD(VII)/C.IV/L.2	8 (*d*)	
TD/L.308	General assessment: text submitted by Belgium on behalf of the States members of Group B	8	
TD/L.309	Report of Committee I: amendments to TD(VII)/C.I/L.2	8 (*a*)	
TD/L.310	Address by H.R.H. Crown Prince Hassan Bin Talal of the Hashemite Kingdom of Jordan, at the 212th plenary meeting, on 27 July 1987		See *Proceedings*, volume II
TD/L.311	Statement by Mr. Norberto González, Executive Secretary of the Economic Commission for Latin America and the Caribbean		*Ibid.*
TD/L.312	Resources for development, including financial and related monetary questions: policies and measures, submitted by Cuba on behalf of the States members of the Group of 77	8 (*a*)	Withdrawn; see part two above, para. 22
TD/L.313	Commodities: policies and measures, submitted by Cuba on behalf of the States members of the Group of 77	8 (*b*)	*Idem*
TD/L.314	International trade: policies and measures, submitted by Cuba on behalf of the States members of the Group of 77	8 (*c*)	*Idem*
TD/L.315	Commodities—programme for improved processing in developing countries: proposal submitted by Japan	8 (*b*)	
TD/L.316 and Add.1-6	Draft consolidated text submitted by the President of the Conference (Final Act of UNCTAD VII)	8	See part one above, section A.1
TD/L.317	Commodities: draft proposal submitted by Cuba, on behalf of the States members of the Group of 77; Poland, on behalf of the States members of Group D; and the People's Republic of China	8 (*b*)	Adopted; see part one above, section A.3
TD/L.318	Statement by Mr. Kenneth K. S. Dadzie, Secretary-General of UNCTAD, at the closure of the Conference, on 3 August 1987		See *Proceedings*, volume II

C. DOCUMENTS IN THE NON-GOVERNMENTAL ORGANIZATION SERIES

Document No.	Title
TD/NGO/26	Note by the UNCTAD secretariat transmitting documents submitted by the International Chamber of Commerce
TD/NGO/27	Note by the UNCTAD secretariat transmitting a document submitted by the World Trade Federation of Trade Unions
TD/NGO/28	Note by the UNCTAD secretariat transmitting a document submitted by the World Association of Former United Nations Internes and Fellows, Inc.
TD/NGO/29	Note by the UNCTAD secretariat transmitting a document submitted by the World Federation of Industry Workers
TD/NGO/30	Note by the UNCTAD secretariat transmitting a document submitted by the International Confederation of Free Trade Unions
TD/NGO/31	Note by the UNCTAD secretariat transmitting a document submitted by non-governmental organizations
TD/NGO/32	Note by the UNCTAD secretariat transmitting a document submitted by the International Organization of Consumers Unions
TD/NGO/33	Note by the UNCTAD secretariat transmitting a document submitted by non-governmental organizations

D. DOCUMENTS IN THE INFORMATION SERIES

Document No.	Title	Observations and references
TD/INF.23	Information for participants	
TD/INF.24 and Corr.1	Calendar of UNCTAD meetings for the remainder of 1987	See part one above, section A.4, (*c*)
TD/INF.25	List of participants in the seventh session of the Conference	

Document No.	Title	Agenda item	Observations and references

E. DOCUMENTS IN THE BUREAU SERIES

TD(VII)/BUR.1	Letter to the President of the Conference at its thirty-third regular session and fifteenth special session from Mr. Saad Alfarargi, President of the Trade and Development Board		

F. DOCUMENTS IN THE MISCELLANEOUS SERIES

TD(VII)/Misc.1	Note by the UNCTAD secretariat transmitting the resolution adopted by the Economic and Social Commission for Asia and the Pacific at its forty-third session, April 1987, entitled "Implementation of the Substantial New Programme of Action for the 1980s for the Least Developed Countries"		
TD(VII)/Misc.2	Note by the UNCTAD secretariat transmitting the report of the Intergovernmental Group of 24 on International Monetary Affairs entitled "The role of the International Monetary Fund in adjustment with growth"		
TD(VII)/Misc.3 and Rev.1 and Rev.1/Add.1 and Rev.2	Provisional list of participants in the seventh session of the Conference		See TD/INF.25
TD(VII)/Misc.4	Programme of the inaugural ceremony for the seventh session of the Conference, Thursday, 9 July 1987 at 3.00 p.m.		
TD(VII)/Misc.5	Check-list of documents by provisional agenda item		
TD(VII)/Misc.6	Enterprise Symposium: note by the UNCTAD secretariat		
TD(VII)/Misc.7	Tentative schedule for the week 20-24 July 1987: note by the UNCTAD secretariat		
TD(VII)/Misc.8	Communication from the Minister for Development Co-operation of the Netherlands to the President of the Conference		

G. COMMITTEE DOCUMENTS

Committee I

TD(VII)/C.I/L.1	Proposals on policies and measures, submitted by Peru on behalf of the States members of the Group of 77	8 (a)	See annex V.B above, part II, section I. Also subsequently issued as TD/L.312
TD(VII)/C.I/L.2	Draft report of Committee I	8 (a)	Adopted as amended by TD/L.309; see part two above, paras. 130-147
TD(VII)/C.I/CRP.1	Statement by Denmark on behalf of the European Economic Community and its member States	8 (a)	
TD(VII)/C.I/CRP.2	Views of the Nordic countries (Finland, Norway and Sweden)	8 (a)	
TD(VII)/C.I/CRP.3 and Rev.1 and 2	Chairman's non-paper: debt problems	8 (a)	
TD(VII)/C.I/CRP.3/Add.1 and Rev.1 and 2	*Idem*: external resources for development	8 (a)	
TD(VII)/C.I/CRP.3/ Add.2 and Rev.1	*Idem*: domestic resources for development, including non-financial resources	8 (a)	
TD(VII)/C.I/CRP.3/ Add.3 and Rev.1	*Idem*: introduction	8 (a)	
TD(VII)/C.I/CRP.3/Add.4	*Idem*: related monetary questions	8 (a)	

Committee II

TD(VII)/C.II/L.1	Proposals on policies and measures, submitted by Ethiopia on behalf of the States members of the Group of 77	8 (b)	See annex V.B above, part II, section II. Also subsequently issued as TD/L.313
TD(VII)/C.II/L.2	Draft report of Committee II	8 (b)	Adopted as amended by TD/L.306; see part two above, paras. 148-161
TD(VII)/C.II/CRP.1	Organization of work of the Sessional Committee: proposal submitted by the Group of 77	8 (b)	
TD(VII)/C.II/CRP.2	Items of work in the Sessional Committee on commodities submitted by the Chairman of the Committee	8 (b)	

Document No.	Title	Agenda item	Observations and references
TD(VII)/C.II/CRP.3	Working paper submitted by Switzerland on behalf of the States members of Group B	8 (b)	See part two above, chapter V, section B.4, appendix II
TD(VII)/C.II/CRP.4	Policies and measures: text submitted by the Chairman	8 (b)	
TD(VII)/C.II/CRP.5	Paper submitted by Norway on behalf of the Nordic countries (Finland, Norway and Sweden)	8 (b)	
TD(VII)/C.II/CRP.6	Paper submitted by Denmark on behalf of the European Economic Community and its member States	8 (b)	
TD(VII)/C.II/CRP.7	Commodities—programme for improved processing in developing countries: proposal submitted by Japan	8 (b)	Subsequently issued as TD/L.315
TD(VII)/C.II/CRP.8	Position paper submitted by the United States of America	8 (b)	
TD(VII)/C.II/CRP.9	Paper submitted by Australia	8 (b)	

Committee III

Document No.	Title	Agenda item	Observations and references
TD(VII)/C.III/L.1 and Corr.1	Proposals on policies and measures, submitted by India on behalf of the States members of the Group of 77	8 (c)	See annex V.B above, part II, section III. Also subsequently issued as TD/L.314
TD(VII)/C.III/L.2	Draft report of Committee III	8 (c)	Adopted as amended by TD/L.303; see part two above, paras. 162-186
TD(VII)/C.III/CRP.1	Statement by the representative of the Federal Republic of Germany on behalf of the States members of Group B	8 (c)	See part two above, chapter V, section C.4, appendix II
TD(VII)/C.III/CRP.2	Statement by the representative of Hungary on behalf of the States members of Group D and Mongolia	8 (c)	
TD(VII)/C.III/CRP.3	Statement by the representative of India on behalf of the States members of the Group of 77	8 (c)	*Idem*, appendix III
TD(VII)/C.III/CRP.4	Promotion of trade and economic co-operation among countries having different economic and social systems, with particular consideration given to the interests of developing countries: statement by the representative of the Sudan on behalf of the States members of the Group of 77	8 (c)	*Idem*, appendix IV
TD(VII)/C.III/CRP.5	Statement by the representative of Bulgaria on behalf of the States members of Group D on trade relations among countries with different social systems	8 (c)	
TD(VII)/C.III/CRP.6	Statement by the representative of Sweden on behalf of the Nordic countries (Finland, Norway and Sweden)	8 (c)	
TD(VII)/C.III/CRP.7	Working paper submitted by the Federal Republic of Germany on behalf of the States members of Group B	8 (c)	*Idem*, appendix V
TD(VII)/C.III/CRP.8	Information brief by the UNCTAD secretariat on UNCTAD technical co-operation activities in international trade and related fields	8 (c)	
TD(VII)/C.III/CRP.9 and Corr.1	Text submitted by the Chairman	8 (c)	

Committee IV

Document No.	Title	Agenda item	Observations and references
TD(VII)/C.IV/L.1	Proposal on policies and measures, submitted by Bangladesh on behalf of the States members of the Group of 77	8 (d)	See annex V.B above, part II, section IV. See also part two above, para. 22
TD(VII)/C.IV/L.2	Draft report of Committee IV	8 (d)	Adopted as amended by TD/L.307; see part two above, paras. 187-205
TD(VII)/C.IV/CRP.1	Statement by the representative of Bangladesh on behalf of the States members of the Group of 77	8 (d)	See part two above, chapter V, section D.4, appendix III
TD(VII)/C.IV/CRP.2 and Rev.1	Statement by the representative of the German Democratic Republic on behalf of the States members of Group D	8 (d)	*Idem*, appendix IV
TD(VII)/C.IV/CRP.3	Statement by the representative of the Netherlands on behalf of the States members of Group B	8 (d)	*Idem*, appendix V
TD(VII)/C.IV/CRP.4	Schedule for the second week, 20-24 July 1987, submitted by the Chairman	8 (d)	*Idem*, appendix VI
TD(VII)/C.IV/CRP.5	Statement by the representative of Denmark on behalf of the European Economic Community and its member States	8 (a)	*Idem*, appendix VII
TD(VII)/C.IV/CRP.6	Views of the Nordic countries (Finland, Norway and Sweden)	8 (d)	*Idem*, appendix VIII

Document No.	*Title*	*Agenda item*	*Observations and references*
TD(VII)/C.IV/CRP.7 and Add.1	Report by Sessional Committee IV to the President's Contact Group: Chairman's draft	8 (*d*)	*Idem*, appendix I
TD(VII)/C.IV/CRP.8	Amendments proposed by the representative of China to TD(VII)/C.IV/CRP.7 and Add.1	8 (*d*)	*Idem*, appendix IX
TD(VII)/C.IV/CRP.9	Proposal by the Netherlands on behalf of the States members of Group B	8 (*d*)	*Idem*, appendix X

Contact Group

TD(VII)/CG/CRP.1 and Corr.1	Commodities: text submitted by the Working Group on Commodities	8 (*b*)	
TD(VII)/CG/CRP.2	Resources for development, including financial, and related monetary questions: text submitted by the Working Group on Resources	8 (*a*)	
TD(VII)/CG/CRP.3	International trade: text submitted by the Chairman of the Working Group on International Trade	8 (*c*)	